INTERNATIONAL AND COMPARATIVE
INDUSTRIAL RELATIONS

The Industrial Relations Research Centre (IRReC) is based at the University of New South Wales and was established in 1980 with the assistance of a federal government General Development Grant to the University. The Centre's function is to focus and stimulate industrial relations research, and to facilitate publication of research results. The policy of IRReC is to promote the use of research results in industrial relations practice, and to sponsor projects in applied research, the results of which will help inform public debate and policy making. Books to date in the Australian Studies in Industrial Relations Series are:

Industrial Action (Frenkel)
Wage Indexation (Plowman)
Arbitrator at Work (Dabscheck)
Unions against Capitalism? (Frenkel and Coolican)
Control, Consensus or Chaos? (Niland and Turner)
Wage Fixation in Australia (Niland)
Alternatives to Arbitration (Blandy and Niland)

International and Comparative Industrial Relations

A Study of
Developed Market Economies

EDITED BY GREG J. BAMBER AND
RUSSELL D. LANSBURY

London
ALLEN & UNWIN
Sydney   Boston

To Val and Gwen,
Alex, Katie, Owen and Nina

George Allen & Unwin (Publishers) Ltd
40 Museum Street, London WC1A 1LU, UK

George Allen & Unwin (Publishers) Ltd
Park Lane, Hemel Hempstead, Herts HP2 4TE, UK

Allen & Unwin Inc.
9 Winchester Terrace, Winchester, Mass 01890 USA

Allen & Unwin Australia   •
8 Napier Street, North Sydney NSW 2060 Australia

Allen & Unwin New Zealand Limited
60 Cambridge Terrace, Wellington, New Zealand

British Library Cataloguing in Publication Data

International and comparative industrial relations:
    a study of developed market economies.
    1. Industrial relations
    I. Bamber, Greg   II. Lansbury, Russell D.
    331   HD6961
    ISBN 0-04-331116-4
    ISBN 0-04-331117-4 Pbk

Set in 10/11 Times by Best-set Typesetter Limited, HK
Printed in Singapore by Koon Wah Printers

Contents

Tables

Figures

Preface

We discovered the need for this book, while trying to teach our Masters students about comparative industrial relations, both in Australia and Britain. The book is a product of extensive international co-operation. Many institutions have kindly helped us to work on it including, in Australia: the Labour–Management Studies Program (Macquarie University) and the Industrial Relations Research Centre (University of New South Wales); in Britain: the Australian Studies Centre and Durham University Business School; and in the USA: the Sloan School of Management (Massachusetts Institute of Technology). Most of the secretarial work was conducted cheerfully and efficiently in Durham by Chris Harper and Wendy Musgrave and in Sydney by Lisa McLeod. We owe each of them a great debt.

In editing such a book, we are especially grateful to Roger Blanpain and the authors from the various countries who have collaborated with us. They have kindly tolerated our rewriting and sometimes reinterpreting their original material. Most of them had collaborated with us before (see G.J. Bamber and R.D. Lansbury eds, 'Technological Change and Industrial Relations: An International Symposium', a Special Issue of the *Bulletin of Comparative Labour Relations*, 12, 1983).

Many people have commented helpfully on some or all of the draft manuscript of this book, including: Frances Bairstow, Jeff Bridgford, Willy Brown, Duncan Bythell, Ron Callus, Jon Clark, Oliver Clarke, Steve Deery, Yves Delamotte, Djelloul Djeldjli, Ron Dore, David Dror, Bill Ford, John Goodman, Winton Higgins, Johannes Juttner, Ev Kassalow, Peter Kaim-Caudle, Solomon Levine, David Lewin,

Richard McMahon, Denis MacShane, Rod Martin, Doug Miller, Dick Miller, Gerry Phelan, Alan Ponak, Bob Price, Derek Sawbridge, Jim Scoville, Jean-Jacques Silvestre, Siegi Steininger, Barry Thomas, Keith Thurley, Lord Wedderburn, Morris Weisz, Bob Woodward and several others. We are grateful to them all, but especially to Ed Davis, Patrick Gallagher and John Niland in Australia, and to Ed Snape and John Ritchie in England.

Much of the statistical data cited in the text and the Appendix was supplied by Ken Walsh, Institute of Manpower Studies, University of Sussex and John Evans, Organisation of Economic Co-operation and Development (OECD). Unless otherwise specified, currencies cited throughout the book are in US$ at current exchange rates, as in Appendix Table A.6. Greg Bamber compiled the Appendix, but also used data from other sources, particularly the International Labour Organisation and the Bureau of Labor Statistics. We appreciate the help of all of these people and institutions, though of course the usual disclaimers apply.

We are already planning to improve the next edition, so would be glad to hear any suggestions or corrections to any of the inevitable errors which have crept into this edition please, c/o George Allen & Unwin, PO Box 764, North Sydney, NSW 2060, Australia. They originally commissioned this book in their series with the Industrial Relations Research Centre, University of New South Wales.

Our greatest debt is to our immediate families, to whom this book is dedicated.

G.B. and R.L.
Durham and Sydney
June 1986

Contributors

Greg Bamber teaches at the Durham University Business School, England, where he is the Director of Research. He is a part-time Arbitrator for the Advisory, Conciliation and Arbitration Service (ACAS) and a Research Associate, Industrial Relations Research Centre, University of New South Wales, Sydney. He has also been a Visiting Fellow at Macquarie University, Sydney. In the 1970s, he worked for the Commission on Industrial Relations, London, and the Steel Industry Management Association, Yorkshire. He holds degrees from the University of Manchester Institute of Science and Technology, and Heriot-Watt University, Edinburgh. Dr Bamber's book, *Militant Managers?* was published by Gower, Aldershot, in 1986 and he has also published on technological change, unions, retail distribution and workers' participation.

Roger Blanpain is Professor at the Law School, University of Leuven and Visiting Professor at the European Institute of Business Administration (INSEAD), Fontainebleau. He is President of the International Industrial Relations Association, Editor in Chief of the *International Encyclopaedia for Labour Law and Industrial Relations*, the *Bulletin of Comparative Labour Relations* and the textbook, *Comparative Labour Law and Industrial Relations* (all published by Kluwer). He heads the Belgian delegation in the International Investment and Multinational Enterprises Committee of the Organisation for Economic Co-operation and Development (OECD), which monitors the OECD Guidelines for Multinational Enterprises.

Edward Davis is a senior lecturer in Industrial Relations at the Department of Industrial Relations, University of New South Wales. He holds a Master of Arts and Certificate of Education from Cambridge University, England, a Master of Economics from Monash University, and a PhD from La Trobe University, Australia. His recent research and publications have been mainly on technological change and on the democracy and government of Australian unions. He is co-editor with Russell Lansbury of *Technology, Work and Industrial Relations*, Longman Cheshire, 1984 and *Democracy and Control in the Work Place* (also with Russell Lansbury), Longman Cheshire, 1986.

Friedrich Fuerstenberg was born in Berlin. After receiving a doctorate in Economics at Tubingen University (1953) he was a member of the Human Relations Research Group at the New York State School of Industrial and Labor Relations, Cornell University (1953–54). In 1956–57, he conducted research on Joint Consultation in the British Civil Air Transport Industry, being affiliated with the London School of Economics and Political Science under a British Council grant. After working as Superintendent of the Central Training Department at Daimler–Benz AG in Stuttgart and as Managing Director of the Research Institute for Co-operatives in Erlangen, he was appointed as a full Professor at the Technical University in Clausthal in 1963. From 1966 until 1981 he was Professor of Sociology at Linz University, Austria and Head of the Sociological Division of the Austrian Institute for Labour Market Research. From 1981 until 1986 he has been Professor of Sociology, Bochum University, West Germany. Since 1986 he is Professor of Sociology, Bonn University, West Germany. He was President of the International Industrial Relations Association, 1983–86.

Janine Goetschy graduated as a political scientist and holds a doctorate in Organizational Sociology from the Institut d'Études Politiques of Paris. In 1976, she was appointed as a researcher at the *Centre de Recherche en Sciences Sociales du Travail* (University Paris XI) and presently, she is Senior Research Fellow with the *Centre National de la Recherche Scientifique* (CNRS, Paris). She has published several reports and numerous articles in the field of comparative industrial relations and industrial sociology. She is currently carrying out comparative research on the developments in industrial democracy and collective bargaining in the 1980s.

Olle Hammarström received an MBA from Gothenburg School of Economics and Business Administration in 1967, and worked as a consultant in personnel administration before joining the Sociology Department of Gothenburg University. He worked as a researcher and change-agent during the first generation of industrial democracy experiments in Sweden 1969–74, and later joined the Ministry of Labour as a policy adviser in the field of Industrial Democracy and Work Environment, and as a liaison officer with labour market organisations. He spent 15 months in Australia 1976–77, as an exchange officer with both the Australian Department of Employment and Industrial Relations, and the Australian Department of Productivity. He joined the *Arbetslivcentrum* (Swedish Work Life Centre) as a Research Director in 1978. Since June 1981 he has been the Head of the Research Department, Swedish Union of Clerical and Technical Employees in Industry (SIF). He has published several books and articles on industrial democracy and industrial relations.

Yasuo Kuwahara is a Professor of Economics at Dokkyo University and Senior Research Associate at the Japan Institute of Labour in Tokyo. He is a graduate of Keio University (Tokyo) and the New York State School of Industrial and Labor Relations, Cornell University (USA). Previously, he worked at Nippon Light Metal Co. Ltd as a planning officer, and at the Organisation for Economic Co-operation and Development as a consultant and adviser. He has lectured at Yokohama National University, St Paul University, and Hosei University as a Visiting Lecturer. He has published over fifty papers and books on technological change, foreign direct investment, equal employment opportunities and industrial relations.

Russell Lansbury is Professor of Industrial Relations at the University of Sydney, Australia. He holds degrees in Psychology and Political Science from the University of Melbourne and a doctorate from the London School of Economics. Professor Lansbury has worked in personnel and industrial relations for British Airways in London, and has held visiting positions at various universities in Europe and North America. In 1984 he was a Senior Fulbright Scholar at both MIT and Harvard University in the United States. He has acted as a consultant to governments in Australia and the International Labour Organisations on industrial relations issues. He is author and editor of numerous academic articles and books on topics such as industrial democracy, technological change and the role of management in industrial relations.

Claudio Pellegrini graduated in Labour History at the University of Rome in 1972. Subsequently he worked for an Italian union (CGIL) as an editor, labour educator, and collective bargaining representative at the national level. Between 1978 and 1984 he studied in the USA for a PhD in Industrial Relations from the University of Wisconsin, Madison. He currently teaches at the University of Rome in Italy. He has published several articles on industrial relations in the construction industry, on collective bargaining and on management and union rights.

Jacques Rojot holds a doctorate in Management from both the University of California at Los Angeles and the University of Rennes (France). He holds a Chair in Management in the French university system where he teaches Human Resources Management, Labor Law and Industrial Relations. He also holds a position at INSEAD, where he teaches comparative industrial relations. He is the author of several books and numerous articles on comparative industrial relations. He has served a consultant to OECD and an expert with EEC and is presently a member of the Executive Council of the International Industrial Relations Association, as well as being a correspondent of the US Academy of Arbitrators.

Ed Snape is a lecturer in Economics at Teesside Polytechnic, England and an Honorary Research Associate at Durham University Business School. He has a BA in Economics from Durham and an MScEcon in Industrial Relations from University College, Cardiff. Previously,, he worked at Sheffield City Polytechnic, England, as a research assistant and associate lecturer, and also as a school teacher. His research interests include the industrial relations of managerial and professional employees.

Mark Thompson received his PhD from the New York State School of Industrial and Labor Relations, Cornell University, USA. He taught at

McMaster University and then, since 1971, in the Faculty of Commerce, University of British Columbia. In addition, he spent two years as a member of the Research and Planning Department, International Labour Office, Geneva, Switzerland. He has been a visiting scholar at the University of Texas, El Colegio de Mexico, Cornell University and University of Warwick. He was appointed William M. Hamilton Professor of Industrial Relations in 1985. He is a member of the National Academy of Arbitrators and has served on the executive of the Industrial Relations Research Association (USA). His research interests include public sector industrial relations, labor relations in Mexico and the role of management in Canadian industrial relations. He has published articles in *Relations Industrielles*, *British Journal of Industrial Relations*, *Industrial Relations*, and *Industrial and Labor Relations Review*.

Hoyt Wheeler is an American. After obtaining a BA in Political Science at Marshall University and a law degree from the University of Virginia, he practised labour law as a partner in a law firm from 1961 to 1970. He received his PhD in 1974 from the University of Wisconsin. He taught at the University of Wyoming from 1973 to 1976; during this time he became an active labour arbitrator. From 1976 to 1981, he taught at the University of Minnesota. In 1981, he became Professor of Industrial Relations in the College of Business Administration, University of South Carolina, where he has helped to establish a new graduate programme in personnel and industrial relations and a local chapter of the Industrial Relations Research Association, of which he is currently President. He has just completed a book, *Industrial Conflict: An Integrative Theory*, which was published by the University of South Carolina Press in 1985.

Foreword

I warmly welcome this timely book, which complements several other works with which I am associated, including *Comparative Labour Law and Industrial Relations* (1985) and the *International Encyclopaedia for Labour Law and Industrial Relations* (both published by Kluwer, Deventer).

Greg Bamber and Russell Lansbury and their collaborators have written an excellent introductory text. In spite of the immense difficulties of working across different languages, cultures and disciplines, this collaboration has been a success, thanks to the perseverance of all those concerned with it.

As Shakespeare's Hamlet put it: 'Brevity is the soul of wit'. And this book is relatively concise, so is reasonably accessible to a wide range of readers including students and working people, as well as to the industrial relations practitioners in international companies, unions and government agencies. Many such people will find the book useful to them.

This book begins by showing why international and comparative industrial relations is an important area of study. It goes on to consider some of the relevant methodological problems and to evaluate the various theories in this field. The book focusses on 'western' capitalist market economies, with a chapter devoted to each of nine selected countries which all belong to the 'rich man's club', the Organisation for Economic Co-operation and Development (OECD). Four of these countries have comparable English-speaking traditions: Britain, the USA, Canada and Australia. Another four are from the European continent: two of which are Latin countries, with strong post-war traditions of Communist and Catholic unionism: Italy and France. The other two share some North-West European traditions of social partnership: West Germany and Sweden. In view of its important trading and industrial links with all of the other countries, I am pleased that the book also considers Japan. Thus it starts with the country which industrialised first (Britain), and finishes with one which did so more recently (Japan).

In relation to each country, there is a good introduction to the historical, social, economic and political context of industrial relations; this is followed by a discussion of the main economic actors: the unions, employers and governments. Each chapter also explains the most important industrial relations processes, such as collective bargaining and arbitration. These chapters also discuss such current issues as labour law reform, industrial democracy, technological change and incomes policies. At the end of each chapter there is a glossary of abbreviations, list of references and a chronology of the major developments in industrial relations, which is a helpful way of putting current events into perspective. The chapters also include comments on particularly important disputes (for example, the 1984–85 British miners' strike in chapter 2 and the 1984 German metalworkers' dispute about shorter working hours in chapter 8). Chapter 9 describes the process of local bargaining in Sweden and chapter 10 illustrates how industrial relations in Japan differ fundamentally between large and small firms. The Appendix includes a useful collection of comparative international data on these nine countries. The challenge for readers is to compare, contrast and to begin to explain the issues which emerge—and some which do not emerge—from these countries.

All in all, I can thoroughly recommend this book, especially as much of the collaboration arose from meetings of the International Industrial Relations Association!

Professor Roger Blanpain
President, International Industrial Relations Association
Director, Institute of Labour Relations
University of Leuven, Belgium

I
Introduction

1 | Studying international and comparative industrial relations

GREG BAMBER AND RUSSELL LANSBURY

The field of industrial relations has been defined in many different ways. It is fundamentally concerned with the behaviour of working people, particularly as members of organised groups. A narrow definition may focus on various aspects of job regulation and rule-making about work, while a broader view may portray industrial relations as one aspect of power and conflict in the wider society.

There has been a move away from a traditional, institutional orientation which focussed on the means by which work relationships are regulated, to an alternative approach which seeks to examine and explain the effects of wider economic and social influences on the interactions between workers, employers, their collective organisations and the state. Therefore, understanding industrial relations requires an interdisciplinary approach which uses analytical tools drawn from several academic fields, including law, economics, history, psychology, sociology and politics. Nevertheless, industrial relations is an independent field of study in its own right.

Adopting a comparative approach to industrial relations not only requires insights from several disciplines, but also knowledge of different cultural settings. It is useful to distinguish between 'comparative' industrial relations and 'international' studies in this field. Bean (1985:3) notes that 'comparative industrial relations is a systematic method of investigation relating two or more countries which has analytic rather than descriptive implications'. By contrast, argues Bean, international industrial relations deals with 'those institutions and phenomena which cross national boundaries, such as the industrial relations aspects of multinational companies or the international

3

labour movement'. In this book, the emphasis is on a comparative approach to industrial relations through the analysis of nine different countries, although some attention is also paid to international industrial relations. Each chapter uses a similar framework of analysis, so that comparisons can readily be made between the countries.

In this first chapter we begin by examining the important reasons for studying industrial relations in various countries, analyse the difficulties and problems in this field, highlight some of the major issues and review the main theoretical approaches which can help to explain different national patterns of industrial relations.

The emergence of international industrial relations

Multinational enterprises   Several factors have been influential in promoting the 'internationalisation' of industrial relations, especially since the Second World War. The growth of multinational enterprises has eroded the significance of national boundaries and weakened the ability of either governments or unions in a single country to insulate themselves from external influences. Such firms have often played an important role in 'exporting' personnel management policies and practices from one country to another, especially from their 'home' country to various 'host' countries in which they operate.

In some countries, particularly those which are competing for capital investment by providing cheap labour, laws governing pay and conditions may be changed to attract multinationals. Although it is argued that multinationals often provide good pay and working conditions for their employees in Third World countries, some of these firms have used 'offshore' manufacturing locations to evade the higher pay and stricter regulation of working conditions which have been achieved by unions in their home country. There are, of course, considerable differences in the degree to which a multinational can impose its will on a host country. As Blanpain (1982:18) notes: 'the entities of a multinational enterprise located in various countries are subject to the laws of these countries ... [and have to] manage their business within the framework of law, regulations and prevailing labour relations and employment practices, in each of the countries in which they operate'. Thus, there is a two-way influence between a firm and the countries in which it operates. A multinational must adapt to the local laws and practices, yet it may also use its influence to achieve certain changes in accordance with its own self-interest.

International trade union organisations   The union movement has also developed strategies in an attempt to counter the influence of multinational enterprises. For example, there have been international trade union secretariats for particular crafts or industries since 1889 (Northrup and Rowan, 1979). There are now three main international union confederations: the International Confederation of Free Trade Unions (ICFTU), the World Federation of Trade Unions (WFTU) and the World Confederation of Labour (WCL). The demarcation between them is mainly in terms of political ideology.

The ICFTU is generally anti-communist in its orientation. The American Federation of Labor–Congress of Industrial Organizations (AFL–CIO) rejoined in 1981 after an absence of twelve years, and most of the main union confederations in the nine countries discussed in this book belong to the ICFTU. Most ICFTU activities fall into one of three categories. First, in its representational activities, the ICFTU calls attention to injustices committed by governments or employers. Second, its services, and especially its organisational activities, are largely directed to Third World countries where trade unionism is weak. Third, the ICFTU has fairly self-sufficient regional organisations for Asia and for North and South America, but it is weak in Africa (Windmuller, 1982) and its regional organisation in Europe was disbanded in favour of a more all-inclusive European Trade Union Confederation (ETUC—see below).

The two other main international confederations are the WFTU and the WCL. The principal constituents of the WFTU are in the centrally-planned economies, mainly of Eastern Europe. However, the French Confédération générale du travail (CGT) is also a member. The WCL now has few major members among unions in the western market economies and is much smaller than the other two world bodies. The WCL formerly had a Christian identity, but now has a secular radical socialist ideology. The Confédération française démocratique du travail (CFDT), the second largest French confederation, used to be a major constituent but no longer belongs to the WCL.

There is another small confederation in Europe: the Confédération internationale des cadres (CIC). It aims to represent executive and professional staffs as a 'third force' between capital and labour (Bamber, 1986). However, it includes only a few Western European managerial unions among its membership and has generally been shunned by the mainstream unions at national and international level.

In spite of the activities of these and many other international union organisations, the union movement has found it extremely difficult to exercise much influence over the activities of multinationals. Nevertheless, most unions are concerned about the growing power of multinationals, and consequently their international activities are increasing.

The international trade secretariats (ITSs) bring together individual national unions in particular sectors of industry. They are sometimes referred to as the industrial internationals, since they focus on particular industries or occupations and concentrate on sectors or major companies, rather than wider political issues. For instance, they co-ordinate research on health and safety hazards and new technology in their sectors. They also aim to gather information and to maintain international union solidarity in relation to certain large multinationals. However this is an almost impossible task, as workers' interests in one country often seem to conflict with those in another. The ITSs are autonomous and self-governing organisations, but follow the ICFTU on broad policy issues. Mergers and recruitment have considerably increased the size of the main ITSs in recent years. There are currently 16 ITSs, the largest of which is the International Metalworkers' Federation (IMF) with 168 affiliated unions in 70 countries. Other large ITSs include the Commercial and Clerical Workers (FIET), the Public Service Employees, the Chemical Workers, the Textile Workers and the Transport Workers. A General Conference of ITSs meets about once a year to review common problems and interests.

International governmental organisations   The International Labour Organisation (ILO) is the major forum for international industrial relations activities by governments and employers, as well as by unions. The ILO was founded in 1919 under the First World War peace treaty. The ILO was associated with the League of Nations. Unlike the League, the ILO survived the Second World War and became associated with the United Nations. By 1984, the ILO had 151 member countries. The ILO's structure is illustrated in Figure 1.1.

The ILO has been an important agency for the development of international labour standards (Valticos, 1982:49). Indeed the ILO is the major source of international labour law and of data on international and comparative industrial relations. It has passed about 160 conventions and 170 recommendations, which have had more than 5000 ratifications by over 130 countries. The ILO is also an important source of information on personnel policies and practices throughout the world (Johnston, 1970; Galenson, 1981).[1]

The ILO provides an example of the limits to transferability, despite the fact that it constitutes 'a gigantic exercise in transplantation' (Kahn-Freund, 1976). The ILO, like most other international agencies, is extremely cautious about offending its members and therefore drafts its recommendations in flexible terms. Hence, the obligation on members to promote collective bargaining is tempered by the terms 'by measures appropriate to national conditions' and 'only where necessary'. It is significant that many of the ILO's

Figure 1.1   The structure of the International Labour Organisation

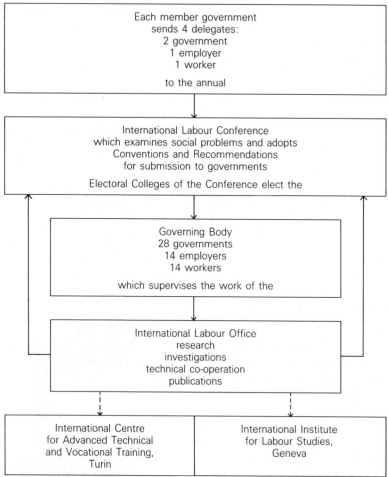

International Labour Organisation

Each member government sends 4 delegates: 2 government 1 employer 1 worker to the annual
International Labour Conference which examines social problems and adopts Conventions and Recommendations for submission to governments Electoral Colleges of the Conference elect the
Governing Body 28 governments 14 employers 14 workers which supervises the work of the
International Labour Office research investigations technical co-operation publications

| International Centre
for Advanced Technical
and Vocational Training,
Turin | International Institute
for Labour Studies,
Geneva |

Source: Reproduced with permission from Smith (1984:23).

conventions and recommendations relate to issues which do not directly impinge upon the power relations between organised labour, employers and governments, such as: protective standards, discrimination in employment and general conditions of work. The ILO cannot compel its members to adhere to particular standards and it is left to governments to decide which ones they will ratify. Furthermore,

the ratification of ILO Conventions by a government does not necessarily mean that it will enforce them and governments may subsequently give a year's notice of deratification.

Within the European Communities (EC) a change in the industrial
relations practices of one country, which results in improved wages
or conditions, can become a precedent used by unions to demand
similar reforms, especially in other member countries. Therefore as
one element in a drive to create a 'common market', the EC aims to
'harmonise' labour laws and fundamental industrial relations practices within the member countries. Both the EC and the Organisation
for Economic Co-operation and Development (OECD) also conduct
research and hold conferences on industrial relations practices which
are relevant to their member countries. Compared with the ILO,
however, industrial relations is not such a major consideration for the
EC and OECD.

Nonetheless, the EC provides another example of the limits to
transferability of industrial relations regulations and processes. The
member countries have generally preserved their separate approaches
to industrial relations despite their attempts to move towards similar
social and economic policies in other spheres (Blanpain, 1982:30).
However, since industrial relations involve issues of the distribution
of power between organised groups in society, any change which
threatens to alter the existing balance of power is likely to meet
resistance from those who feel threatened. Thus, multinationals
strongly opposed both the EC draft (fifth) directive on workers'
participation which was first proposed in 1972, and the 1980 proposal
for a (Vredeling) directive on employees' consultative rights in
multinational enterprises. In each of these cases, the multinationals
feared that they would be unduly constrained by the proposed
reforms. Consequently, by 1986, neither of these directives had been
enacted.

International employers' associations   International employers' organisations generally have a shorter history and play a less prominent
role than their union counterparts. Unlike many employers' organisations at national level, those at the international level began
less as a response to the growth of unions and more as a reaction to
the growth of supranational governmental agencies (Oechslin, 1982).
The origins of the International Organisation of Employers (IOE),
the most prominent employers' group, can be traced back to the first
ILO conference in 1919. The IOE's role has grown since the Second
World War, although its main activities are still focussed on
representing employers' interests at the ILO (see Windmuller and
Gladstone, 1984).

As a parallel to the situation in many individual countries, there is another employers' confederation which places more emphasis on trade and economic matters: the International Chamber of Commerce (ICC). There is a broad division of responsibilites between the IOE and ICC, with the former concentrating on industrial relations issues, but the division is not always clear. Both the IOE and ICC, for example, are concerned about the various attempts to constrain multinationals by unions, governments and international agencies. The employers are less prone than the unions to be divided in terms of political ideology, but the IOE does not admit members from the centrally-planned countries.

There are also regional organisations of employers. The establishment of the EC prompted the formation of the Union of Industries of the European Community (UNICE). Similarly, at the OECD, employers are represented by the Business and Industry Advisory Committee (BIAC).

Prospects and problems

There are many ways in which comparative studies can contribute to knowledge about industrial relations. One of the main reasons why we study the experiences of other societies is to gain a better insight into our own institutions and practices. 'If one's environment never changes in the course of one's life', argues Kahn-Freund, 'one tends to assume that an institution, a doctrine, a practice, a tradition, is inevitable and universal, while in fact it may be the outcome of specific social, historical or geographical conditions of the country' (1979:3).

The study of industrial relations practices in other countries may provide the basis for *reforms* in one's own country and have important implications for public policy. Most countries are confronting social change, whereby institutions, not least those relating to industrial relations, are required to adapt to new circumstances. Labour issues have become increasingly important in international relations. Many countries send labour attachés to their most important foreign embassies. The growth of international commercial and industrial links have made it imperative for governments, employers and unions to be aware of the industrial relations situation prevailing in other countries. For example, the Japanese steel companies aim to forecast their future needs for raw materials to be sure of obtaining appropriate supplies. Therefore, these companies have studied industrial relations in the Australian iron-ore mines and docks, and exploited Australian industrial disputes to their own advantage when negotiating contracts with Australian suppliers (Hill et al., 1983).

A problem which pervades the field of comparative industrial relations is the choice of 'what' and 'how' to compare. As Schregle (1981:16) argues: 'international comparison in industrial relations requires the acceptance of a reference point, a scale of values ... a third factor to which the industrial relations systems or phenomena of the countries being compared can be related'. He illustrates his argument by considering three examples: labour courts and labour disputes, collective agreements, and collective bargaining. In each case there are problems of distinguishing the formal institutions themselves from the functions which they perform. Thus, a comparative study of labour courts in Western European countries immediately encounters the problem that the functions of these bodies differ so markedly. In France, for example, the labour courts deal with individual as distinct from collective disputes, while the Swedish labour court is competent to deal only with disputes arising out of the interpretation of collective agreements. Hence, it is important to compare the *functions* performed by particular institutions, irrespective of the terminology used.

The collection of comparative data also poses problems for those studying this field. For example, the definition of industrial disputes differs between countries (see Appendix, Table A.18). Some authorities distinguish between lockouts by employers and strikes by workers, and between strikes which are officially recognised by a union executive and those which are not. Other countries distinguish between legal and illegal strikes, between plant strikes and industry strikes, or between strikes which are constitutional and those which are not (i.e. in breach of disputes procedures previously agreed between the parties). The criteria used by different countries for collecting statistics on work stoppages also varies. Japan, for example, excludes disputes which last less than four hours and does not take into account the working days lost by workers not directly involved in the dispute. Before 1975, Italy did not count days lost due to political strikes, while France excludes certain industries from its statistics. Australia, on the other hand, includes stoppages which may last for only a few hours that would not be counted either in Britain or the USA. For such reasons, Shalev (1978) cautions against 'lies, damn lies and strike statistics'. Moreover in 1981, the USA increased the minimum size threshold for inclusion in its strike statistics from five workers to 1000. Thus international comparisons became even more difficult (Edwards, 1983:392). Such distinctions make it difficult to compare strike patterns between countries.

Neither in Australia nor Britain is there any distinction between conflicts of right and of interest. But in the USA, Sweden and a growing number of other countries, there is such a distinction. Conflicts of right concern the interpretation of an *existing* rule or award, for example, about which pay grade applies to a particular group of workers. However, conflicts of interest arise during collective bargaining about a *new* claim, for example, for a general pay increase or a reduction in working hours.

In practice, conflicts of interest are usually collective disputes. In France, Italy and many other countries, conflicts of right are further divided into individual and collective disputes. The general intention is that different settlement procedures will apply to the different types of dispute. For example, only conflicts of interest can lead to strikes or other forms of sanction, but conflicts of right must be settled by a binding decision of a labour court or similar body (ILO, 1985:49).

In some countries, a distinction is made between stoppages about *industrial* issues and those which arise over *political* or non-industrial matters. Such distinctions create confusion when attempting to make comparisons.

The lack of a common language and terminology creates other problems. As Blanpain (1982:27) points out: 'identical words in different languages may have different meanings, while corresponding terms may embrace wholly different realities'. He notes that the term 'arbitration' (or 'arbitrage' in French) which usually means a binding decision by an impartial third party, can also signify a recommendation by a government conciliator to the conflicting parties. There can also be difficulties in distinguishing between the law and the actual practice. For example, while Australia has formally practised 'compulsory arbitration' since the beginning of this century, there is relatively little 'compulsion' in practice and the arbitration tribunals rely mainly on advice and persuasion.

A comparative approach can facilitate industrial relations reform by indicating alternative institutions or procedures which other countries have used to solve particular problems. But, programmes of reform based on the experience derived from another context can have unanticipated consequences. As shown in chapter 2, the British government introduced an Industrial Relations Act in 1971 which was based partly on American experiences (such as enforceable contracts, unfair industrial practices etc.). Among other objectives, the Act aimed to constrain unions and thereby reduce the number of disputes. However, the failure of this Act demonstrates the difficulty of attempting to graft industrial relations practices derived from one country on to another.

We cannot take for granted that rules or institutions are transplantable . . . any attempt to use a pattern of law outside the environment of its origin continues to entail the wish for rejection

... Labour law is part of a system, and the consequences of change in one aspect of the system depends upon the relationship between all elements of the system. Since the relationships may not be similar between the two societies, the effects of similar legislation may differ significantly as between the two differing settings' (Kahn-Freund, 1974:27).

An illustration of the way in which institutions are reshaped by different environments may be seen in the former British colonies. Although many of these countries inherited the English legal system and other institutions from Britain, most of them have subsequently modified or transformed this legacy. Many of the American (chapter 3), Canadian (chapter 4) and Australian (chapter 5) approaches to industrial relations are as different from each other as they are from Britain's (chapter 2).

As shown in chapter 10, in Japan, following the Second World War, the occupying forces tried to impose American-type labour laws and managerial techniques. These were not completely rejected, but were subsequently *reshaped* by the Japanese to suit their particular circumstances (Shirai, 1983; Gould, 1984).

Theoretical approaches to comparative industrial relations

Many researchers have criticised the relative lack of theory in the study of industrial relations. This is partly a reflection of the contribution of policy-makers, practitioners and academics, many of whose studies have tended to be predominantly descriptive and without much of an analytical framework. It also reflects the problem of having to amass a large amount of detail of a wide range of countries, before being able to make generalisations. There has also been a tendency to focus on the formal legal structures as a basis for comparison, rather than to address the more complex informal practices and processes of industrial relations. A comparative approach to the study of industrial relations is important not only for policy-formulation, however, but may also assist in the construction of theory in industrial relations. Such an approach can be a useful way of verifying hypotheses or of producing generalisations derived from research findings in a variety of national contexts.

The Webbs (1897) and Commons (1910) laid the foundations for the academic study of industrial relations in the early 1900s in Britain and the USA. Other scholars subsequently added greater depth to industrial relations as a field of study; for example Perlman (1928) and Dunlop (1958) in the USA, and Flanders (1970) and Clegg (1976) in Britain. Nevertheless, there is still no generally accepted theory of industrial relations and we are far from having an agreed analytical approach to international and comparative industrial relations. Walker (1967) urged that we should transcend the dominant descriptive approaches to foreign industrial relations systems and concentrate on identifying the role, importance and interaction of different factors which shape and influence industrial relations in different national contexts. Those who have approached this herculean task are inevitably influenced by their cultural backgrounds.

Ideology is also significant in shaping the framework within which research questions are formulated (Korpi 1981:186–7). Industrial relations research in the English-speaking countries, for example, tends to focus on procedural and institutional approaches to problem-solving, predominantly within a pluralist framework. Some American and British writers have also tried to formulate broader theories to explain similarities and differences between countries. Within a radical left perspective, industrial relations issues tend to be seen as only one component of a larger concern with economic and social change and relationships between classes. In some countries (such as Sweden and France), there is a combination of approaches, so that Marxist-oriented research is tempered by a pragmatic orientation towards public policy (Doeringer et al. 1981). Another approach has been developed by political economists working in the USA. In the next section of this chapter we illustrate these approaches and indicate their strengths and weaknesses.

Systems theory Following Parsons and Smelser (1956), Dunlop (1958) developed an approach based on a notion of an 'industrial relations system'. This includes three sets of actors and their representative organisations ('the three parties'): employers, workers, and the state. These parties' relations are determined by three environmental contexts:

1 the technology;
2 market forces; and
3 the relative power and status of the parties.

Dunlop defined *the network of rules* which govern the workplace (e.g. the web of rules about pay and conditions) as the output of the industrial relations system.

Dunlop's (1958) approach has been influential among scholars in the English-speaking countries and elsewhere, and it was an important attempt to identify a theoretical framework for industrial relations. Other scholars have also modified or developed Dunlop's basic approach (e.g. Blain and Gennard, 1970; Craig, 1975). Various critics accept that Dunlop's framework is useful as 'a model within which facts may be organised, but stress that it must not be understood as having a predictive value in itself' (Gill, 1969). Criticisms of the systems approach include its neglect of the importance of such behavioural variables as motivations, perceptions and attitudes (Bain and Clegg, 1974); moreover, it tends to concentrate on the rule-making institutions and the settlement of conflict, rather than examining the causes of conflict and the role played by people in making decisions about the employment relationship (Hyman, 1975).

Convergence theories   A more ambitious American theory argued that industrial societies will gradually tend to become more alike. Although first published in 1960, the arguments of Kerr et al. (1973) remain influential, especially in the English-speaking countries. Their core proposition was that there is a world-wide tendency for techno-logical and market forces associated with industrialisation to push national industrial relations systems towards uniformity or 'conver-gence'. They argued that there is a logic of industrialism, even though the process has various patterns in different countries. Among the 'universals' of the logic are the development of a concentrated, disci-plined work force with new and changing skills, and a larger role for governments in providing the infrastructure required for industrial-isation. An essential part of the logic of industrialism is the growth or imposition of a pluralistic consensus which provides an integrated body of ideas and beliefs. Each industrialising society develops an industrial relations system, which becomes increasingly tripartite as industrialisation proceeds.

Figure 1.2 illustrates schematically the logic of industrialism, showing how the various social changes are related to the prime cause: technology. Convergence between advanced industrial so-cieties occurs most readily at the technological level, at plant and industry levels, or urban levels and then ultimately at national levels. However, Kerr et al. did concede that total convergence was unlikely because of the persistence of political, social, cultural and ideological differences. Kerr later (1983) modified his views and argued that convergence is a *tendency* that is not likely to precipitate identical systems among industrialised countries. He also noted that while advanced industrial societies at the macro-level might appear to be similar, differences at the micro-level could be quite profound. Furthermore, industrialisation on a world-wide scale is never likely to be total, because the barriers to it in many less-developed countries are insurmountable. Nevertheless, he still held the central assump-tions of the original study, namely, that the basic tensions inherent in the process of industrialisation had been overcome by modern industrial societies and that there would be a growing consensus around liberal–democratic institutions and the pluralist mixed eco-

Figure 1.2   The logic of industrialism

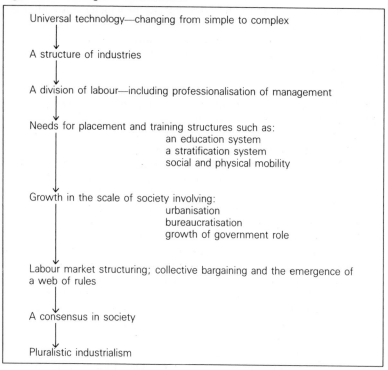

Universal technology—changing from simple to complex

A structure of industries

A division of labour—including professionalisation of management

Needs for placement and training structures such as:
an education system
a stratification system
social and physical mobility

Growth in the scale of society involving:
urbanisation
bureaucratisation
growth of government role

Labour market structuring; collective bargaining and the emergence of a web of rules

A consensus in society

Pluralistic industrialism

Source: Reproduced with permission from Brown and Harrison (1978:129).

nomy. Relations between 'managers and the managed' would be increasingly embedded in a web of rules agreed to by both parties, so that industrial conflict would 'wither away' (see Ross and Hartman, 1960).

Many writers have criticised the 'liberal–pluralist' approach of Kerr et al. For example, Chamberlain (1961) saw their book as

> long on categories and classifications and impressionistic observations, but ... short on analysis. It is perhaps best described as a latter-day descendant of the 19th century German school of economic history, whose hallmark was a literary exposition of the transition from one idealized state of economic development to another.

Other critics have focussed on the 'deterministic view of the future' represented by industrialisation as an 'invincible process' (Cochrane, 1976). According to Bendix (1970:273), 'seldom has social change been interpreted in so *magisterial* a fashion, while all contingencies of action are treated as mere historical variations which cannot alter the logic of industrialism'. Arguably, Kerr et al. were too concerned with maintaining the *status quo*, controlling conflict, defending the existing institutions and imposing an ethnocentric, American perspective on the rest of the world.

Partial convergence theories   Doeringer (1981) is less critical, but argues that convergence should be seen in a different form from that envisaged by Kerr et al. Doeringer argues that countries develop alternative solutions to problems common to all industrial relations systems. Thus, all industrialised countries show a tendency to institutionalise their arrangements for making the rules of industrial relations, even though their particular approaches vary. Differences between countries, therefore, are not simply random but rooted in their individual responses to the underlying compulsions of industrialisation. He analyses convergence using a three-part framework: firstly, as the result of responses to problems common to all industrial relations systems; secondly, as the process by which gaps in areas in the institutional arrangements of industrial relations systems are filled; and thirdly, as the realisation that, over time, all industrial relations systems selectively respond to multiple and often incompatible goals. Hence, what may appear as differences between systems may be due simply to differences in the goals which are being pursued at a particular point in time.

Another American writer also doubts that the thesis is a general theory of comparative industrial relations. Thus Piore (1981) observes that certain aspects of industrial societies tend to converge while others diverge, depending upon time and circumstances. An alternative approach suggested by Piore is to focus on the role of regulatory institutions in the industrial relations of different societies. He argues that capitalist economies pass through a distinct series of regulatory systems in the course of their historical development. As technology and industry change over time, they outgrow the regulatory structures initially adopted and the system has increasing difficulty maintaining itself in balance. The result is an economic and social crisis which can only be resolved by the development of a new set of institutions.

Kassalow argues that there will still be 'vast differences as between labour relations institutions in communist and capitalist countries' even if convergence takes place. Hence he concludes that 'the largest work of comparative labour study lies in exploring and explaining these differences, even more than the similarities' (1976:302).

In comparison with the work of Kerr et al. and that inspired by it, Dore (1973) has a more modest approach. He too aims to account for international differences, but he focusses on Japan and Britain. Dore places less emphasis on technology than Kerr et al., and highlights the importance of other factors: the emergence of giant corporations and the spread of democratic ideals of egalitarianism.

In examining Japanese industrial relations, Dore identifies a 'late-comer' effect; since Japan industrialised relatively late (half a century after Britain), it was able to learn from the experience of the countries which had already industrialised. Thus, Dore argues that late-developers have been able to adopt organisational forms and institutions which are more suited to industrialisation than are those of countries which industrialised relatively early. Dore concludes that employment systems are becoming more alike, but it is Japan, rather than any Western country, which is the model to which other countries are converging. There have been general criticisms of Dore's thesis and specific criticisms of some of his detailed interpretation. However, his overall approach has considerable potential in this field. According to Shalev: 'by concentrating on only two country cases and dealing with these cases in a consistently and systematically comparative fashion, Dore succeeded in minimising the danger of lapsing into either vacuous description or superficial comparison' (1980:40).

Collective bargaining approaches Dunlop's systems approach has influenced several other writers who, in comparison with the convergence theorists, have focussed on particular institutions. For example, Clegg (1976) concentrates on unions and on collective bargaining. Drawing on data from six of the nine countries represented in this book, he argues that variations in the dimensions of collective bargaining are the main influences on union behaviour. Clegg defines union behaviour as: their density of membership, external structure, internal government, workplace organisation, strikes, attitudes to industrial democracy and political action.

For Clegg, collective bargaining covers both the negotiation and the administration of agreements. In spite of the usual distinction between collective bargaining and arbitration, many arbitration awards in Australia are in fact the outcome of collective bargaining (see our chapter 5 and Niland, 1978). Thus the distinction is not between collective bargaining and arbitration, but between collective bargaining and either political action or unilateral regulation.

Clegg identifies six dimensions of collective bargaining, as follows: extent, level, depth, union security, degree of control and scope. He contends that:

> The extent and depth of collective bargaining and the degree of union security offered by collective bargaining are the three dimensions which influence trade union density. The level of

bargaining accounts for the extent of decentralisation in union government, including the power and independence of workplace organisations, and decentralisation in turn helps to explain the degree of factionalism within unions . . . (1976:118).

Clegg argues that the dimensions of collective bargaining are themselves mainly determined by the structures of management and of employers' organisations; 'but where the law has intervened in the early stages, it may have played an equally important part, or even a more important part, in shaping collective bargaining' (1976:118). He submits that the theory is confirmed by data from five countries. However, it is not so applicable in France, 'because collective bargaining is not the main method of trade union action there' (1976:119). Political action is more important for French unions, but Clegg fails to find a simple explanation for this.

Clegg's approach is narrower than Dunlop's, as Clegg seems to ignore the economic, social and technological environment, while concentrating on collective bargaining and the 'web of rules'. Clegg holds that collective bargaining is the principal influence on union behaviour, yet unions are part of collective bargaining. Thus, it is unclear which is cause and which is effect in Clegg's theory. While Clegg does not provide an adequate theory of union behaviour, his approach does provide a stimulus for those who wish to construct theories of comparative industrial relations. Ideally, however, such theories would also have to explain the behaviour of managers, employers' organisations and governments, rather than accepting it as given, as Clegg does.

Radical approaches Most of the writers mentioned in the paragraphs above could be described as liberal pluralists, in terms of their ideological presuppositions. The most far-reaching critique of the orthodox pluralist approaches to the study of industrial relations has been made by radical scholars (e.g. Mills, 1959; Mandel, 1969). Such critics argue that the orthodox approaches are parochial and generally ignore the world outside a narrow definition of industrial relations. They hold that, at most, the wider society is included in the pluralist's models only through narrowly circumscribed channels of 'adjustment' and 'feedback' (Hyman, 1980).

Most Marxists, for example, generally see industrial relations merely as derivative of the patterns of economic ownership, political domination and of relations of production. Therefore much Marxist research has been concerned with examining such broader issues as capital accumulation and class struggle.

Largely inspired by Braverman (1974), however, there has been a revival of radical analyses of the labour process, sometimes in a comparative perspective (e.g. Littler, 1982). Yet Marxists tend not to see it as either desirable or possible to formulate a Marxian theory of industrial relations:

> To argue thus would be to accept the theoretical coherence of 'industrial relations' as an area of analysis: to endorse the material and theoretical *autonomy* of institutionalised management–union relations. For the same reason, any search for a radical *redefinition* of 'industrial relations' must be self-defeating (Hyman, 1980:55).

In spite of this view Marxists have contributed important work on issues which impinge on our field. For example, Beynon (1984) vividly illustrates how a powerful multinational enterprise may behave in a host country. Miliband (1977) and others have focussed on the increasingly pervasive role of the state in capitalist production and in the conduct of labour–management relations.

Radical writers have analysed forms of segmentation of the labour market into, for example, primary and secondary markets (e.g. Edwards et al., 1975); women and migrants are usually confined to the secondary segments. Marxists have also demonstrated that the practical struggles of women and migrants should not be located merely within the framework of a 'national industrial relations system'. The position of women demands analysis not only in the world of work, but also in terms of the more general processes of social production and reproduction in the wider society (Brown, 1984).

Like Kerr et al., Marxists have tended to foresee a convergence of industrial societies. However they see it as a 'logic of capitalism', fuelled by its own contradictions. Most Marxists have not explicitly focussed on the detailed strategies and tactics of unions, employers and governments in the labour market. We generally have to infer the Marxist interpretations of industrial relations from writing which is addressed to other issues.

Political economists' approaches: towards divergence? Recent work by certain political economists has drawn upon social, political and economic theory in an attempt to compare some aspects of industrial relations. They have argued that the pluralists have either ignored or denied the interaction between politics (or power relations) and industrial relations, while the Marxists have not provided a satisfactory framework for analysing the labour market and associated political processes.

Several political economists who have contributed to this field are associated with the Harvard Centre for European Studies. In two volumes which deal with union strategy and political economy in five Western European countries (Lange et al., 1982; Gourevitch et al.,

1984), the Harvard group has put a strong case in favour of a 'divergence thesis', arguing that, in those sectors where it has representation, the union movement has responded to the economic crisis since the early 1970s in quite different ways (also see Goldthorpe, 1984). Four broad approaches are identified in the responses of Western European unions. First a *maximalist* response is associated with some of the French unions, especially those on the left, as demonstrated by their refusal to play any role in the 'management of the crisis' at the firm, sectoral or national levels. This is seen as an illustration of the subordination of union policy to the strategic and tactical interests of the French Communist Party, with the CGT playing the role of a 'transmission belt' for the Party (see our chapter 7). Second, an *interventionist* approach characterises some of the Italian unions, which have tried to intervene at the firm, sectoral and national levels in order to develop incremental policies to relieve the economic crisis (see our chapter 6). Third, a *defensive–particularistic* strategy occurs where groups of workers seek to protect themselves, in the face of income and job insecurity, using rank and file power bases to veto changes. This is seen as characteristic of some British unions (see our chapter 2). Fourth, a *corporatist* strategy is associated with unions which collaborate with the state and employers in areas such as incomes policies and broader economic and social programmes. This approach is epitomised by unions in Sweden and, to some extent, in West Germany, especially during periods of Social Democratic government (see our chapters 8 and 9). These categories are not intended to fit different national union movements with precision, but are merely intended as ideal–typical illustrations of how unions differ both within and between the countries of Western Europe.

Lange et al. also outline four different characteristics which distinguish these union movements: market strength, political influence, inter-union relationships and expectations. While these writers are able to demonstrate the existence of important differences between the union movements of Western Europe, they rather neglect such areas of common interest as confronting multinationals and defending members' job security. They also focus on a rather limited period, namely 1945–80 in general and the 1970s in particular. Indeed, events since the publication of the first volume, concerning for example the accommodation between some of the French unions and the Mitterrand government, illustrate the current difficulty of predicting even a few years ahead. A more important limitation of this approach, however, is the focus on the macro-level and the neglect of perspectives from the 'rank and file'. For this reason, they emphasise the role of the state and the role of union confederations, which although important are only two elements in the wider spectrum of industrial relations.

Strategic choice: a new direction? There is another recent approach from the pluralist tradition of collective bargaining specialists. Kochan et al. (1984) is notable, because although it focusses on the changing patterns of American industrial relations, it does have a comparative application. Kochan et al. argue for the addition of a dynamic component to existing forms of analysis, which they call 'strategic choice'. They also advance a model or framework that differentiates between three levels of decision-making within employer, union and government organisations and which identifies the relatively independent effects of these levels on industrial relations.

The concept of strategic choice is not new and has previously been used in economics and organisational behaviour, but there are considerable differences in the way the concept is used. Kochan et al. use a matrix to encompass the three levels of strategic decision-making. As shown in Figure 1.3, the columns of the matrix represent the three key parties who make strategic decisions. The rows represent the levels at which these decisions are made. The effects of particular decisions, however, may appear at levels other than those where the decisions are made.

Examples of strategic decisions made at different levels are illustrated in Figure 1.3. Strategic choices in the bottom row are those associated with individual workers or work groups and their relations with the immediate work environment. In the middle row are decisions associated with the practice of collective bargaining and implications of personnel policy. Strategic choice in the top row is concerned with macro or organisation-wide matters. For instance, Kochan et al. point out that in view of their job control traditions in the USA, unions have not generally emphasised decisions at this highest level, although this may change in the future. By contrast, Western European unions have been more involved in the decisions at the highest level, within the tradition of tripartite discussions between governments, unions and employers.

The emphasis given by the different parties to decisions at various levels tends to change according to circumstances. The greater attention given by American employers to macro-level strategy in recent years has initiated a fundamental change in industrial relations in the USA (see chapter 3). Shifts in business strategies, for example, are affected by the current state of industrial relations which in turn affect future industrial relations outcomes at all three levels.

A strategic choice model of industrial relations may provide a framework for examining differences in industrial relations practices

Figure 1.3 Industrial relations strategy matrix

| Decision level | Nature of decisions | | |
	Employers	Unions	Government
I Macro or global level for the key institutions	The strategic role of human resources; policies on unions; investments; plant location; new technology; and outsourcing	Political roles (e.g. relations with political parties and other interest groups); union organizing (e.g. neutrality and corporate campaigns); public policy objectives (e.g. labor law reform); and economic policies (e.g full employment)	Macro economic and social policies; industrial policy (protection vs. free trade)
II Employment relationship and industrial relations system	Personnel policies and negotiations and strategies	Collective bargaining policies and negotiations strategies (employment vs. income)	Labor and employment standards law; direct involvement via incomes policies or dispute settlement
III Work place: individuals and groups	Contractual or bureaucratic; and individual employee/ workgroup participation	Policies on employee participation; introduction of new technology; work organization design	Regulations of worker rights and/or employee participation

Source: Reproduced with permission from Kochan, McKersie and Cappelli (1984:23).

at the levels of national and corporate policy-making, collective bargaining and workplace interactions. The model is not a substitute for studying the dimensions of collective bargaining and the broader social and political context, but it can help us to understand the dynamics of industrial relations. The importance of strategies developed by employers, unions or government varies between countries in accordance with the prevailing values, ideologies and power relationships. Furthermore, the strategies which dominate industrial relations in a particular firm, industry or country vary over time. Therefore, though not yet a complete theory with testable propositions, this model may provide a step on the way to developing a new framework for the study of comparative industrial relations.

Towards a new typology for comparative studies?

Drawing upon studies of the impact of technological change on industrial relations in various countries, Bamber and Lansbury (1983) suggest that in societies which have a predominantly adversarial approach to industrial relations (such as Britain, Australia, and perhaps the USA and Canada too), the parties find it more difficult to cope with technological change than those which have more of a social partnership approach to industrial relations (such as West Germany, Sweden, Norway and Denmark). For the convenience of discussion, they label the former as Type I countries and the latter as Type II.

Although each of the countries within each group differ in many respects, Type I countries share a common inheritance of occupationally-based unionism, relatively weak central union and employer associations, a less consistent role played by governments in industrial relations (depending upon which political party holds office) and adversarial traditions of labour–management relations, which mean that their negotiations tend to concentrate on how the wealth is to be *distributed* in society.

By contrast, the Type II countries tend to have industry-wide unions (except for Denmark), strong central union and employer organisations, and generally a more consensual approach to industrial relations. These Type II countries have had a tradition of social partnership since the Second World War. This has enabled unions to become more involved in the process of wealth *creation*. There has also been a higher degree of agreement, planning and co-ordination in the Type II countries. By contrast, in the Type I countries, unions and governments have not often achieved such a broad consensus on incomes policies and on issues such as the introduction of technological change and employee participation in the management of enterprises.

Of course the pattern of industrial relations in a particular country is not immutable. A change of government and dominant political ideology may induce a shift in a country which formerly had a pre-dominantly adversarial (or Type I) tradition to one which has more of a social partnership (or Type II) approach. As shown in chapter 5, this happened to an extent in Australia after 1983, where the incoming Labor government concluded an 'Accord' with the trade union movement on a range of economic and political issues and sought to develop a social partnership approach to industrial relations (Lansbury, 1985). Other countries may almost fit either Type I or II. Hence, while the English-speaking countries can be described as Type I, others such as Italy and France have some similar characteristics. By contrast, while the northern European countries are prime examples of Type II, perhaps Japan also shares some similar characteristics.

The challenge of explanation

Having discussed several theoretical approaches, it is apparent that none is yet completely adequate. Various pluralists provide some categories which are useful ways for organising our work, but they tend to have a restricted focus and make naive assumptions about the inevitability of consensus. Certain radical writers usefully focus attention on some current issues and on the rank and file workers themselves, but Marxists tend to over-emphasise the 'inevitability' of greater class conflict in capitalist societies. They also tend to deny any autonomy to industrial relations processes, while the pluralists tend to exaggerate such autonomy. The reality is that class and industrial relations issues are both important, as shown by the work of political economists.

Each approach is partial. The political economists show how there has been a growing divergence, even between Western European nations. They provide some convincing explanations of national union strategies in the polity, but neglect the increasing initiating role played by employers. On the other hand, the importance of managerial strategies is highlighted by the work of Clegg (1976) and Kochan et al. (1984), and by some recent analyses of the labour process. Some of the most illuminating studies of the detail and actual processes on the shop floor have been by Dore (1973) and by some of the more sensitive analysts of the labour process.

When analysing the patterns of labour–management relations in their own countries, our authors have generally been most influenced by the pluralist approaches. But readers should themselves draw selectively from other approaches in an attempt to make sense of the various aspects of the complex realities of the real world. That is the challenge ahead for students of international and comparative industrial relations.

Abbreviations

AFL–CIO	American Federation of Labor–Congress of Industrial Organizations
BIAC	Business and Industry Advisory Committee (OECD)
CFDT	Confédération francaise démocratique du travail (French Democratic Federation of Labour)
CGT	Confédération générale du travail (General Confederation of Labour)
CIC	Confédération internationale des cadres (International Confederation of Executive Staffs)
EC	European Communities
ETUC	European Trade Union Confederation
FIET	Fédération internationale des employés techniciens et cadres (International Federation of Commercial, Clerical, Professional and Technical Employees)
ICC	International Chamber of Commerce
ICFTU	International Confederation of Free Trade Unions
ILO	International Labour Organisation
IMF	International Metalworkers' Federation
IOE	International Organisation of Employers
ITS	International Trade Secretariat
OECD	Organisation for Economic Co-operation and Development
TUAC	Trade Union Advisory Committee (OECD)
UNICE	Union of Industries of the European Community
WCL	World Confederation of Labour
WFTU	World Confederation of Trade Unions

Note

1 Apart from the many publications of the ILO and its International Institute for Labour Studies, Bennett and Fawcett (1985) is one of the most useful sources of references on international and comparative industrial relations. Selected references are cited on each of the countries in this book, at the end of the appropriate chapter.

References

Bain, G.S. and Clegg, H.A. (1974) 'A Strategy for Industrial Relations Research in Great Britain' *British Journal of Industrial Relations* 12, 1 (Mar.), pp. 91–113

Bamber, G.J. (1986) *Militant Managers? Managerial Unionism and Industrial Relations* Aldershot: Gower

Bamber, G.J. and Lansbury, R.D. (1983) 'A Comparative Perspective on Technological Change and Industrial Relations' *Proceedings of the 36th Conference of the Industrial Relations Research Association* Madison: IRRA. pp. 92–9

Barrett, B., Rhodes, E. and Beishon, J. eds (1975) *Industrial Relations and the Wider Society* London: Collier Macmillan

Bean, R. (1985) *Comparative Industrial Relations* London: Croom Helm

Bendix, R. (1970) *Embattled Reason* New York: Oxford University Press

Bennett, J. and Fawcett, J. eds. (1985) *Industrial Relations: An International and Comparative Bibliography* London: Mansell/British Universities Industrial Relations Association

Beynon, H. (1984) *Working for Ford* 2nd edn Harmondsworth: Penguin

Blain, A.N. and Gennard, J. (1970) 'Industrial Relations Theory: A Critical Review' *British Journal of Industrial Relations*, 8, 3(Nov.), pp. 389–407

Blanpain, R. (1982) 'Comparativism in Labour Law and Industrial Relations' in Blanpain et al. (1982), pp. 17–33

Blanpain, R. et al. eds (1982) *Comparative Labour Law and Industrial Relations* Deventer: Kluwer (2nd edn, 1985)

Braverman, H. (1974) *Labor and Monopoly Capital* New York: Monthly Review Press

Brown, D. and Harrison, M.J. (1978) *A Sociology of Industrialisation* London: Macmillan

Brown, R.K. (1984) 'Work: Past, Present and Future' in K. Thompson ed. *Work, Employment and Unemployment* Milton Keynes: Open University Press, pp. 261–75

Chamberlain, N.W. (1961) Book review of Kerr et al. (1960) in *American Economic Review* (June)

Clegg, H.A. (1976) *Trade Unionism Under Collective Bargaining: A Theory Based on Comparisons of Six Countries* Oxford: Blackwell

Cochrane, J.L. (1976) 'Industrialism and Industrial Man in Retrospect: A Preliminary Analysis' in Stern and Dennis (1977), pp. 274–87

Commons, J.R. (1910) *A Documentary History of American Industrial Society* Cleveland: Clark

Craig, A. (1975) 'The Framework for the Analysis of Industrial Relations Systems' in Barrett et al. (1975), pp. 8–20

Doeringer, P.B. (1981) 'Industrial Relations Research in International Perspective' in Doeringer et al. (1981), pp. 1–21

Doeringer, P.B. et al. eds (1981) *Industrial Relations in International Perspective: Essays on Research and Policy* London: Macmillan

Dore, R. (1973) *British Factory, Japanese Factory: The Origins of National Diversity in Industrial Relations* London: George Allen & Unwin

Dunlop, J.T. (1958) *Industrial Relations Systems* New York: Holt, Rinehart & Winston

Edwards, P.K. (1983) 'The End of American Strike Statistics' *British Journal of Industrial Relations* 21, 3 (Nov.), pp. 392–4

Edwards, R.C. et al. (1975) *Labor Market Segmentation* Lexington: Heath

Flanders, A. (1970) *Management and Unions: The Theory and Reform of Industrial Relations* London: Faber

Galenson, W. (1981) *The International Labour Organization: An American View* Madison: University of Wisconsin Press

Gill, J. (1969) 'One Approach to the Teaching of Industrial Relations' *British Journal of Industrial Relations* 7, 2 (Jul.), pp. 265–72

Goldthorpe, J.H. (1984) 'The End of Convergence: Corporatist and Dualist Tendencies in Modern Western Societies' in J.H. Goldthorpe ed. *Order and Conflict in Contemporary Capitalism: Studies in the Political Economy of Western European Nations* Oxford: Clarendon, pp. 315–44

Gould, W.B. (1984) *Japan's Reshaping of American Labor Law* Cambridge, Mass.: MIT Press

Gourevitch, P. et al. (1981) 'Industrial Relations and Politics: Some Reflections' in Doeringer et al. (1981) pp. 401–16

Gourevitch, P. et al. (1984) *Unions and Economic Crisis: Britain, West Germany and Sweden* London: George Allen & Unwin

Hill, J.D. et al. (1983) *Industrial Relations: An Australian Introduction* Melbourne: Longman Cheshire

Hyman, R. (1975) *Industrial Relations: A Marxist Introduction* London: Macmillan

—— (1980) 'Theory in Industrial Relations: Towards a Materialist Analysis' in P. Boreham and G. Dow eds *Work and Inequality Vol. 2: Ideology and Control in the Labour Process* Melbourne: Macmillan, pp. 38–59

ILO (1985) *World Labour Report 2: Labour Relations, International Labour Standards, Training, Conditions of Work, Women at Work* Geneva: International Labour Office

Johnston, G.A. (1970) *The International Labour Organisation: Its Work for Social and Economic Progress* London: Europa

Kahn-Freund, O. (1974) 'On Uses and Misuses of Comparative Law' *The Modern Law Review* 37, 1 (Jan.), pp. 1–27

—— (1976) 'The European Social Charter' in F.G. Jacobs ed. *European Law and the Individual* Amsterdam: North Holland, pp. 181–211

—— (1979) *Labour Relations: Heritage and Adjustment* Oxford: Oxford University Press

Kassalow, E. (1976) Discussion of Kerr et al. (1960) in Stern and Dennis (1977), pp. 298–302

Kerr, C. (1983) *The Future of Industrial Societies: Convergence or Continuing Diversity?* Cambridge, Mass.: Harvard University Press

Kerr, C. et al. (1960) *Industrialism and Industrial Man: The Problems of Labour and Management in Economic Growth* Harmondsworth: Penguin (Rev. edn, 1973)

Kochan, T.A. (1980) *Collective Bargaining and Industrial Relations* Homewood: Irwin

Kochan, T.A. et al. (1984) 'Strategic Choice and Industrial Relations Theory' *Industrial Relations* 23, 1 (Winter), pp. 16–39

Korpi, W. (1981) 'Sweden: Conflict, Power and Politics in Industrial Relations' in Doeringer et al. (1981), pp. 185–217

Lange, P. et al. (1982) *Unions, Change and Crisis: French and Italian Unions and the Political Economy, 1945–1980* London: George Allen & Unwin

Lansbury, R.D. (1981) 'Prospects for Industrial Democracy under Liberal

Capitalism' in R.D. Lansbury ed. *Democracy in the Work Place* Melbourne: Longman Cheshire, pp. 228–41

—— (1985) 'The Accord Between the Unions and Government in Australia: A New Experiment in Industrial Relations?' *Labour and Society* 10, 2, pp. 223–34

Littler, C. (1982) *The Development of the Labour Process in Capitalist Societies: A Comparative Study of the Transformation of Work Organisation in Britain, Japan and the USA* London: Heinemann

Mandel, E. (1969) *A Socialist Strategy for Europe* Institute for Workers' Control Pamphlet No 10, Nottingham: IWC

Marx, K. and Engels, F. (1958) *Selected Works* Moscow: Foreign Languages Publishing House

Miliband, R. (1977) *Marxism and Politics* Oxford: Oxford University Press

Mills, C. Wright (1959) *The Sociological Imagination* New York: Oxford University Press

Niland, J.R. (1978) *Collective Bargaining and Compulsory Arbitration in Australia* Sydney: New South Wales University Press

Northrup, H.P. and Rowan, R.L. (1979) *Multinational Collective Bargaining Attempts: The Record, the Cases and the Prospects* Philadelphia: Industrial Research Unit, The Wharton School, University of Pennsylvania

Oechslin, J. (1982) 'Employers Organisations' in Blanpain et al. (1982), pp. 190–205

Parsons, T. and Smelser, N.J. (1956) *Economy and Society: A Study in the Integration of Economy and Social Theory* London: Routledge & Kegan Paul

Perlman, S. (1928) *A Theory of the Labor Movement* New York: Augustus Kelley

Piore, M.J. (1981) 'Convergence in Industrial Relations? The Case of France and the United States' *Working Paper* No 286, Department of Economics, Cambridge, Mass: Massachusetts Institute of Technology

Reynaud, J.D. (1981) 'Industrial Relations Research in France 1960–75: A Review' in Doeringer et al. (1981), pp. 246–86

Ross, A.M. and Hartman, P.T. (1960) *Changing Patterns of Industrial Conflict* New York: Wiley

Schregle, J. (1981) 'Comparative Industrial Relations: Pitfalls and Potential' *International Labour Review* 120, 1 (Jan.–Feb.), pp. 15–30

Shalev, M. (1978) 'Lies, Damned Lies and Strike Statistics: the Measurement of Trends in Industrial Conflict' in Crouch, C. and Pizzorno, A. eds *The Resurgence of Class Conflict in Western Europe Since 1968, Vol 1: National Studies* London: Macmillan, pp. 1–20

—— (1980) 'Industrial Relations Theory and the Comparative Study of Industrial Relations and Industrial Conflict' *British Journal of Industrial Relations* 18, 1 (Mar.), pp. 26–43

Shirai, T. ed. (1983) *Contemporary Industrial Relations in Japan* Madison: University of Wisconsin Press

Smith, F. (1984) 'What is the International Labour Organisation?' *International Labour Reports* 6 (Nov.–Dec.), pp. 23–4

Stern, J.L. and Dennis, B.D. eds (1977) *Proceedings of the Twenty-ninth*

Annual Winter Meetings, Industrial Relations Research Association Series Madison: IRRA

Valticos, N. (1982) 'International Labour Law' in Blanpain et al. (1982), pp. 49–64

Walker, K.F. (1967) 'The Comparative Study of Industrial Relations' *Bulletin of the International Institute for Labour Studies* 3 (Nov.), pp. 105–32

Webb, S. and Webb, B. (1897) *Industrial Democracy* London: Longman

Windmuller, J.P. (1982) 'International Trade Union Movement' in Blanpain et al. (1982), pp. 98–116

Windmuller, J.P. and Gladstone, A. eds (1984) *Employers Associations and Industrial Relations: A Comparative Study* Oxford: Oxford University Press/International Institute of Labour Studies

II
English-speaking countries

2 | British industrial relations

GREG BAMBER AND ED SNAPE

In this chapter, we begin by putting British industrial relations into context. We discuss unions and employers and go on to look at collective bargaining as the most important form of job regulation in Britain. We then examine the role of the state and conclude with a review of some issues of current and future importance.

Britain[1] has a total population of 56 million people; 42 per cent of them are in civilian employment (see Appendix). It has relatively fewer people employed in agriculture (2.6 per cent of civilian employees) than any other OECD country. About 33 per cent of its civilian employees work in industry; the remaining 64 per cent work in the services sector. There has been a greater decline in the industrial sector since 1970 than in any of the other countries in this book. The decline has been most acute since 1979 and was probably exacerbated by Britain's economic policies (see later) and by it becoming an oil producer in 1975, which tended to boost its exchange rate. In spite of the relative growth of the services sector, there has been a steep rise in unemployment, from 1.4 per cent of the working population in 1965, to 4.1 per cent in 1975 and over 13 per cent by 1986. In 1985, Britain had a higher unemployment rate than any other country covered in this book.

Britain's GDP was US $438 billion by 1985. Its annual average increase in GDP for the period 1978–83 was 0.8 per cent, less than in any of the other eight countries, and its GDP per capita in 1984 was $7495. (This appears to be less than in any of the other countries except Italy: $6114.)

Britain's average annual increase in consumer prices during the

33

English-speaking countries

Table 2.1   The governing party in Britain from 1945–

1945–51	Labour
1951–64	Conservative
1964–70	Labour
1970–74	Conservative
1974–79	Labour
1979–	Conservative

Source: Whitaker (1984:319)

period 1979–84 (9.5 per cent) was just above average of the countries included in this book (8.9 per cent). However, Britain's relative position had been worse in the 1970s. By 1985, its annual rate of inflation had fallen to 5.7 per cent per annum.

Government revenue is 43 per cent of GDP, which is about average for the nine countries. However, the average take-home pay in Britain is only 73 per cent of gross earnings. This is about the same as in West Germany, but is a lower percentage than in any of the countries except Sweden (66 per cent).[2]

British politics have been dominated by two political parties since the First World War. Table 2.1 summarises the pattern of party government since the Second World War. The Conservative Party is on the right of the political spectrum. Its support is strongest in the more prosperous south of England, and more generally amongst the business and farming communities which provide much of its income. The Labour Party is on the left of British politics. Its support is strongest in Wales, Scotland and the north of England, particularly in manual working-class communities. The Labour Party is mainly funded by the unions.

There are several other political parties. In 1981 a few Labour Members of Parliament broke away to set up the Social Democratic Party. They formed an electoral Alliance with the small, but long-established Liberal Party, with the aim of ending the domination of the two main parties and establishing a force in the centre of British politics. In the 1983 general election, the share of the popular vote was 44 per cent Conservative, 28 per cent Labour and 26 per cent Alliance. This represents a rapid growth for the Alliance and a considerable decline in the Labour share, since its all-time high of 49 per cent in 1951. However, the British Parliament is elected on the basis of 'first past the post' in each constituency and since the Conservative and Labour parties' votes are concentrated in particular strongholds, the Alliance has found it difficult to win many parliamentary seats.

Although the Alliance had made some significant gains in local elections and had received considerable support in opinion polls and in the media, in 1983 it won only 3.5 per cent of the seats. Thus it had not yet made an electoral breakthrough sufficient to be generally seen as a credible contender for national government, though it could perhaps win the balance of power in a future general election.

There are nationalist parties in Wales and Scotland. They each had two seats in Parliament in 1986. Their degree of electoral success was greater in the 1970s, but they have generally been a minor force in British politics.

Britain has a very small Communist Party, which has no seats in Parliament. Nevertheless, it has been influential in some unions, and it contributes to policy debates on the left. Compared with Italy and France, relatively few people in the British labour movement have embraced revolutionary political ideologies. In spite of some rhetoric, leading members of most unions and of the Labour Party have generally been committed to reforming, rather than abolishing, the market economy.

The industrial relations parties

The bonding between 'masters' and 'men' which once held British society together was collapsing by the sixteenth century. Even before industrialisation, the early capitalists were changing the basis of society. Workers were seen as 'hands', as expendable resources for whom the employer had no responsibility beyond the legal obligations of contract (Fox, 1985). Workers responded to this view and by the early nineteenth century had begun to organise collectively to defend themselves in unions (see the Chronology at end of chapter). Unlike the position in Sweden, Japan and some other countries which industrialised relatively late, in Britain the notion of a 'vertically-bonded works community' hardly developed; industrial relations were generally adversarial rather than paternalistic.

The unions   Since industrialisation began earlier in Britain, and since unions grew as a response to industrialisation, they have older traditions in Britain than elsewhere. Many British unions can trace their roots back to the mid-nineteenth century or earlier.

The earliest unions were formed by skilled craftsmen. Widespread unionisation of semi-skilled and unskilled manual workers began in the late nineteenth century, whilst few white-collar workers joined a union until after the Second World War. British unions can be classified as craft, general, industrial or white-collar (depending on their origins and predominant membership), although this categorisation has become blurred as unions have gained members in more than one category. It may be more useful to see unions as either 'closed' or 'open', according to whether or not they restrict recruitment to particular categories of workers (Turner, 1962).

Although there were about 1000 known unions in Britain in 1940, there were only 400 by 1983. Then, their average size was about 30 000 members, but there was still much variation between unions: 'over half the unions have less than a thousand members; together they account for under half of one per cent of total members. At the other extreme, the seven largest unions accounted for over half the total; while the 22 with over 100 000 members together contained 80 per cent of all trade unionists' (Hyman, 1985:108).

There is a complex structure of multi-unionism in many industries, reflecting the long and continuous history of British unions. Many have grown in an *ad hoc* manner, recruiting wherever the opportunities arose. Union mergers have further complicated the structure, since they have often brought together disparate occupational and industrial groups (as illustrated in Table 2.2).

It might simplify collective bargaining structures if British unions were organised by industry, with one union representing the workers in each main industry. Indeed, this structure was recommended by a British union delegation which advised on the reconstruction of the West German unions in the late 1940s (see chapter 8). There are some quasi-industrial unions in Britain, for example in steel, railways and coal-mining, but within these industries, certain occupations such as craftsmen, engine drivers, white-collar and supervisory workers may still be organised by separate unions. We are unlikely to see the development of industrial unionism in the near future, not least because most union leaders would probably resist the loss of members involved in such a reorganisation.

The complexity of union structure is especially evident in private-sector manufacturing industry; workers may belong to different unions depending on their job, skill level and whether they are manual or non-manual employees. Membership patterns vary between establishments, employers and localities. Therefore, an employer may deal with several unions within one establishment, even on behalf of a group of workers with similar jobs. There have been inter-union disputes in some industries, but the possible problems associated with multi-unionism have increasingly been offset by the practice of having multi-union negotiating committees, both at workplace and industry levels.

Unlike most other European countries, Britain has only one main union confederation: the Trades Union Congress (TUC). In 1985, 92 unions (including most of the large ones), representing around 90 per cent of British union members, were affiliated to the TUC. It was originally set up in 1868 to lobby governments and this has remained a primary role. However, since the Second World War in particular, it has nominated union representatives to various quasi-governmental

Table 2.2 The fifteen largest British unions

Union	Membership (000s) 1978	Membership (000s) 1983	% change 1978 to 1983	Summary description
Transport and General Workers Union	2073	1547	−25	General/open; has white-collar section
Amalgamated Union of Engineering Workers	1494	1224	−18	Ex-craft; now fairly open. White-collar section split from the union in 1985.
General, Municipal, Boilermakers and Allied Trades Union	965	875	−9	General/open; has white-collar section.
National and Local Government Officers' Association	729	780	+7	Public services; white-collar.
National Union of Public Employees	712	689	−3	Public services; mainly manual.
Association of Scientific, Technical and Managerial Staffs	471	410	−13	White-collar, in private and public sectors.
Electrical, Electronic, Telecommunication and Plumbing Union	438	405	−8	Ex-craft; now fairly open; has white-collar section.
Union of Shop, Distributive and Allied Workers	462	403	−13	Fairly general, but based in retailing.
National Union of Mineworkers	371	318	−14	Coal-mining industry non-managerial workers.
Union of Construction, Allied Trades and Technicians	325	260	−20	Building industry union; some craftsmen elsewhere.
National Union of Teachers	293	250	−15	Largest schoolteachers' union.
Royal College of Nursing	134	231	+72	'Professional union' for nurses; the only 'top 15 union' not in TUC.
Confederation of Health Service Employees	215	223	+4	Health service staff.
Society of Graphical and Allied Trades	202	217	+7	Ex-craft union in printing/paper industries.
Union of Communication Workers	197	196	−1	Post Office and British Telecom workers.
Total membership of top 15 unions	9,084	8,029	−12	
Total membership of all other unions	3,970	3,271	−18	
Total membership of all unions	13,054	11,210	−13	

Source: Calculated from Certification Office for Trade Unions and Employers' Associations

agencies and tripartite bodies, such as the Manpower Services Commission and the Health and Safety Commission. The TUC has no
direct role in collective bargaining and it cannot itself implement
industrial action. British unions have generally been too jealous
of their own autonomy to allow the TUC a more powerful role. It
has, however, played an important role in regulating inter-union
relations, conciliating in major industrial disputes and training union
representatives.

Besides setting up the TUC to lobby governments, the unions have
also sought direct representation in Parliament. This led to the
establishment of the Labour Party in 1906. It was seen as a necessary
complement to the industrial activities of the unions, particularly
after a series of adverse legal judgements meant that new legislation
was required to establish union rights.

Individual unions may affiliate to the Labour Party, contributing
to its funds through a 'political levy' on members, from which
individuals may 'contract out' if they wish. Also, unions often
sponsor individual candidates in parliamentary and local government
elections, usually Labour. In 1983, 47 unions were affiliated to the
Labour Party, providing nearly 80 per cent of the party's income.
Links between the Labour Party and the unions continue to be close,
not least because many union activists are also Labour Party members. Joint TUC–Labour Party committees discuss various aspects
of economic and social policy.

The level and density of union membership has increased since
1945. We can identify three broad phases (Bain and Price, 1983).
Firstly, between 1948 and 1968, membership grew, but at a lower rate
than the growth in potential membership, hence density fell slightly.
This was due to structural shifts within the economy, as low union
density industries increased their share of employment and the proportion of women and white-collar employees increased. Secondly,
the level and density of membership grew rapidly in the decade 1969
to 1979, as workers were attracted to unions by the 'threat' effect of
declining real wages and the 'credit' effect of rapid pay increases in a
period of high inflation. Also, the period was notable for a legal and
political climate generally favourable to union growth, particularly
under the 1974–79 Labour government, so that density rose to an all-
time high of 59 per cent in 1979 (according to the definitions adopted
in the Appendix, Table A.17).

The beginning of the third phase coincided with the return of a
Conservative government in 1979 and the onset of a severe economic
recession. The rise in unemployment reduced union membership,
largely because the unemployed tended to allow their membership to
lapse. By 1984, membership density had fallen to about 50 per cent.

This decline was particularly significant when compared with the rapid growth of the preceding decade. Union density in Britain was still higher than in the other countries in this book except Sweden and Australia.

Manual workers are much more likely to be unionised than non-manual staff. In spite of this, by 1979, non-manual workers constituted about 40 per cent of total union membership, compared with only 23 per cent in 1948 (Bain and Price, 1983). Much of this growth took place in separate white-collar unions, and some unions also organised managerial and professional employees, especially in the public sector (Bamber, 1986). The increasing importance of non-manual unions is helping to change the style of union leadership and may have implications for the future political allegiance of unions, since their members and officials may lack the Labour traditions of manual-worker trade unionists.

Union density is higher among men (about 60 per cent) than women (about 40 per cent). There are significant differences in density between industries. Thus the private services (including insurance, banking and finance, entertainment, distribution and miscellaneous services) have a union density of less than 17 per cent, compared with a density of 70 per cent in manufacturing industry as a whole.

The closed shop is an important feature of British industrial relations. In a closed shop, workers must join a union either before (pre-entry) or soon after (post-entry) starting a job. The number of closed shops increased significantly during the 1970s. By 1978, at least 25 per cent of all employees were covered, the majority by post-entry closed shops. Most manual unions prefer closed shops wherever possible, to reinforce their power. Many employers have also welcomed such an arrangement, to ensure that stewards[3] speak for the whole workforce, and as a means of stabilising industrial relations, for example by controlling union structure in the workplace (McCarthy, 1964; Dunn and Gennard, 1984).

The employers The plurality and fragmentation of the employers' associations is at least as complex as that of the unions. Employers began to form their own collective organisations during the nineteenth century, largely as a reaction to growing levels of unionisation. One of the largest employers' associations, the Engineering Employers' Federation, was established in 1896 and in the following year it led a national lockout of workers in opposition to union calls for an eight-hour day.

Employers' associations are not merely reactive. They have taken important initiatives in the development of industrial relations procedures, especially in the early twentieth century. They still operate procedures for resolving industrial disputes, provide advisory and consultancy services, and lobby governments. Increasingly, employers' associations also provide a range of services relating to trading activities, though in many sectors, such services are provided by separate trade associations (Armstrong, 1984).

Most employers' associations have traditionally engaged in collective bargaining on a multi-employer, industry-level basis. In recent years there has been a trend towards single-employer bargaining in such sectors as chemicals and engineering. Some larger firms have left their associations, largely because multi-employer bargaining had apparently failed to neutralise union activity at the workplace (Sisson, 1987). Nevertheless, there is little evidence that employers' associations are disappearing. On the whole, they are retaining their membership, and firms still value at least some of their services, in particular, disputes procedures, advice and consultancy.

The Confederation of British Industry (CBI) is the employers' equivalent of the TUC. The CBI has more resources than the TUC, though it is younger. It was formed in 1965, following a merger between two separate employers' confederations. It has individual firms and employers' associations in membership and more than half of Britain's workers are employed by CBI members. The CBI has become an important lobbyist on behalf of employers but, like the TUC, its powers are limited and it does not participate in collective bargaining.

The decline of multi-employer bargaining arrangements in some sectors has meant that many employers have tried to play a more direct role in industrial relations. By the 1960s, many first-line supervisors were involved in negotiations with stewards, usually on an informal basis. More recently, formal collective bargaining has increasingly taken place at company, division or workplace level. Employers have taken initiatives in determining the level at which bargaining takes place. Personnel management became a more important and specialised function in Britain, particularly in the larger firms. The 1970s saw a growth in the relative number, pay and status of personnel specialists, although this trend may have been reversed in the 1980s.

Collective bargaining

In general, collective bargaining in Britain is voluntary. Private-sector employers are under no legal obligation to bargain. The content of collective agreements is for the parties themselves to determine, although they typically include procedures, as well as substantive agreements on terms and conditions of employment.

Collective agreements are not legally enforceable; they are backed only by the relative power of the bargaining parties and their wish to maintain mutual goodwill.

Compared to American contracts (see chapter 3), most British agreements are concise, extending to only a few pages, and they do not usually specify a fixed-term duration. However, most general pay rates are reconsidered annually, and most procedural agreements specify the period of notice which either party agrees to give before terminating the agreement.

Collective bargaining is the most important method of pay determination in Britain. The basic pay of at least 75 per cent of all employees is determined by collective bargaining. Those working in smaller private-sector establishments are the least likely to be covered, whilst coverage is greatest in the public sector. There are some broad differences between bargaining arrangements in private-sector manufacturing industries, the public sector, and private-sector services. We discuss each in turn.

Multi-employer bargaining was established in Britain by the early 1920s. In some industries, such as engineering, this had developed in the late nineteenth century. In others, 'joint industrial councils' were set up after the First World War to conduct industry-level bargaining between employers' associations and unions. Most of the major industries were covered. Such industry-level machinery was encouraged by the government, as a way of constructing orderly procedures between the parties. Bargaining regulated pay and conditions as well as establishing negotiating and disputes procedures. Agreements were usually in writing, while negotiations and dispute-settlement followed formally agreed procedures. This industry-level process rarely included a role for stewards. Bargaining was usually conducted by full-time union officers and was not carried out at the workplace. In most unions, stewards were not mentioned in the union rules as much more than the collectors of union subscriptions.

However, after the Second World War, stewards increasingly became involved in bargaining with management within the workplace, particularly where piecework pay systems existed. This was partly because the tight labour markets of the immediate post-war years enhanced workers' bargaining power. Stewards derived much of their power from their ability to pressurise local managers into making concessions, sometimes under the threat of industrial action.

In the mid-1960s, there was an upward trend in the number of unofficial strikes outside the coal-mining industry.[4] Many commentators were denigrating Britain as a strike-prone country, with chaotic industrial relations. This prompted some employer interests to call for 'something to be done'. (In fact, in so far as it is possible to compile an international 'league table' of strike-proneness, Britain was near the middle of it in the mid-1960s, just as it was in 1974–83; see Appendix, Table A.19). Unions were also increasingly concerned about the courts making changes in the labour law which threatened the ability of unions to engage in lawful industrial action (Davies and Freedland, 1984:738 ff.). Therefore, in 1965, the government set up a Royal Commission, chaired by Lord Donovan, to study industrial relations, 'with particular reference to the Law' (Donovan 1968:1). The Donovan Report concluded that Britain had two systems of industrial relations. On the one hand, there was industry-level bargaining, but on the other hand, this was extensively supplemented by workplace bargaining. The latter involved local managers and stewards bargaining over pay and conditions, individual grievances and job control issues. Employers' associations, senior management and full-time union officials tended not to be involved in workplace bargaining, which led to verbal agreements and implicit understandings, rather than to formal written agreements and procedures.

In certain sectors, industry agreements set a 'floor' to pay levels, substantial additions to this being negotiated at the workplace. Workplace bargaining was also concerned with detailed issues such as piece rates and working practices, which industry-level negotiations could not regulate effectively. According to Donovan, the 'informality' of workplace bargaining was a cause for concern. It increased the likelihood of local unofficial industrial action and made managing more difficult. Donovan's prescription was a formalisation of workplace bargaining, which should thereby avoid the potential disorder of informality. Donovan put the onus on managers to reform their own bargaining practices, and recommended the establishment of a government agency to promote reform (Palmer, 1983:189 ff.).

Donovan's analysis focussed on manufacturing, particularly engineering, thus tending to understate the diversity of bargaining arrangements. Nevertheless, the Donovan reforms have to some extent been realised, with workplace bargaining becoming more formalised. The organisation of stewards within the workplace has become more elaborate, with more convenors[5] and stewards' committees being established. At most workplaces, the parties have formalised their grievance-handling and negotiation procedures; nevertheless these are still less formal than North American collective bargaining or Australian arbitration (see chapters 3–5).

During the 1970s, single-employer bargaining developed at the expense of multi-employer arrangements in some industries. In such cases the significance of industry-wide pay bargaining has so declined that Donovan's analysis is no longer relevant. However, multi-employer bargaining at industry-level continues to be significant in some industries and even where its relevance in determining pay levels has declined, it often continues to be important for determining issues such as hours of work, holidays, overtime and shift-premia. The public sector is rather different. Union density is higher, mainly because the state has obliged public-sector employers to bargain with unions. Bargaining has usually been centralised and workplace representatives did not generally become important until the 1970s, following widespread militancy in the public sector. This was largely because traditional pay relativities with the private sector were being disturbed by government incomes policies. Even so, the development of workplace bargaining in the public sector has been uneven and bargaining is still more highly centralised than in most private manufacturing industries.

The private-sector service industries have the lowest union densities and the least developed system of bargaining. Where it exists, bargaining is more centralised than in manufacturing industry, with single-employer bargaining at the level of the firm (rather than the establishment) being the norm.

Particularly in manufacturing and the public sector, the *scope* of bargaining typically involves a wide range of issues, including remuneration, hours of work, holidays, overtime and shift-working arrangements, pensions, and other working conditions. In addition, unions often bargain over issues such as staffing arrangements, recruitment, retrenchment and working practices.

Some union activists have wanted to extend the scope of bargaining to include the wider issues of corporate policy, such as investment, marketing and product strategies. For example, in the mid-1970s, a multi-plant 'combine group' of stewards from Lucas Aerospace devised an alternative corporate plan (Wainwright and Elliott, 1982). However, employers have usually seen such issues as management prerogatives and have rarely been willing to negotiate on them.

The role of the state

Throughout much of the nineteenth century the law was/hostile to unionism and many trade unionists are still wary of legal intervention. Since the nineteenth century, the law has tended to provide only a minimum framework, within which voluntary collective bargaining has taken place between employers and unions. This is the British tradition of 'voluntarism' in industrial relations. The law has had less influence on industrial relations than in most other countries. There is no law setting out a specific right to strike; instead, unions and employees have certain statutory immunities protecting them from liability when invoking sanctions.

For most of this century, governments have encouraged the parties to develop voluntary collective bargaining arrangements. Governments have, however, legislated to provide individual rights for employees. These include the right to have contracts of employment, redundancy payments, protection from unfair dismissal, healthy and safe workplaces, maternity arrangements, and protection from victimisation for union activity. Most of these rights were established by Labour governments since 1964; Conservative legislation has amended certain details. Nevertheless, until the 1980s, there was a broad consensus about the desirability of most of the provisions.

The issue of equal opportunities in the labour market has attracted increasing attention, though perhaps less so than in Sweden, Australia and North America. Under various British laws enacted since 1970, discrimination in employment on the grounds of race or sex is illegal. However, it is often difficult to enforce these laws. As with unfair dismissal cases, enforcement largely depends on individuals complaining to an industrial tribunal.[6] The government has also established the tripartite Commission for Racial Equality and Equal Opportunities Commission to provide information and to help monitor and enforce these laws.

The state has a limited role in regulating pay and conditions in certain industries. It began setting up wages boards or councils in 1909, whereby representatives of employers and unions, along with independent members, determine legally enforceable minimum terms and conditions for their industry to be monitored by a 'wages inspectorate'. Such institutions were set up where effective collective bargaining had failed to develop, for example, in agriculture, clothing manufacture, retailing, hairdressing, hotels and catering.

The purpose of wages councils has been to 'plug the gaps' in the coverage of voluntary bargaining arrangements rather than to establish a comprehensive statutory system or a general minimum wage, as there is in many other countries. In recent years several wages councils have been abolished, occasionally on the initiative of the unions, who sometimes argue that the presence of a wages council may discourage the development of voluntary arrangements. Large firms have often opposed abolition, arguing that the absence of statutory minima allows smaller firms in particular to undercut prices by driving pay down. Wages councils survive in a number of industries where there are poor prospects for the development of voluntary collective bargaining. At their peak, in the late 1940s, wages councils covered over 15 per cent of workers, but by 1985 this had fallen to under 12 per cent.

British governments have also acted in a third party role in pursuing incomes policies designed to control inflation. Such policies have been prompted by accelerating inflation and balance of payments difficulties. The form of such a policy tends to depend on the political complexion of the current government. Some governments have opted for a statutory policy, often with a quasi-independent body to vet proposed pay increases with penalties for those breaking the norm. Other governments have preferred to follow a voluntary approach, seeking to win the support and compliance of unions and employers by persuasion.

Incomes policies have not been particularly successful in containing pay increases over the longer term. Periods of restraint have often been followed by periods of 'catching up' as unions have sought additional pay increases to compensate. Incomes policies have been criticised by some on the right because they may distort the pay structure and so impede the efficient functioning of the labour market. In contrast, some on the left have argued that incomes policies are unacceptable, because they have been used to control pay, while non-pay incomes and prices have been less effectively controlled.

Incomes policies have been particularly controversial in the public sector. If the government is unable to control the pay of its own employees, it is unlikely to be able to control pay in the private sector. Thus public sector pay has often been singled out for particular attention by governments.

The state has made various attempts to reform industrial relations in general. By the 1960s there was increasing concern at Britain's relatively poor economic performance, with slow growth, high inflation and recurrent balance of payments difficulties. Some commentators argued that Britain's industrial relations system was largely to blame, with restrictive working practices and unofficial strikes making industry uncompetitive. Accordingly industrial relations reform has been high on the political agenda since the mid-1960s.

As we have seen, the Donovan Commission argued for voluntary reform to formalise workplace bargaining; to some extent such reform was implemented in the 1970s. Nevertheless, since the 1960s, successive governments have also resorted to various forms of legislation. The Conservatives' 1971 Industrial Relations Act sought to legislate for reform. Following the US example, this Act even included provisions which aimed to make collective agreements into legally enforceable contracts. The unions boycotted much of the Act, thereby rendering it largely ineffective. The Act was repealed by Labour in 1974.

The British state has long intervened in industrial relations by acting as a third party in employer–employee relations. Conciliation and arbitration services were formerly provided by a government department. By the 1970s the government was so committed to pay restraint, however, that many felt that these services should be more independent of the government. Hence, the Labour government established the Advisory, Conciliation and Arbitration Service (ACAS) in 1974. ACAS is governed by a tripartite council consisting of employer and union nominees and government-nominated academics. Thus, the government sought to distance itself from the settlement of industrial disputes. The services of ACAS are a supplement to, rather than a substitute for, collective bargaining. ACAS services are free, and include the provision of advice to employers and unions on all aspects of industrial relations and employment policies. ACAS officials carry out conciliation, but they appoint academics and other independent experts as mediators and arbitrators. Unlike the position in Australia, arbitration is not usually compulsory or legally binding in Britain.

The post-1974 Labour government also introduced a 'social contract', offering pro-union legislation and Keynesian economic policies in exchange for voluntary pay restraint, in an accord with the TUC. This was effective in so far as there was a temporary reduction in the number of stoppages. But the social contract collapsed after about three years, under an onslaught of industrial action in the 'winter of discontent' of 1978–79.

Current and future issues

In most European countries, governments have tried to promote industrial democracy. Leaving collective bargaining aside, however, there have been fewer attempts at developing formal channels of industrial democracy in Britain than in most other Western European countries. Proposals for worker directors have had a mixed reception from the unions, which tend to fear that worker directors elected outside union channels (as in West Germany, see chapter 8), might provide a rival channel of representation. In the private sector, worker directors are sometimes opposed by unions as representing an unacceptable compromise between labour and capital, with labour being offered responsibility without real power.

Employers have often been openly hostile to industrial democracy proposals. However, many employers are introducing briefing groups, quality circles and more direct forms of communications in an attempt to increase levels of commitment and productivity. Such schemes have often bypassed the unions. One employers' aim is often to forestall any future calls for more rigorous forms of industrial democracy, which might come from future governments or the European Communities (Bamber and Snape, 1986).

The 1970s saw a renewed development of joint consultative committees within many firms. These provide a forum for labour–management discussions on a range of issues, often including items such as health, safety and welfare facilities which may be beyond the scope of collective bargaining. These committees differ from collective bargaining institutions, in that issues are discussed, but not formally negotiated. Joint consultation has not necessarily grown at the expense of collective bargaining, indeed it has often developed furthest alongside high levels of union activity, particularly in the public sector. However, in some private-sector establishments, management seems to have fostered direct employee communications and joint consultation, in an attempt to forestall unionisation and collective bargaining.

During the early 1980s, many unions sought to extend the scope of collective bargaining to regulate technical change. They attempted to negotiate 'technology agreements' which would oblige employers to involve unions in decision-making. Employers would be required to disclose information about their plans, they would usually have to avoid redundancies and new health hazards, whilst providing retraining where appropriate. Unions also demanded a reduction in lifetime hours of work, joint regulation of any personal data that might be collected and training for their own 'technology stewards', who would negotiate and monitor these innovations (Bamber, 1985). British unions were influenced by similar policies adopted by several Scandinavian unions (see chapter 9). Some British unions did negotiate technology agreements but, in general, employers were not willing to concede to the spirit of such demands. Most technical change was introduced unilaterally by employers. They might *consult* with employees, but they were reluctant to *negotiate* with unions on such issues (Davies, 1984).

Following the general election of 1979, the incoming Conservative government rejected much of the post-war consensus on economic policy. The reduction of inflation, through monetarist policies, was accorded a higher priority than the maintenance of full employment. The Conservatives argued that the unions had become too powerful and that legislation was needed to shift the 'balance of power' in industrial relations. Accordingly, laws were introduced to restrict picketing, industrial action, and unions' political activities. The Conservatives also sought to promote secret ballots in unions (see the Chronology at end of chapter). The impact of all this legislation was greater than that of the 1971 Act, partly because it was introduced more gradually and was accompanied by a steep rise in unemployment, with a consequent decline in union power.

The coverage of the closed shop has been reduced since 1979; the Conservative government opposed it as an infringement of individual liberties. They also saw wages councils as preventing 'flexibility' in the labour market and 'pricing people out of jobs' by keeping pay levels 'artificially' high. Young people were removed from regulation by wages councils, whose powers were restricted to the setting of a single minimum hourly rate and overtime rate, for workers over 20 years old. Nevertheless, the government hesitated about wholesale abolition, partly because of the employers' views, mentioned earlier. Also, having previously ratified the International Labour Organisation (ILO) minimum wage-fixing convention (see chapter 1), Britain was obliged to have some such procedure for establishing minimum wage levels in low-paid manufacturing and commercial trades (and in particular homeworking trades) where there were no effective alternative procedures. Although this convention has been ratified by 97 countries, none of which have deratified it, the British government decided to deratify it in 1985, though this involved giving a year's notice. The government also reduced the wages inspectorate, thereby limiting the effectiveness of wages councils. Similarly, in the early 1980s, it reduced the staff of ACAS and the Health and Safety Executive, and abolished several other tripartite agencies.

In this context, by the 1980s some employers were seeking concessions from unions. These ranged from pay cuts, to the introduction of more flexible working practices. Particularly in those industries hit by foreign competition or the recession, such changes were often introduced with very little, if any, union resistance.

Several unions made concessions at new sites to gain bargaining rights, and hence extra members. Some unions saw such forms of recruitment as increasingly important during a period of generally declining union membership. These new agreements often gave sole bargaining rights to the union concerned, sometimes in exchange for an undertaking not to invoke sanctions, but rather to submit any disputes to a relatively new form of final-offer (pendulum) arbitration on disputes of interest; Japanese multinationals pioneered such agreements in Britain. They tended to be concluded with unions with right-wing leaderships, who saw them as part of a 'new realism' amongst unions in a period of recession. Critics on the left often condemned them as 'sweetheart deals'.

After a decade of growth and increasing influence in the 1970s, the unions were on the defensive in the mid-1980s. The prospects for future growth looked bleak. Higher unemployment, along with lower inflation than in the 1970s, meant that the economic situation did not favour a resumption of union growth. The political situation was also unfavourable, with the Conservatives re-elected for a further term in 1983. In this general election less than 40 per cent of union members voted Labour. The Social Democratic Party's Alliance with the Liberals contributed to Labour's defeat.

The unions were facing increasingly assertive and sophisticated employers, who were bolstered by a government committed to shifting the industrial balance of power in their favour. This involved dismantling much of the labour law, especially that enacted by the 1974–79 Labour government, in an attempt to deregulate the labour market, following the US example. Under these circumstances the unions tended to be reactive and to experience difficulty in capturing the industrial and political initiative. This was reflected in the 1984–85 miners' strike (Beynon, 1985), the most significant industrial dispute in Britain since the general strike of 1926, which had also centred on the coal-mining industry.

Coal-mining is a relatively strike-prone industry in most countries. In Britain, the industry was nationalised by a Labour government in 1947, to form the National Coal Board (NCB). Since then, the industry's workforce has declined, as capacity has been reduced and productivity increased. The National Union of Mineworkers (NUM)[7] had generally accommodated this decline, partly because the NCB had developed a close working relationship with the union, and also perhaps because of the general availability of alternative employment until the early 1970s. There was, however, a growing frustration amongst miners about the decline, and against this background the NUM elected a radical left-wing leader, Arthur Scargill, in 1981.

By the early 1980s, the NCB's management was becoming more aggressive and commercial in its approach and large-scale pit closures seemed likely. This set the scene for confrontation. In 1983 the NUM began a ban on overtime working as a reaction to the NCB's current pay offer and its threat of further pit closures. The strike began in March 1984, following the NCB's announcement of two particular closures and its intention to reduce capacity further.

A full national strike would have required a national ballot of the members, under the NUM's own rules. It did not hold such a ballot, however, in spite of the calls from some members and many outsiders. The union's strategy was to allow the more militant local area unions to declare their own strikes and then for others to follow their example, forcing them to do so by picketing if necessary. The strike was therefore a series of local area strikes. The leaders reasoned that a majority of members might not vote for a strike, because it would appear that only a minority were threatened by the closures. Moreover, the NCB, government and media propaganda could sway members to vote against a strike.

Early in the strike, some miners tried to force other areas out and to close power stations, steelworks and other coal-using plants by mass picketing. This attracted much public attention due to the sometimes violent confrontations between pickets and police. Some pit villages were divided between strikers and non-strikers, with cases of violence and intimidation.

By March 1985, several sets of negotiations had broken down acrimoniously. The NUM refused to accept the closure of 'uneconomic pits', whilst the NCB insisted on its 'right to manage' and to implement its planned reductions in capacity. Thanks to imported coal and oil, and to the high level of coal stocks, no power cuts had been necessary. The miners were supported by donations of food and money from community groups and other unions. Nevertheless, the strike was increasingly presented as a failure in the media; more and more of the NUM's funds were being seized by the courts, few other unions had given active support, and a drift back to work developed. Therefore, the NUM signalled a unilateral end to the strike, although it declared that the 'guerilla war' would continue.[8]

The strike illustrates many of the features of British industrial relations in the mid-1980s: a tougher management style; legal interventions; the weakness of the labour movement; and, in the number of working miners and the increasing unpopularity of the strike, a public mood out of sympathy with militant union action. Also, the policing of the strike aroused some concern from the civil liberties movement, with roadblocks and unprecedented national police co-ordination being used to deal with the picketing. Although the government sought to distance itself from the dispute, it played an important role in influencing the NCB and police policies.

As a major employer, the state's employment policies are important, both directly and also through their influence as an example to other employers. Traditionally, the state has been a 'good' employer, offering secure employment and reasonable terms and conditions. It has generally encouraged union membership. However, the Thatcher government has begun to change these traditions. Parts of the public sector are being privatised by selling off whole corporations or divisions and by subcontracting such services as transport, cleaning and catering. The effect is to reduce the number of public-sector employees and also to undermine union organisation, job security, pay and other conditions of employment.

In January 1984, the government announced the withdrawal of union membership and employment protection rights for staff at the Government Communications Headquarters (GCHQ). It claimed that this was necessary for 'national security'. Existing GCHQ staff were offered £1000 in return for the loss of their rights. Whilst only a few actually refused the offer, many seemed to accept reluctantly, and the unions claimed that staff morale was badly affected by the controversy.

The unions reacted angrily to the government's action, unsuccessfully challenging its legality in the courts. The unions claimed that the government had breached the ILO convention on freedom of association and protection of the right to organise. One union also complained to the European Commission on Human Rights. The whole issue contributed to a further deterioration of relations between the government and the unions, with the TUC boycotting the tripartite National Economic Development Council for a period, in protest.[9]

Conclusion

Following its set-backs in the mining industry and at GCHQ, for example, there are signs that the labour movement is beginning to formulate new strategies to cope with conditions in the late 1980s and beyond. British unions are probably too well established for membership densities to fall to, say, the American or French levels in the foreseeable future, and it seems unlikely that the unions will lose all the ground won in the 1970s. They will almost certainly continue to play an important role in industrial and political affairs.

The Conservatives are aiming to continue their step-by-step changes to labour law. A future Labour government would herald a different approach. It would modify much of the early-1980s legislation and generally pursue policies more favourable to the unions. If the Alliance held the balance of power, any such change would probably be more gradual. Whichever party is in government, it seems likely that the law will continue to play a key role, and the trend away from the British tradition of 'voluntarism' will continue.

Some British employers are trying to import American techniques of 'human resource management' (see chapter 3), but in view of the greater institutionalisation of collective bargaining in Britain, relatively few British employers have tried to copy the 'union busting' initiatives of their American counterparts. In many sectors, British firms are facing tough product market competition and a slack labour market. This along with the development of more professional styles of personnel management, may mean that the employers retain much of the initiative in British industrial relations in the foreseeable future.

Abbreviations

ACAS	Advisory, Conciliation and Arbitration Service
CBI	Confederation of British Industry
GCHQ	Government Communications Headquarters
GDP	gross domestic product
ILO	International Labour Organisation
NCB	National Coal Board
NUM	National Union of Mineworkers

OECD   Organisation for Economic Co-operation and Development
TUC   Trades Union Congress

A chronology of British industrial relations

1349	Ordinance of Labourers set up pay determination machinery; the first recognisable labour legislation.
1563	Prohibition of workers' 'conspiracy' and 'combination' to raise wages.
1780–1840	Period of primary industrialisation.
1799–1800	Combination Acts, provided additional penalties against workers' 'combinations'.
1811–14	'Luddites' began smashing machines.
1824–25	Repeal of Combination Acts.
1829	Grand General Union of Operative Spinners formed.
1834	'Tolpuddle martyrs' transported to Australia for taking a union oath.
1851	'New model unions' formed, mainly of skilled craftsmen.
1868	First meeting of TUC.
1871	Trade Union Act gave unions legal status.
1880s–90s	Growth of militancy and development of 'new unionism' amongst unskilled workers.
1899	TUC set up Labour Representation Committee, which became the Labour Party in 1906.
1901	House of Lords' Taff Vale Judgement held that a union could be liable for employers' losses during a strike.
1906	Trades Disputes Act gave unions immunity from such liability, if acting 'in contemplation or furtherance of a trade dispute'.
1909	House of Lords' Osborne Judgement ruled that unions could not finance political activities.
1913	Trade Union Act legalised unions' political expenditure if they set up a separate fund, with individuals able to 'contract out'.
1917–18	Whitley reports recommended joint industrial councils.
1926	General strike and nine-month miners' strike.
1927	Subsequent legislation restricted picketing and introduced criminal liabilities for political strikes.
1945–50	Nationalisation of the Bank of England, fuel, power, inland transport, health, steel etc.
1946	Repeal of 1927 Act.
1962	National Economic Development Council established.
1964	House of Lords' Rookes and Barnard Judgement held that union officials threatening industrial action could be sued for 'intimidation'.
1965	Trades Disputes Act overturned the 1964 decision.

1968	Donovan report advocated voluntary reform of industrial relations.
1969	Labour Government proposed legal reforms, but was successfully opposed by the unions.
1970	Equal Pay Act.
1971	Industrial Relations Act legislated for reform; most unions refused to comply. It also introduced the concept of 'unfair dismissal'.
1974	A miners' strike contributed to the fall of the Conservative government.
1974	Trade Union and Labour Relations Act replaced the 1971 Act, but retained the 'unfair dismissal' concept, set up ACAS and signalled a new Social Contract.
1974	Health and Safety at Work etc. Act.
1975	Employment Protection Act extended the rights of workers and unions.
1975	Sex Discrimination Act.
1976	Race Relations Act.
1978–79	'Winter of discontent'.
1980	Employment Act restricted unions' rights to enforce closed shops, picket and invoke secondary action; it weakened individuals' rights (e.g. in relation to unfair dismissal, maternity leave etc.).
1981	Social Democratic Party formed.
1982	Employment Act restricted closed shops, strikes and union-only contracts.
1984	Trade Union Act required regular secret ballots for the election of officials, before strikes, and to approve the continuance of political funds.
1984–85	Miners' strike.

Notes

1 Britain includes England, Scotland and Wales, whilst the United Kingdom includes Britain and Northern Ireland. Although Northern Ireland has much in common with Britain, some important elements of industrial relations are different. This chapter concentrates on Britain, although some of the statistics here and in the Appendix refer to the United Kingdom as a whole.

2 These take-home pay data relate to manufacturing industry and are after tax and social security contributions, but excluding family benefits. Unless otherwise specified, these comparative data all relate to 1983–84 and are from OECD sources, especially the *OECD Observer*, March 1986. It used 1 January 1986 exchange rates in relation to GDP per capita; thus fluctuations in the values of currencies do distort such international comparisons; see Table A.6.

3 A steward (also known as a shop steward or union representative) is not a

union employee, but usually has some time off work to represent fellow union members in the workplace where he or she is employed (see Goodman and Whittingham, 1969).
4 An unofficial strike takes place without the official approval of the union hierarchy. This is not necessarily illegal in Britain.
5 A 'convenor' is the senior steward in a workplace. The convenor is usually chosen by the stewards.
6 An industrial tribunal is a form of local labour court established to deal with cases brought under various employment legislation. The tribunals are meant to be less formal than the law courts, and consist of a legally qualified chairman, along with nominees from panels of employers' and employees' representatives.
7 The NUM represents the manual workers. There are also two other unions in the mainstream of the NCB: the British Association of Colliery Management, representing middle and senior managers and the National Association of Colliery Overmen, Deputies and Shotfirers, which represents first-line supervisors.
8 In 1985, in the aftermath of the strike, there was a breakaway by some sections of the NUM, to set up a rival Union of Democratic Mineworkers.
9 The National Economic Development Council provides a national forum for representatives of employers, unions and government to meet to discuss economic and industrial issues on a regular basis.

References

Advisory, Conciliation and Arbitration Service (annually) *Annual Report* London: HMSO
—— (1980) *Industrial Relations Handbook* London: HMSO
Armstrong, E.G.A. (1984) 'Employers Associations in Great Britain' in J.P. Windmuller and A. Gladstone eds *Employers Associations and Industrial Relations: A Comparative Study* Oxford: Oxford University Press, pp. 44–78
Bain, G.S. ed. (1983) *Industrial Relations in Britain* Oxford: Basil Blackwell
Bain, G.S. and Price, R.J. (1983) 'Union Growth in Britain: Retrospect and Prospect' *British Journal of Industrial Relations* 11, 1, pp. 46–68
Bamber, G.J. (1985) 'Some "Knowns" and "Unknowns" about Management, Industrial Relations and Technical Change' in B.R. Williams and J.A. Bryan-Brown eds. *Knowns and Unknowns in Technical Change* London: Technical Change Centre
—— (1986) *Militant Managers? Managerial Unionism and Industrial Relations* Aldershot: Gower
Bamber, G.J. and Snape, E.J. (1986) 'British Routes to Employee Involvement' in E.M. Davis and R.D. Lansbury eds *Democracy and Control in the Workplace* Melbourne: Longman Cheshire
Beynon, H. ed. (1985) *Digging Deeper: Issues in the Miners' Strike* London: Verso

Bright, D. et al. (1984) 'Industrial Relations in North East England' *Employee Relations* 6, 4, pp. 1–34

Brown, R.K. (1983) 'From Donovan to Where? Interpretations of Industrial Relations in Britain since 1968' in A. Stewart ed. *Contemporary Britain* London: Routledge & Kegan Paul, pp. 129–53

Brown, W. (1981) *The Changing Contours of British Industrial Relations* Oxford: Basil Blackwell

Certification Office for Trade Unions and Employers' Associations (annually) *Annual Report of the Certification Officer* London: The Office

Clegg, H.A. (1979) *The Changing System of Industrial Relations in Great Britain* Oxford: Basil Blackwell

Daniel, W.W. and Millward, N. (1983) *Workplace Industrial Relations in Britain: The DE/PSI/SSRC Survey* London: Heinemann Educational Books

Davies, A. (1984) 'Management–Union Participation During Microtechnological Change' in M. Warner ed. *Microprocessors, Manpower and Society: A Comparative Cross-national Approach* Aldershot: Gower, pp. 149–70

Davies, P. and Freedland, M. (1984) *Labour Law: Text and Materials* London: Weidenfeld & Nicolson

Department of Employment (monthly) *Employment Gazette* London: HMSO

Donovan Commission (1968) *Royal Commission on Trade Unions and Employers' Associations*—Report Cmnd 3623 London: HMSO

Dunn, S. and Gennard, J. (1984) *The Closed Shop in British Industry* London: Macmillan

Flanders, A. (1970) *Management and Unions: The Theory and Reform of Industrial Relations* London: Faber & Faber

Fox, A. (1985) *History and Heritage: The Social Origins of the British Industrial Relations System* London: George Allen & Unwin

Goodman, J.F.B. and Whittingham, T.G. (1969) *Shop Stewards in British Industry* London: McGraw-Hill

Hyman, R. (1985) 'Class Struggle and the Trade Union Movement' in Coates, D. et al. eds *A Socialist Anatomy of Britain* Cambridge: Polity Press, pp. 99–123

Industrial Relations Services (twice monthly) *Industrial Relations Review and Report* London: IRS

Johnston, T.L. (1981) *Introduction to Industrial Relations* Plymouth: MacDonald & Evans

McCarthy, W.E.J. (1964) *The Closed Shop in Britain* Oxford: Blackwell

Marsh, A. (1979) *Concise Encyclopedia of Industrial Relations* Aldershot: Gower

Palmer, G. (1983) *British Industrial Relations* London: George Allen & Unwin

Pelling, H. (1971) *A History of British Trade Unionism* 2nd edn Harmondsworth: Penguin

Sisson, K.F. (1987) *The Management of Collective Bargaining: An International Comparison* Oxford: Blackwell

Turner, H.A. (1962) *Trade Union Growth, Structure and Policy: A Comparative Study of the Cotton Unions* London: George Allen & Unwin
Wainwright, H. and Elliott, D. (1982) *The Lucas Plan: A New Trade Unionism in the Making* London: Allison & Bushby
Webb, S. and Webb, B. (1897) *Industrial Democracy* London: Longman
Whitaker, J. (1984) *Whitaker's Almanack 1985* London: Whitaker

3 | Management–labour relations in the USA

HOYT WHEELER

Diversity and complexity, two of the main attributes of the American industrial relations system, make it difficult to understand. Yet, a full comprehension of industrial relations in industrialised market economies requires an understanding of the USA's system. This requirement stems from two sources: the relative power of the American economy, and the influence of its managerial and industrial relations models on other countries. It is also of considerable interest in its own right.

The great magnitude of the American economy is apparent from its GDP of US \$3 865 billion and population of 237 million, both by far the largest of any country covered in this book. The impact of American influence can be observed in the other national systems reported in other chapters. These influences derive in part from the early development of professional management techniques in the USA. This has been facilitated by the USA's guidance and financing of the post-Second World War recovery; and by the size and world-wide scope of American multinational corporations.

The American context

The industrialisation of the USA, which was somewhat later than that of Britain, began in the period 1810–1840. From the mid-1820s to 1860, manufacturing developed in a broad range of industries, with textiles being among the most significant (Lebergott, 1984:130, 136). Prior to the 1850s, however, production was mainly in small shops and in workers' homes. This extensive use of part-time home-

57

working ameliorated the labour shortage that existed throughout this period (Taylor, 1951:215). From the 1790s, skilled craftsmen began to form unions in response to the downward pressures on pay, produced by the growing and increasingly competitive markets. The character of American unions was deeply and permanently influenced by the nature and practical goals of these early, pre-factory unions.

The establishment of the factory system in the 1850s and 1860s brought into the industrial system large numbers of native rural women and children, and eventually many immigrants from Ireland, Britain, Germany and other countries. Their pay was generally comparable to American farm earnings and higher than for factory workers in Europe. This is one reason for the historically low rate of unionisation of factory workers in the USA. In addition, repression of unionisation by employers, either directly or through government action, inhibited unionisation. It may also be that the high rate of worker mobility to other jobs, and considerable social mobility, hindered the development of solidarity among workers, sufficient to facilitate the widespread organisation of unions (Lebergott, 1984: 373, 386–7; Wheeler, 1985). However, craftsmen did form national unions in the 1860s, and the social reform-oriented Knights of Labor grew to prominence in the 1880s, organising a somewhat broader range of workers.

Around 1900, building upon a large home market made accessible by an improved transportation system, large corporations achieved dominance in American industrial life. These complex, impersonal organisations required systematic strategies for managing their workers. In response to this need, Frederick Taylor, the father of 'scientific management', and his disciples the industrial engineers, began to have a powerful influence on the ideology and practice of management (Hession and Sardy, 1969:546–7). These ideas first became widely accepted in the USA, before they were accepted in Europe and other areas of the world. By declaring 'scientific' principles for the design of work and pay, the Taylorists undermined the rationale for bargaining organisations such as unions. Added to this was the continuing vigorous opposition of the capitalists, who had both enormous power and high prestige. By the 1920s these factors, along with employer use of company-dominated unions and a hostile legal framework, meant that the labour movement was very weak.

It was during the Great Depression of the 1930s that American unions penetrated mass production industry, organising large numbers of factory workers for the first time. Deteriorating working conditions and pay, a changed political environment, and the strategy of mass organising campaigns, led to unionisation of cars, steel, rubber, coal and other industries (Wheeler, 1985). In the 1940s and 1950s the unions continued to grow, and to develop the collective bargaining system. Since the 1950s they have organised large numbers of government employees, but have generally declined in strength. In the 1980s, American unions cover less than 20 per cent of the work force. Nevertheless, they have been fairly militant, as is indicated by the relatively high number of working days lost due to industrial stoppages in the USA (see Table A.19).

Employment patterns in the USA are rather distinctive. Forty-three per cent of the population is engaged in civilian employment. The services sector employs 68 per cent of civilian employees (along with Canada this is a higher percentage than any other OECD country); 28 per cent are employed in industry; and only 3.3 per cent in agriculture (less than any of the other countries in this book, except Britain).

The level of unemployment in the USA has tended to be higher than that in Australia, Japan and most of Western Europe. However, in the early 1980s the unemployment rate fell while it was rising in many European countries. By 1985, the USA had a lower unemployment rate (7.1 per cent) than all of the other eight countries except Sweden and Japan. During 1979–84 the average annual increase in consumer prices was 7.4 per cent. This rate was less than the crude average for the nine countries: 8.9 per cent (see Table A.7).

Although the USA is heavily engaged in international trade, exports of goods constitute only 6.1 per cent of its GDP—smaller than any other OECD country. The relative unimportance of exports to the economy reflects the USA's large home market which creates a greater potential for self-sufficiency than exists in most other countries. However, in recent years large international trade deficits have become a major problem for the economy.

American politics is largely politics of the centre. The two major parties, Republicans and Democrats, which dominate national politics, have generally avoided sharp divisions over policy, and have absorbed and moderated the ideas of more extreme groups. However during the Great Depression of the 1930s, Franklin Roosevelt's Democrats moved some distance to the left, and in the early 1980s, Ronald Reagan's Republicans moved to the right. Even in these instances, substantial segments of the other major party moved in the direction set out by the party in power, thereby shifting the centre. Unlike most political parties in other English-speaking countries, party discipline is weak, making it difficult to reliably label the parties.

Nevertheless, the two political parties *do* differ with respect to the area of the centre which they occupy. The Democrats, while not a labour party, are clearly more leftward inclined than the Republicans. In general, they have more 'liberal' political goals, and are more supportive of government action to achieve social and economic justice. As a party, the Democrats enjoy the support of the unions, with only the renegade Teamsters and a few other unions supporting the Republican party on a regular basis. Under Ronald Reagan, the Republicans have moved to the right, drawing upon traditional American notions of individualism and distrust of 'big government', reaction to the demands of blacks, rising religious fundamentalism, appealing to patriotism to salve the wounds to national pride inflicted by the Vietnam War, and utilising a new blend of economic policies.

Since the 1950s management–labour relations issues have not often been high on the national agenda, although at the local level and occasionally the national level, the unionisation of government employees and strikes have each been important. The general lack of prominence of these issues has several causes. First, at least until the 1980s, there was a widespread impression that the collective bargaining system was relatively stable and needed little attention. Second, and perhaps most importantly, even at the peak of their strength, unions have not been overwhelmingly powerful. Union membership has remained relatively small. Neither economic nor political action by labour has been of such a magnitude or nature to hold national attention for any length of time. Third, as the collective bargaining system is localised, and national government involvement in it is minimal, it is difficult for national policy to focus on collective bargaining. There has, however, been no lack of debate and legislative action in the broad area of industrial relations, as questions of race and sex discrimination in employment, worker safety and health, pension plans and minimum wage laws have all attracted national attention.

Nature of industrial relations   The industrial relations system in the USA consists of two rather distinct sectors: a unionised sector and a non-union sector. These two sectors interconnect in many ways, and share common legal and social underpinnings, but do differ significantly.

The *unionised sector* is characterised by openly adversarial relations between labour and management (Barbash, 1981:1–7). Both unions and management perform the functions of serving rather discrete, and fundamentally opposed interests. The conflict between unions and management is circumscribed, however, by the limited goals of American unions. As the unions are still mainly concerned with the 'pure and simple' goals of the founders of the American labour movement, i.e., better wages, hours and conditions of work, and do not wish to be broadly involved in management, their challenge to management has been rather constrained. They have been willing to enter into what the old radical trade unionists called a 'treaty with the boss', a collective bargaining agreement covering those matters which concern them, even giving up the right to strike for the duration of this 'treaty'. Conflict in the unionised sector is further bounded by the recognition by managers and unions that there are some broad areas of mutual interest.

The end result in the unionised sector is a rather stable situation where conflict is legitimate but bounded as to grounds, timing, and emotional intensity. The main threat to its stability is endemic managerial resistance to unions, which from time to time results in efforts to move establishments from the unionised sector to the non-union sector—either by disestablishing a union in an existing location or moving the work to a southern or western location where unions are weak.

The *non-union sector* is characterised by broad management discretion and control over the terms and conditions of employment. This is limited only by labour market constraints, protective labour legislation, the desire of managers to avoid unionisation, and the strong influence of a managerial philosophy of 'personnel welfarism'. Managers in this sector widely espouse 'positive' managerial views which hold that the firm 'should' offer favourable conditions of employment to employees. A unity of interests between managers and non-managerial workers is held to make unions unnecessary. This sector includes private white-collar employment, electronics, small firms, and most of the textile industry. The main threat to the stability of this sector are the sporadic efforts of unions to organise it.

The environment of industrial relations The *economic* environment has always had a powerful influence upon the American industrial relations system. The predominant employers are large private-sector enterprises. American unions were created to deal with, and have adapted to operating in a capitalist economy. Government's limited role in the system is precisely what one would expect in such an economy, and has changed as the economy has evolved. In addition, economic growth has helped to produce relatively favourable terms and conditions of employment for the majority of workers in the USA since the Second World War.

A reduction in demand for American goods followed the general decrease in demand during the post-1974 recession, and the competition from high quality goods produced in other countries. In the home market, competition from higher quality and lower cost foreign goods has particularly affected major industries such as cars, textiles and steel. In these and other industries, improvements in technology have caused workers to be replaced by machines. To further complicate matters, the type of labour demanded has been changed both by new technology and the shift of the American economy from manufacturing to services. All of this has weakened the bargaining power of labour. In periods of relative economic growth, collective bargaining demands, and perhaps results, are generally more favourable to labour. Upon a return to prosperity, wages may resume their historic upward movements in major industries.

The *political* environment in the United States, with its representative democratic institutions, has historically provided a structure for the development of free trade unions and free management. The political strength of capital and its representatives has always been sufficient to preserve broad areas of managerial discretion from government regulation. The balance of political forces has also permitted the development of reasonably strong trade unions and the imposition of some governmental constraints upon managerial freedom in the industrial relations arena. The government endorsed the formation of private sector unions during the period 1935–47, and of public sector unions in the 1960s and 1970s.

During the early 1980s the political environment appears to have accentuated the trend toward greater management power in industrial relations. A conservative national administration has 'deregulated' the transport industry, increasing competition and placing downward pressure on wages. It has lessened the influence of government upon employers generally by moderating the enforcement of laws protecting workers from health and safety hazards and employment discrimination. Its appointees to the agency responsible for ensuring workers the right to organise (the National Labor Relations Board) have instituted major policy changes that are unfavourable to unions.

The major participants in industrial relations

In the USA, all of the actors in the industrial relations system are influential. It is the employers, however, who are generally more powerful than the other actors.

Employers and their organisations An American scholar, Kochan has written, 'Management is the driving force in any advanced industrial relations system' (1980:179). This derives, at least in part, from the crucial function of management in ensuring the efficiency of the work organisation. It may further stem from the high general social status of managers or their relatively high position in the organisational hierarchy.

In the 1980s the non-union sector of the American work force includes more than 80 per cent of workers. Throughout most of this sector, redundant workers can be laid off in whatever order the employer desires, and terminated for any, or no reason. Furthermore, the conditions under which employment takes place are essentially employer-determined.

The power of the employer to set terms and conditions of employment in the non-union sector is, of course, limited by labour market forces. Also, employee preferences may prevail in those few occupations where, because of scarce skills or other reasons, the individual worker's bargaining power equals or exceeds that of the employer. The ability of the non-union employer to set terms and conditions of employment is also restricted somewhat by protective labour legislation, which is described below.

In some non-unionised firms, the conditions of employment are quite favourable to employees. 'Personnel welfarism' has been a strong movement in the USA since the early years of the twentieth century. Modern personnel practice is oriented toward 'human resources management', the notion that the labour factor of production is valuable, worth investing in, and worth preserving (Heneman et al., 1980:6). In this 'enlightened' view, it is in the interests of the corporation as a whole to attract, retain and improve workers. It is a unitary perspective which sees no necessary conflict between the interests of managers and other workers (Feuille and Wheeler, 1981: 255–7).

Employer organisations are relatively unimportant in the USA (Adams, 1980:4). In contrast to many other countries, there have never been national employers' confederations engaging in a full range of industrial relations activities. However, there have long been employer organisations in the non-union sector for the purpose of avoiding the unionisation of their members. The National Association of Manufacturers was formed for this purpose in the nineteenth century. At both the regional and national levels, the Chamber of Commerce includes union avoidance within the range of its activities. These employer groups and others engage in anti-union litigation, lobbying, and publicity campaigns. They, along with management consultants, engage in the lucrative business of educating employers in techniques of union avoidance.

There has been a considerable increase in employer anti-union activities since the mid-1970s. These actions have ranged from locating plants in non-union areas in the south and west (the so-called 'Sun-Belt'), to openly violating the labour laws, to providing higher pay than the union range. The reasons for this increase are not entirely clear. It may be, at least in part, the result of a movement arising from the lower levels of management in protest against the strictures which unions impose on the performance of work (Piore, 1982:8). This is especially ironic, as many union rules were developed in the context of management application of Taylorist notions of scientific management (Taylor, 1964). Another cause of increased employer resistance may be managers seizing the opportunity to defeat their historic adversary when it is weak. The acceptance of unions by American managers has always been somewhat grudging, and based upon necessity rather than choice. It may also be that the old pluralist American notion of the legitimacy of groups such as unions freely pursuing their self-interest is suffering a general decline in popularity.

The unions   The fundamental characteristics of the American labour movement are as follows:

1 goals which are largely those of 'bread and butter' unionism;
2 a strategy which is mainly economic;
3 collective bargaining as a central well-developed activity;
4 relatively low total union density;
5 strength vis-à-vis the employer on the shop floor;
6 an organisational structure in which the national union holds the reins of power within the union;
7 financial strength;
8 leadership drawn largely from the rank-and-file.

Selig Perlman long ago argued that the American labour movement exhibited a 'Tom, Dick and Harry' idealism—an idealism derived from the ordinary worker (1970:274–5). Perlman believed that unions, because they reflected the aspirations of their members, adopted those goals which seemed most important to the workers. These goals, said Perlman, had nothing to do with the imagined utopia of the Marxist 'intellectuals', but rather with the 'pure and simple' matters espoused by such labour leaders as Samuel Gompers, the 'father' of the American labour movement. Perlman's argument well describes the American labour movement. Although American unions have also pursued wider goals, what has endured has been their emphasis upon the improvement of wages, hours and conditions of work. Of course, unions in other countries have also sought 'bread and butter', but the American unions have focussed more closely upon this outcome than have most others.

The ideology of American unions is still much as it was expressed in 1911 by Samuel Gompers:

The ground-work principle of America's labour movement has been to recognize that first things must come first. The primary essential in our mission has been the protection of the wage-workers, now; to increase his wages; to cut hours off the long workday, which was killing him; to improve the safety and the sanitary conditions of the workshop; to free him from the tyrannies, petty or otherwise, which served to make his existence a slavery (Gompers, 1919:20).

American unions have relied upon collective bargaining, accompanied by the strike threat, as their main weapon. This strategy has influenced the other characteristics of the American labour movement. It has provided the basis for an effective role on the shop floor, as the day-to-day work of administering the agreement requires this. It has required unions to be solvent financially in order to have a credible strike threat. It has resulted in an organisational structure in which the power within the union is placed where it can best be used for collective bargaining, the national union (Barbash, 1967:69). Centralisation of power over strike funds in the national union has been a crucial source of union ability to develop common rules and to strike effectively. It has facilitated, and perhaps even required an independence from political parties which might be tempted to subordinate the economic to political. It is one reason why there is a relatively low total union density, as collective bargaining organisations have a concern about density only as it pertains to their individual economic territories. It has contributed to one of the concommitants of low density, weak political power.

Although American unions have emphasised collective bargaining, they have also engaged in politics. Their political action has for the most part taken the form of rewarding friends and punishing enemies among politicians, avoiding the formation of a labour party, and lobbying for legislation. The American Federation of Labor–Congress of Industrial Organizations (AFL–CIO) Committee on Political Education (COPE) and similar union political agencies are major financial contributors to political campaigns. The goals of such political activity have often been closely related to unions' economic goals, being aimed at making collective bargaining more effective. However, the American labour movement has also been a major proponent of progressive political causes such as laws on civil rights, minimum wages, and other subjects of benefit to citizens generally.

Why is the USA unique among the countries in this book in having no labour party? First, it would be difficult to operate as an independent national political force when representing only 20 per cent or so of the work force. Second, American workers have traditionally been highly independent politically, often voting in ways other than those desired by their union leaders. Third, the American experience with separate labour parties has not been very favourable. Formed in 1828, the Working Men's Party was arguably the first labour party in the world. Its collapse, and the problems which it engendered were long remembered. Later attempts were not much more successful. Fourth, the idea of a labour party is one which has often been urged by left-wing unionists who were the losers in struggles for control of unions in the 1930s and 1940s, and were purged during the 'Red-scare' years of the 1950s. Yet, in the mid-1980s, the AFL–CIO seems to be moving toward greater identification with a party (the Democratic Party) than has been the case in the past. This move is accompanied by many statements by labour leaders which provide evidence of a new aware-ness of the importance of politics. It is possible that having Ronald Reagan as President has helped to move them to this conclusion.

The structure of the American labour movement is rather loose compared to that of other Western union movements. The AFL–CIO is a federation of national unions which include approximately 80 per cent of American union members. In addition to serving as the chief political and public relations voice for the American labour move-ment, it resolves jurisdictional disputes among its members and enforces codes of ethical practices and policies against racial and sex discrimination. It is also the main link to the international labour movement.

The national unions have been described as occupying the 'kingpin' position in the American labour movement (Barbash, 1967: 69). They maintain ultimate power over the important function of collective bargaining, in large part through their control of strike funds. The national unions can establish or disestablish local unions, and can withdraw from the AFL–CIO if they wish. The presidents of the national unions are generally considered to be the most powerful figures in the American labour movement.

The local unions perform the day-to-day work of the labour move-ment. They usually conduct the bargaining over the terms of new agreements and conduct strikes. They administer the agreement, performing the important function of enforcing the complex set of rights which the American collective bargaining agreement creates. Social activities among union members take place at the local level, where there exists what there is of a union culture in the USA (Barbash, 1967: 26–41).

By 1984, unions organised about 19 per cent of civilian employees in employment, compared with 31 per cent in 1970 (see Table A.17). According to a survey conducted by the US Bureau of Census, unions lost 891 000 members between 1979 and 1980. This trend has con-tinued into the 1980s.

Since 1978, government and service employee unions such as the American Federation of Teachers, the Communication Workers of America, the American Federation of State, County and Municipal Employees, and the United Food and Commercial Workers, have experienced substantial growth. It is in the manufacturing sector that union membership has been lost, as unions such as the United Rubber Workers, the Oil, Chemical and Atomic Workers, the United Automobile Workers, and the Amalgamated Clothing and Textile Workers have experienced heavy membership declines (Gifford, 1982).

The composition of the American labour movement has gradually come to include more white-collar and female workers since 1973. Then, 24 per cent of organised workers were white-collar workers. By 1980, this figure was 35 per cent. In 1973, 23 per cent of organised workers were female—in 1980, 30 per cent. As one would expect, there has been a reduction in the proportion of manufacturing workers as the majority of union members now work in non-manufacturing occupations.

The American labour movement has long been considered an exceptional case because of its apolitical 'business unionism' ideology, focussing rather narrowly on benefits to existing membership. The most convincing explanations for this are historical (Kassalow, 1974). There is no feudal tradition in the USA, which has made the distinctions among classes less obvious than in much of Europe. American capitalism developed in a form that allowed fairly widespread prosperity. The great diversity of the population has always hampered the organisation of a broad-based working-class movement. The early establishment of voting rights and free universal public education eliminated those potential working-class issues in the nineteenth century. Social mobility from the working class to the entrepreneurial class blurred class lines, creating a basis for the widely-held belief in the 'log cabin to White House' myth. In consequence, the American labour movement has seldom defined itself in class terms. Additionally, the historic experience of American trade unionists was that class-conscious unions, i.e., those that assumed the 'burden of socialism', tended to be repressed by the strong forces of American capitalism.

Government Government has three main roles in industrial relations: the direct regulation of terms and conditions of employment; regulation of the manner in which organised labour and management relate to each other; and as an employer.

The direct regulation of terms and conditions of employment is in the areas of employment discrimination, worker safety, unemployment compensation, minimum wages and maximum hours, and retirement (Ledvinka, 1982). Since 1964, the government has acted to prohibit discrimination in employment on the grounds of race, colour, sex, religion, national origin or age. It has also proscribed discrimination against disabled persons and Vietnam War veterans.

The government has addressed problems of worker safety, mainly through the Federal Occupational Safety and Health Act of 1970

(OSHA), state health and safety laws, and state workers' compensation laws. OSHA mandates a safe workplace, both by imposing a general duty of safety upon employers and by providing a detailed set of regulations for each industry. Employers violating safety and health standards are subject to fines and remedial orders. Workers' compensation laws provide for medical care and income protection for workers injured on the job. They encourage safety indirectly by increasing the insurance rates for employers which experience a large number of on-the-job injuries.

Unemployment compensation is provided for on a state-by-state basis, but with some federal control and funding. It involves payments to persons who have become involuntarily unemployed but are seeking work. The duration of payments is less than in most of the other countries in this book. It is usually limited to a period of 26 weeks, although this may be extended (Commerce Clearing House, 1983:4409). Federal and state wage and hour laws provide a level of pay and a premium rate of pay for overtime work. In 1985 the minimum pay level was US $3.35 per hour. Employers are required to pay one and a half the employee's regular rate of pay for hours worked in excess of 40 in a particular work week. In addition, the national government uses its power as a purchaser of goods and services to require those doing business with it to pay the prevailing rates of pay in their region, and one and a half the regular rate of pay for all hours worked in excess of eight in a work day.

Retirement benefits are regulated in two main ways. First, through the Social Security system, employers and employees are required to pay a proportion of wages (6.7 per cent each in 1984) into a government fund. It is out of this fund that pensions are paid by the government to retired employees who are covered (Social Security Act). The second way in which government controls pension benefits is through regulation of private pension funds set up voluntarily by employers. The Employee Retirement Income Security Act of 1974 requires retirement plans to be financially secure, and insures these plans. It also mandates that employees become vested in their retirement rights after a period of time.

There are a number of long-standing issues in the area of government regulation of conditions of employment. A major public policy debate has taken place over the minimum wage laws. As in Britain, many economists believe that such laws tend to create unemployment, particularly among the young. This belief has led to proposals for a sub-minimum wage for this group of workers, for whom unemployment has been particularly high. Opponents of this idea see it as creating unemployment for adults and greater employer exploitation of low-wage workers.

In the field of sex discrimination laws, the concept of 'comparable worth' has been much debated. This is the notion that different jobs should carry equal rates of pay if they are worth the same to the employer. That is, the job of secretary, which is mostly held by women, should pay as well as that of truck driver, which is mostly held by men, if its worth is comparable. The chief argument against this theory is its difficulty of application. In addition, occupational safety and health laws and pension regulations have been challenged because of their cost to employers and their alleged ineffectiveness.

Government regulation of the labour–management relationship consists largely of a set of ground rules through which these actors establish, and work out the terms of their relationship. Through the National Labor Relations Act of 1935, as amended in 1947 and 1959, government provides a structure of rules which establishes certain employee rights with respect to collective action. The right to organise and bargain, as well as the right to refrain from organising and bargaining, is set out in the law. These rights are made effective through the establishment of an election process for workers to choose whether they want union representation, and the prohibition of certain 'unfair labour practices' on the part of employers and unions.

Since the late 1970s, there has been a continuing debate over the adequacy of laws protecting workers' rights to form and join unions. Management spokespersons have argued, and a large portion of the public seems to agree, that unions are too powerful and should not be encouraged by more benevolent organising rules. To the contrary, citing numerous violations of employee rights by many employers, the unions have argued for reforms which would facilitate the enforcement of laws against discrimination against workers for union activity, and expedite the process of choosing union representation. The reality is that employers can violate the labour laws with impunity, knowing the enforcement mechanisms are too weak to do them much damage. The unions tried to correct these problems in their support of the proposed Labor Law Reform Act of 1977. The failure of this legislative initiative in 1978 was a crushing blow to the political credibility of organised labour. This was one of the main spurs to increased union political activity in the 1984 Presidential election.

Since 1959, the government has regulated the internal affairs of unions. Federal law creates a 'Bill of Rights' for union members, requiring that unions accord them rights of free speech and political action. It also punishes union officials who mishandle union funds and outlaws certain anti-democratic practices by unions.

Government is an employer of considerable consequence. In 1980 it employed 15.3 million workers. At the state and local level, government employment increased by 36 per cent between 1968 and 1980. In 1980, 26 per cent of state government workers, 37 per cent of local government workers, 74 per cent of federal postal workers and 19 per cent of federal non-postal workers were unionised (Bureau of Labor Statistics).

The rapid increase in public sector unionisation in the 1960s and 1970s is probably the most important development in the American labour movement since the 1930s. Teachers initiated this, as they successfully protested about declines in their salaries and benefits relative to those of other workers. Unionisation spread rapidly through most areas of government employment. As a result of this wave of unionising, there has been an important change in the composition of the American labour movement, with public employee unions now representing approximately one-third of union members. It remains to be seen to what degree this will affect the basic goals and activities of the movement.

The main processes of industrial relations

In the non-union sector, employers have devised a set of personnel management practices to systematically determine pay and conditions of work. With respect to compensation, a combination of job evaluation and individual performance evaluation systems has become common. Particular employees are assigned wage rates within ranges determined by job evaluation, depending upon seniority, performance, or other factors. In addition to pay, fringe benefits such as health insurance, pensions, vacations and holidays are determined by company policy. All of this is done with an eye to the external labour market, with total compensation having to be adequate to attract and keep needed workers.

With respect to conditions of work, non-union employers establish job design and conditions in two principal ways. First, there is what has been called the 'conventional management theory' approach, in which jobs are standardised and specialised, in the spirit of Frederick Taylor (1964). Jobs are designed in such a way as to maximise efficiency. Second, the 'behavioural science' approach, founded in human relations theory, looks to the internal motivation of workers to provide efficient and high quality production. It attempts to design jobs in such a way that a worker can fulfil his goals and the employer's at the same time. The enrichment of jobs, or at least their enlargement to provide more variety, is a major thrust of this notion. Quality circles and other schemes for worker participation in the design of jobs are consistent with this notion.

Collective bargaining, which chiefly determines the outcomes in the unionised sector, is highly developed in the USA. Since the 1940s, collective bargaining has produced a high standard of living for most unionised workers, protection for the worker interest in fair treatment and a complex and detailed set of rules governing the employment relationship, while generally preserving the managerial ability to ensure efficiency.

The collective bargaining structure is highly fragmented. Single company or single plant agreements are the norm in manufacturing. Most collective bargaining takes place at such levels. Even where national agreements exist, as in the car and steel industries, substantial scope is left for local variations. Yet, in this large and diverse country, there is diversity as to this also, and much bargaining occurs at other (higher) levels (Mills, 1978:120–4).

Although there is considerable variety in collective bargaining agreements (contracts), they share certain nearly universal aspects. Most are very detailed, although the craft union contracts are less so. Agreements generally cover wages, hours of work, holidays, pensions, health insurance, life insurance, union recognition, management rights, and the handling and arbitration of grievances. Most agreements have a limited duration, usually of one, two or three years.

A broadly representative sample of 400 major contracts maintained by the Bureau of National Affairs, Inc. (BNA), provides a picture of the scope of American collective bargaining (BNA, 1983). Discharge and discipline provisions, as well as arbitration clauses, are found in 98 per cent of this sample. Holidays, which are provided for in 99 per cent, amount to nine or more days per year in 83 per cent of the contracts. Provisions covering hours and overtime are found in 99 per cent of the contracts, with the eight-hour day being provided for in a very large proportion of these. Life insurance is provided for in 97 per cent of the contracts, hospital insurance in 81 per cent, and dental insurance in 65 per cent (by contrast, such provisions are rare in British collective agreements). Pensions are mentioned in virtually all American contracts, but the details of pension plans are often set out in separate agreements. Seniority rights are established in 89 per cent of the contracts. These rights, which are crucial in American practice, may cover benefits, such as vacations, or the right to retain an existing job or be promoted to another one. Union promises not to strike are found in 94 per cent of the contracts. Vacation provisions are found in 91 per cent of the contracts, with 58 per cent of the contracts providing for a maximum of five weeks vacation per year. All of the contracts in the sample contain wage provisions, and 48 per cent of them contain some form of automatic adjustment in wages to reflect inflation. Safety and health provisions appear in 82 per cent of the contracts. At least for unionised workers, the relative lack of government welfare programmes in the USA is somewhat compensated for by the extensive protections included in these agreements.

One of the more important developments in collective bargaining in the early 1980s was the widespread occurrence of concession bargaining in which unions accepted cuts in pay and benefits previously won. In 1982, twelve per cent of major contracts either froze or cut wages (Mitchell, 1983:83). The United Steelworkers of America and other major unions have accepted such pay cuts. Although many unions received significant management concessions in return, the reduction of wages was previously rare in American collective bargaining. A related development is the agreement to a 'two-tiered' wage system by some unions in which certain workers, generally new employees, receive lower pay for performing the same work as other workers covered by the same contract.

Third party intervention is widespread. In the private sector, government mediators are active in the negotiation of new agreements, and their work is generally admired. In negotiations involving government employees, many state laws provide for binding arbitration of unresolved disputes over the terms of a new agreement. This is especially common where the government employees involved, such as fire fighters or police officers, are considered to be 'essential'. Interest arbitration of the terms of a new agreement is very rare in the private sector. However, in both the private and public sectors, rights arbitration of disputes over the application and interpretation of an existing agreement is nearly always provided for in collective bargaining agreements. Decisions of arbitrators have historically been treated by the courts as final, binding and unappealable, although their finality has been weakened somewhat in recent years (Feuille and Wheeler, 1981:270, 281).

Worker participation in management, other than through traditional collective bargaining, is an idea which has hitherto not been widely favoured in the USA. In the 1980s, however, there is much discussion of the necessity for developing worker participation for the purpose of improving productivity and product quality. Many large firms have established quality circles to serve these purposes. Interest has developed in the concept of 'quality of working life' (QWL). This ranges from programmes for flexible working hours, to 'cafeteria' benefit programmes where individual workers choose from a selection of benefits, to schemes for worker participation in decisions about how work is to be done (Strauss, 1986).

There have long existed in the USA scattered instances of institutionalised co-operation between unions and management. Scanlon and Rucker plans, which share productivity gains with workers, and joint health and safety committees, have long been used. In 1978, co-operative efforts received some impetus from the passage of the Labor–Management Co-operation Act, under which the federal government assists companies and unions in establishing co-operative mechanisms. Also in the 1970s, area labour–management committees were formed in a number of metropolitan areas for the purpose of fostering co-operation between unions and management (Schuster, 1983:415–30).

Issues of current importance

Of the many issues concerning American industrial relations, three are especially important. These are industrial justice, technological change and trade union weakness.

Industrial justice has become one of the most widely discussed issues, chiefly because there has been increasing dissatisfaction with the common law doctrine of employment-at-will. Under this legal doctrine which has prevailed for many years, the employee can terminate the contract of employment at any time and so can the employer. An employee can be dismissed at any time, for any (or no) reason. The only exceptions to this rule are statutory prohibitions against dismissals which discourage union membership or discriminate on forbidden grounds, and any contractual obligations which the employer voluntarily assumes.

In the unionised sector, employers agree to refrain from dismissing or disciplining employees except for 'just cause'. To enforce this, American collective bargaining agreements provide for a multi-step grievance procedure, with the ultimate step being arbitration by an outside neutral, employed jointly by the union and management. The concept of 'just cause' is one which has been reasonably well defined in the decisions of arbitrators. A distinction is made between 'major' offences, such as theft and insubordination, and 'minor' offences. For a major offence a worker can be discharged immediately upon first offence. For a minor offence, 'progressive' discipline must be used. Progressive discipline means the imposition of progressively more severe discipline, ordinarily beginning with an oral warning, and moving to a written warning, suspension, and eventually discharge for repeated offences. An employer is also required to impose discipline evenly across employees (Elkouri and Elkouri, 1973).

The contrast between the protections available to unionised workers and minority employees on the one hand, and other workers on the other hand, has led to proposals for a general system of protection of all workers (Stieber, 1980). There have been a few court decisions which have somewhat weakened the employment-at-will doctrine. One state, South Carolina, has provided state mediation of grievances to ameliorate these problems.

Technological change is an important issue, as it is in the other countries in this book. It has been said that American industry is prepared to make a 'stunning leap' into automation (*Business Week*, 1981:68). Certainly new technology has major implications for American industrial relations.

Management will probably continue to serve as the prime initiator of technological change. In America, the decision of whether to institute a change in technology is almost always in the hands of management. The role of the union has usually been to respond to management actions with respect to technological change or, at most, to be consulted in advance of a change. The union response has been in the main supportive of the introduction of changes, with a strong interest in influencing particular changes and their effects upon workers. The United Steelworkers of America has even favoured new technology to the extent of conditioning a pay cut upon the expenditure of the savings on new machinery in existing industry locales. There will probably be an increasing union emphasis upon retraining, as is the case in the latest collective bargaining agreement between American Telephone and Telegraph Company and the Communication Workers of America. Based on their past behaviour, and studies of union officer attitudes (Weikle and Wheeler, 1984) it appears that most unions are unlikely to engage in large-scale resistance to new technology, or even to insist upon a guarantee of no lay-offs caused by technological change, as have a few American unions and some unions in other countries.

The role of government in technological change is relatively minor. It has adopted tax laws which facilitate capital investment, such as the 1981 revisions of the Internal Revenue Code. There have been government task forces on the subject, and a series of research reports on changes in various industries. By means of labour relations laws, government regulates the collective bargaining relationship through which organised labour and management settle their differences about technological change. As such, the government has generally supported management's right to institute changes, but has, on occasion, approved the use of the strike weapon by unions in opposition to technological change (Wheeler and Weikle, 1983:2).

The weakness of the trade union movement is an issue which is receiving increasing attention in the USA. Never high, union density has slipped substantially in the last decade. A number of reasons are probably associated with its decline, including:

1 the shift in the economy from manufacturing to services;
2 geographical shifts of industry from the north and midwest to the south and west;
3 the increasingly female composition of the labour force (Allen and Keaveny, 1983:631–8).

Furthermore, the recession has hit hardest at unionised basic industry, causing massive losses of union members. It may also be that even more important causes of trade union decline have been the failure of the unions to expend efforts on organising, and the rising tide of employer opposition.

Employer opposition has been especially great since the mid-1970s. Attempts to disestablish unions are at a new high, as are convictions of employers for violating the labour laws in opposing unions. Given the well-known inability of the labour laws to protect workers from employer retribution, it is hardly surprising that unions have experienced difficulty in organising new members.

The crucial question is whether the American labour movement can survive the current difficulties and emerge as a powerful, lively movement. The alternative is for it to slip into a moribund condition, as it did in the 1920s, a period not unlike the 1980s in political and social climate. Another possibility is a slide to the left, changing from an economic orientation to a more political one. However, neither of these outcomes is likely. Although the unions appear to have a new awareness of the importance of politics, it is still politics directed at achieving more widespread and effective collective bargaining. It seems most unlikely that American unions will become as political as those in Western Europe and Australia. It is also unlikely that they will wither away under the various pressures described above. American unions still have millions of members. As those of us who have worked with labour's 'grassroots' can testify, its ranks are filled with energetic, dedicated and intelligent trade unionists who appear to be capable of weathering the storm. In addition, there are still significant pockets of strength such as public employees and an interesting new militant organisation of female white-collar workers—District 925 of the Service Employees International Union.

Conclusions

The American industrial relations system is diverse. It is confronted with tremendous changes. Yet, it retains the distinctive character which it has had for many years. Managers remain the dominant actors. Although the labour movement has grown and remained reasonably strong, there are doubts about the continuing strength of unions. Workers have done reasonably well in terms of pay, but relative to employees in other industrialised countries, are lacking in job security and social welfare benefits. Government has been content to sit on the sidelines for the most part, and seems increasingly reluctant to assert itself to achieve public purposes in the industrial relations system.

The American industrial relations system has a history of 'muddling through'. It was developed, and has changed over the years, in response to practical circumstances. Pragmatism, not ideology, has been its most constant theme. One who wishes to understand the industrial relations system in the USA would do better to study its history, as do the institutional labour economists, than to delve into the ideologies of the parties or grand theories of economics. Fundamental notions of justice, fairness, balance of power, and the common good are deeply involved in the system, but they are seldom articulated, and are at a high level of generality.

The industrial relations system's character reflects the character of the society as a whole. Yankee practicality is a central aspect of the society's nature. The USA shares this characteristic with such other nations as Japan. It is the flexibility which accompanies such pragmatism which gives American industrial relations a good chance of adjusting successfully to the rapidly changing international economic environment.

Abbreviations

AFL–CIO	American Federation of Labor–Congress of Industrial Organizations
BNA	Bureau of National Affairs Inc.
COPE	Committee on Political Education
GDP	gross domestic product
OECD	Organisation for Economic Co-operation and Development
OSHA	Federal Occupational Safety and Health Act of 1970
QWL	Quality of Working Life

A chronology of United States labour–management relations

1794	Federal Society of Cordwainers founded in Philadelphia—first permanent US union.
1828	Working Men's Party founded.
1834	National Trades Union founded—first national labour organisation.
1866	National Labor Union formed—first national 'reformist' union.
1869	Knights of Labor founded. A 'reformist' organisation dedicated to changing society, which nevertheless was involved in strikes

	for higher wages and improved conditions.
1886	Formation of the American Federation of Labor (AFL), a loose confederation of unions with largely 'bread-and-butter' goals. Peak of membership of the Knights of Labor (700 000 members), which then began to decline.
1905	Formation of the Industrial Workers of the World, the 'Wobblies', an anarcho-syndicalist union.
1914–22	Repression of radical unions because of their opposition to war, and during 'Red-scare' after Russian Revolution.
1915	Establishment of the first company-dominated union, Ludlow, Colorado.
1920s	Decline and retrenchment of the American labour movement.
1932	Election of Franklin D. Roosevelt as President of USA—a 'New Deal' for unions.
1934	Wave of major strikes.
1935	National Labor Relations (Wagner) Act, gave employees a Federally-protected right to organise and bargain collectively. Also, formation of Congress of Industrial Organizations (CIO), a federation of industrial unions.
1934–39	Rapid growth of unions covering major mass production industries.
1941–45	Growth of unions and development of the collective bargaining system during the war.
1946	Massive post-war strike wave in major industries.
1947	Enactment of Taft–Hartley Act, prohibited unions from certain organising and bargaining practices.
1955	Merger of AFL and CIO to form the AFL–CIO.
1959	Landrum–Griffin Act, regulating the internal operations of unions.
1960	New York City teachers' strike—the beginning of mass organisation of public employees.
1962	Adoption of Executive Order 10988 by President John F. Kennedy, providing for limited collective bargaining by Federal government employees. Also the beginning of the movement of the National Education Association toward collective bargaining by teachers.
1960–80	Growth of unionism of public employees. Declines of union density in manufacturing.
1977–78	Defeat of Labor Law Reform Bill in Congress, as employer movement in opposition to unions gained strength.
1980	Election of President Ronald Reagan—new Federal policies generally adverse to organised labour.
1984	Re-election of Ronald Reagan as President.

References

Adams, R.J. (1980) *Industrial Relations Systems in Europe and North America* Hamilton, Ontario: McMaster University

Allen, R.E. and Keaveny, T.J. (1983) *Contemporary Labor Relations* Reading, Massachusetts: Addison-Wesley Publishing Co.

Barbash, J. (1967) *American Unions: Structure, Government and Politics* New York: Random House

—— (1981) 'Values in Industrial Relations: The Case of the Adversary Principle' *Proceedings of the Thirty-third Annual Meeting, Industrial Relations Research Association* Madison, Wisconsin: IRRA, pp. 1–7

Bureau of Labor Statistics (1980) *Current Population Survey* Washington: Government Printing Office

Bureau of National Affairs (1983) *Collective Bargaining Negotiations and Contracts*

Business Week (1981) 'The Speedup in Automation' August 3, 1981, pp. 58–67

Commerce Clearing House (1983) *Unemployment Insurance Reports*

Elkouri, F. and Elkouri, E.A. (1973) *How Arbitration Works* 3rd edn, Washington: Bureau of National Affairs

Feuille, P. and Wheeler, H.N. (1981) 'Will the Real Industrial Conflict Please Stand Up?' in J. Stieber, R.B. McKersie and D.Q. Mills eds *US Industrial Relations 1950–1980: A Critical Assessment* Madison, Wisconsin: IRRA, pp. 255–95

Gifford, C.G. (1982) *Directory of US Labor Organizations* Washington: Bureau of National Affairs

Gompers, S. (1919) *Labor and the Common Welfare* New York: Dutton

Heneman, H.G. III, Schwab, D.P., Fossum, J.A. and Dyer, L.D. (1980) *Personnel/Human Resource Management* Homewood, Illinois: Richard D. Irwin

Hession, C.H. and Sardy, H. (1969) *Ascent to Affluence: A History of American Economic Development* Boston: Allyn & Bacon

Kassalow, E.M. (1974) 'The Development of Western Labor Movements: Some Comparative Considerations' in L.G. Reynolds, S.A. Masters and C. Moser eds *Readings in Labor Economics and Labor Relations* Engelwood Cliffs, New Jersey: Prentice-Hall

Kochan, T.A. (1980) *Collective Bargaining and Industrial Relations* Homewood, Illinois: Richard D. Irwin

Lebergott, S. (1984) *The Americans: An Economic Record* New York: W.W. Norton

Ledvinka, J. (1982) *Federal Regulation of Personnel and Human Resource Management* Belmont, California: Kent

Mills, D.Q. (1978) *Labor–Management Relations* New York: McGraw-Hill

Mitchell, D.J.B. (1983) 'The 1982 Union Wage Concessions: A Turning Point for Collective Bargaining?' *California Management Review* 25, 4, pp. 78–92

Perlman, S. (1970) *The Theory of the Labor Movement* New York: Augustus M. Kelley

Piore, M.J. (1982) 'American Labor and the Industrial Crisis' *Challenge* March–April 1982, pp. 5–11

Player, M.A. (1981) *Federal Law of Employment Discrimination* St Paul, Minnesota: West Publishing

Schuster, M. (1983) 'The Impact of Union–Management Cooperation on

Productivity and Employment' *Industrial and Labor Relations Review* 36, 3, pp. 415–30

Stieber, J. (1980) 'Protection Against Unfair Dismissal: A Comparative View' *Comparative Labor Law* 3, 3, pp. 229–40

Strauss, G. (1986) 'Workers' Participation in the US: Where it Stands in 1985' in E.M. Davis and R.D. Lansbury eds *Democracy and Control in the Workplace* Melbourne: Longman Cheshire

Taylor, F.W. (1964) *Scientific Management* New York: Harper & Row

Taylor, G.R. (1951) *The Transportation Revolution* New York: Rinehart

Weikle, R.D. and Wheeler, H.N. (1984) 'Unions and Technological Change: Attitudes of Local Union Leaders' *Proceedings of the Thirty-sixth Annual Meeting, Industrial Relations Research Association* Madison, Wisconsin: IRRA, pp. 100–6

Wheeler, H.N. (1985) *Industrial Conflict: An Integrative Theory* Columbia: University of South Carolina Press

Wheeler, H. and Weikle, R. (1983) 'Technological Change and Industrial Relations in the United States' *Bulletin of Comparative Labour Relations* 12, pp. 19–21

4 | Canadian industrial relations

MARK THOMPSON

Canada has a GDP of US $342 billion, which represents US $13 000 per capita (higher than in any of the other countries in this book except the USA). Canada has a population of 25 million people. Like its dominating neighbour to the south, Canada has developed a service-based employment structure. Out of its total civilian employment of 11 million people, 69 per cent are employed in services, and 5.3 per cent in agriculture. Canadian industry employs only 26 per cent—a smaller percentage than in any other country in this book (see Appendix, Table A.4).

Students of comparative industrial relations have usually ignored Canada, treating it as part of a continental system or a minor variant of United States industrial relations. While the two nations have similar legal regulation of industrial relations, labour movements with formal organisational links, and plant-level collective bargaining, Canadian industrial relations are now a distinctive system. It is extremely decentralised, with high levels of conflict, a growing labour movement, and frequent legislation to deal with labour problems. In the 1970s, industrial relations were often perceived as serious national or regional issues. Although no national consensus on reform emerged, several governments did amend statutes in efforts to regulate conflict.

The environment of industrial relations

The economic, social and political contexts of Canadian industrial relations are different from most other developed nations. The nation

80

enjoys a standard of living equal to the more prosperous nations in Western Europe, but depends heavily on the production and export of raw material and semi-processed products—mineral ores, food grains, and forest products. Although Canada enjoys a comparative advantage in the production of most of these commodities, their markets are unstable and these industries generate limited direct employment. A large manufacturing sector does exist in the central provinces, but government efforts to stimulate its expansion beyond 20 per cent of the gross national product have failed. Canada lacks a large domestic market, and its manufacturers must compete with much larger US firms elsewhere. Early in the 1980s, traditional Canadian manufacturing industries, such as clothing, automobiles, and electrical products suffered severely from offshore competition. Despite these difficulties, Canada usually exports about 23 per cent of its gross national product and imports almost as much. These transactions are dominated by the US, which is Canada's largest trading partner. Apart from proximity and a natural complementarity of the two economies, Canadian–American trade relations are encouraged by extensive US ownership in many primary and secondary industries.

Canada has a mixed economy, with active roles for both public and private sectors, often in the same industries. Older public enterprises typically came into being for pragmatic reasons—provision of a necessary service, development of natural resources or the preservation of jobs. Thus, many public utilities, transportation and communications companies are government-owned. In recent times, government ownership has served nationalistic goals—the reduction of foreign ownership or stimulation of technological development. In general, public sector companies and their industrial relations are run with relatively little political interference.

Canada's most pressing economic problems in the past decade have been inflation and unemployment, difficulties it shared with most other developed nations. Both prices and wages rose sharply in the mid-1970s, while unemployment, always high by international standards, rose steadily, as Table 4.1 demonstrates. During much of that time, unit labour costs rose more rapidly in Canada than in the US, a cause of special concern to exporters and the government.

Two sets of government policies have been adopted to deal with these problems. Between October 1975 and September 1978, the federal government imposed an anti-inflation programme which included comprehensive wage and price controls, limits on growth in government spending and restrictive monetary and fiscal policies. Nine of the nation's ten provinces enacted legislation to put their own public sector employees, normally within provincial jurisdiction,

Table 4.1   Wages, salaries and prices, 1973–1983

Year	Annual rate of change wages and salaries	Annual rate of change consumer price index
1973	7.5	7.7
1974	11.0	10.9
1975	14.2	10.8
1976	12.1	7.5
1977	9.6	7.9
1978	10.6	8.8
1979	10.9	9.2
1980	10.1	10.2
1981	11.9	12.5
1982	10.0	10.8
1983	10.2	5.8
1984	3.0	4.4
1985	4.0	3.5

Source: Statistics Canada, *Canadian Statistical Review*, various issues.

under the federal programme. Although opinions differ about the impact of the programme, the rate of inflation declined during its life, and the rate of wage increases fell even more sharply. However, both labour and management resented the restrictions in the programme, so it was not extended. But in the early 1980s, the national bank adopted a modified monetarist economic policy, which kept interest rates high, restrained the growth in the supply of money and accepted the basic thrust of US economic policy by maintaining a stable relationship between the two nations' currencies. When the recession of the period grew more serious, federal and provincial governments imposed wage controls in the public sector in an effort to reduce government spending and divert revenues to stimulate the private sector. These policies provoked scattered labour disputes and held public sector compensation down, but did little to reduce deficits or stimulate the private sector.

Politically, Canada has a modified two-party system. The Liberal Party has dominated federal politics for the past 50 years, occasionally forming a minority government or yielding power to the Progressive Conservatives, who returned to office with a large majority in 1984. The Liberals are a pragmatic, reformist party, traditionally relying on overwhelming support in Quebec. The Conservatives are a right of centre party, normally drawing votes from the eastern and western regions. Neither party is ideological, and the Conservative government elected in 1984 did not embrace the strong monetarist economic policies of the Reagan or Thatcher administrations. The New Democratic Party (NDP), with a social–democratic philosophy and strong union support has a small number of parliamentary seats and 15 to 20 per cent of the popular vote. None of the federal parties is strong in all the provinces, and purely provincial parties have normally governed in Quebec and British Columbia. In 1977 a pro-independence party was elected in Quebec, though both French and English-speaking citizens voted to remain in Canada in a later referendum.

Official efforts to deal with economic problems have been hindered by the nation's political structure. Like Australia, Canada is a confederation with a parliamentary government. The ten provinces hold substantial powers, including the primary authority to regulate industrial relations, leaving a few industries, principally transportation and communications, to federal authority. The political structure reflects strongly-held regional sentiments, accentuated by distance and language. The second most populous province, Quebec, is predominantly French-speaking and has strong separatist tendencies. The provinces, often led by Quebec, have resisted any efforts to expand federal powers.

In an effort to establish certain guarantees for Quebec, the Liberal government produced the nation's first written Constitution in 1982. It included a Charter of Rights which contained a number of protections for individuals and groups from government action. Among these are freedom of association and speech and the right to live and work any-where in the nation, all of which have potential impact on industrial relations law and practice.

As a 'new' country, Canada has received immigrants throughout its history. The largest source of immigrants has been Britain, followed by other European countries after World War II and citizens of developing Commonwealth nations in the 1960s and 1970s. Most of the immigrants came to improve their economic status, but many also brought a tradition of working-class politics. Simultaneously, the relatively conservative political tradition of the US has been a powerful model to Canadians. These influences, combined with a parliamentary political system and its acceptance of third parties, have combined to produce a value system which includes both the individualism of an expanding capitalist economy and the collectivism of mature industrial nations in Western Europe. Thus, conservative governments occasionally have nationalised private companies and NDP regimes have encouraged small businesses. Even political parties which govern for long periods of time, such as the Liberals nationally, may alternate between conservative and liberal economic policies.

Major participants in industrial relations

The unions The Canadian labour movement has displayed steady, though unspectacular, growth since the 1930s, despite a long-standing tradition of disunity. Membership reached 3.6 million in 1982, which constituted 38 per cent of non-agricultural employees, an increase from 1.4 million and 31 per cent in 1960. This membership was divided among three national centres and a large number of unaffiliated unions.

The greatest penetration of unionism is in primary industries, construction, transportation, manufacturing and government. In the late nineteenth and early twentieth centuries, Canadian unions were established first in construction and transportation, mostly on a craft basis. During the 1930s and 1940s, industrial unionism spread to manufacturing and primary industries without including white-collar workers in the private sector. Since the late 1960s, the major source of growth in the labour movement has been the public sector. First public servants, then health and education workers joined unions. Professionals, notably teachers and nurses, had long been members of their own associations, and these transformed themselves into unions as their members' interest in collective bargaining grew. By 1980, virtually all eligible workers in the public sector had joined unions. In the public sector, junior managers are permitted to unionise, while supervisors in the private sector are effectively denied the right to collective representation. Table 4.2 shows the relative rate of unionisation by industry.

Approximately 220 unions operate in Canada, ranging in size from under 20 to over 200 000 members. Two-thirds are affiliated with one of the centrals (confederations) discussed below, with the remainder, principally in the public sector, independent of any national body. The ten largest unions contain 42.6 per cent of all members. A variety of union philosophies are represented. Most of the old craft groups

Table 4.2 Union members as a percentage of paid workers, 1982

Industry Group	Per cent unionised
Public Administration	68.7
Construction	61.8
Transportation, communication and other utilities	54.0
Fishing and trapping	45.3
Manufacturing	44.3
Forestry	39.3
Mines, quarries and oil wells	32.9
Service industries	26.3
Finance, trade and agriculture	less than 10

Source: Ministry of Supply and Services, *Annual Report of the Minister of Supply and Services Under the Corporation and Labour Unions Returns Act Part II, 1982* Ottawa: Ministry of Supply and Services, 1984.

still espouse apolitical business unionism. A larger number see themselves fulfilling a broader role and actively support the NDP and various social causes. A few groups, principally in Quebec, are highly politicised and attack the prevailing economic system from a Marxist perspective. But rhetoric aside, the major function of all unions is collective bargaining.

The importance of US-based 'international' unions is a unique feature of the Canadian labour movement that has affected its behaviour in many ways. Most of the oldest labour organisations in Canada began as part of American unions—hence the term 'international'. The cultural and economic ties between the two countries encouraged the trade union connection, while the greater size and earlier development of US labour bodies attracted Canadian workers to them. For many years, the overwhelming majority of Canadian union members belonged to such international unions, which often exerted close control over their Canadian locals. But the spread of unionism in the public sector during the 1960s and 1970s brought Canadian national unions to the fore, as internationals were not active among public employees. As a result, the proportion of international union membership declined from over 70 per cent in 1966 to under 45 per cent in 1982.

Persistent complaints about the quality of service in Canada, American labour's support for economic protectionism and increased Canadian nationalism created pressures for change within the labour movement. During the 1970s, a few unions in Canada seceded from internationals, and the largest international in Canada (the United Automobile Workers) separated in 1985. But a more common (and successful) change was agreement to grant special autonomous status to Canadians in international unions. In the past, internationals encouraged a conservative form of business unionism in Canada, discouraged political involvement and exerted powerful influence over the policies of national centres. While their role in these areas will continue, the impact of policies originating in the US is low and seems destined to decline further. Few Americans are concerned about Canada, and many unions seem ready to sacrifice their international ties for domestic political advantage.

The most important central confederation in Canada is the Canadian Labour Congress (CLC), with about 100 affiliated unions who represent 57 per cent of all union members. CLC members are in all regions and most industries except construction. It is the principal political spokesman for Canadian labour, but is weaker than many other national centrals. It has no role in bargaining. Nor does it have any substantial powers over its affiliates, unlike centrals in West Germany and Scandinavia. The CLC's political role is further limited by the constitutionally weak position of the federal government, its natural contact point, in many areas the labour movement regards as important, such as labour legislation, regulation of industry or human rights. In national politics, it officially supports the NDP. In addition, the CLC has chartered federations in each province to which locals of affiliated unions belong. Some of these bodies wield considerable influence in their provinces.

The Confederation of National Trade Unions (CNTU) represents about 6 per cent of all union members, virtually all in Quebec. It began early in the twentieth century under the sponsorship of the Catholic Church as a conservative French-language alternative to the English-dominated secular unions operating elsewhere in Canada. As Quebec industrialised during and after World War II, members of the Catholic unions grew impatient with their lack of militancy and unwillingness to confront a conservative provincial government. Following an illegal strike against a powerful employer supported by the provincial government in 1949, the Catholic unions abandoned their former conservatism and moved into the vanguard of rapid social change in Quebec. In 1960, the federation adopted its present name and severed all ties with the Catholic Church. Since then, it has become the most radical and politicised labour body in North America. It has supported Quebec independence actively and has adopted left-wing political positions. Unlike the CLC, it has a centralised structure which gives officers considerable authority over member unions. Because of its history, current political posture and the large provincial public sector in Quebec, the CNTU membership is concentrated among public employees.

In 1982, a third labour central was formed. A group of construction unions had left the CLC a year earlier for several reasons. They resented pressure from the CLC to grant greater autonomy for their Canadian sections. They also maintained the craft tradition of business unionism and opposed the social and political activism of the CLC leadership. The CLC voting structure favoured public sector unions and reduced the power of construction unions. Ten of the dissident unions, representing over 5 per cent of all union members, formed the Canadian Federation of Labour (CFL). The new group is apolitical, though it quickly established ties with the federal government. Both the CLC and the CFL have avoided any open hostilities since the latter appeared, but the issues separating them remain, so the potential for conflict is great.

Management Canadian managers have limited commitment to collective bargaining and formal labour relations. Non-union firms strive to retain that status, some by matching the wages and working conditions in the unionised sector, others by combinations of paternalism and coercion. A small number of firms have union substitution policies, which replicate many of the forms of a unionised work environment with grievance procedures, quality circles or mechanisms for consultation. A great many unionised firms accept the role of labour grudgingly, although open attacks on incumbent unions are rare. But in industries with a long history of unionism—for example, manufacturing or transportation—unionism is accepted as a normal part of the business environment.

Most unionised firms in Canada have a full-time industrial relations staff, though seldom a large one. Collective bargaining rounds usually occur at intervals of between one and three years, so it is not feasible for most firms to maintain large staffs for that purpose, and many staff have non-industrial relations duties. Many firms rely heavily on lawyers to perform industrial relations staff functions. Major industrial relations decisions, such as decisions to take strikes or the level of first wage offers, are highly centralised, i.e., taken above the plant level. Overall, the expertise of Canadian managers is not high. Few have formal training, the cadre of specialists is not large, and key decisions are often taken by persons with little sensitivity for the issues.

The high degree of foreign ownership in the Canadian economy affects general management, but seldom industrial relations. Over 35 per cent of the assets of all industrial firms are foreign-owned, chiefly by US corporations. Foreign ownership clearly affects a number of strategic managerial decisions, such as product lines or major investments. But the impact of non-Canadians on industrial relations decisions is unclear.

The organisation of employers varies among regions. No national organisation participates directly in labour relations, although several present management viewpoints to government or the public. Since most labour relations law falls under provincial jurisdiction, few industries have national bargaining structures. In two provinces, Quebec and British Columbia, local economic conditions and public policy have encouraged bargaining by employer associations, normally specialised bodies for that purpose. Elsewhere single-plant bargaining with a single union predominates, except in a few industries with many small firms, such as construction, longshoring or trucking, where multi-employer bargaining is the norm.

Government The government in Canada has a dual role in industrial relations: it regulates the actors' conduct and employs large numbers of people, both directly and indirectly.

Government regulation of industrial relations is very specific, although it rests on an assumption of voluntarism. Each province, plus the federal government, has at least one act covering labour relations and employment standards in the industries under its jurisdiction.

Most governments also have separate labour relations statutes for the public sector. Employment standards legislation generally set minima for such areas as wages, vacations or holidays. In a few areas, such as maternity leave, the law has led most employers. Although the details vary considerably, labour relations legislation combines many features of the US National Labor Relations Act (Wagner Act) and an older Canadian pattern of reliance on conciliation of labour disputes. Each statute establishes and protects the right of most employees to form trade unions and sets out a procedure by which a union may demonstrate majority support from a group of employees in order to obtain the right of exclusive representation for them. The employer is required to bargain with a certified trade union. A quasi-judicial labour relations board administers this process and enforces the statute, although the legislation often specifies the procedural requirements in detail. Despite these restrictions, as many as 30 per cent of all stoppages (normally quite brief) occur while a collective agreement is in force.

Labour relations legislation imposes few requirements on the substance of a collective agreement, though the exceptions are significant and expanding. For many years, Canadian laws have effectively prohibited strikes during the term of a collective agreement, while also requiring that each agreement contains a grievance procedure and a mechanism for the final resolution of mid-contract disputes. More recently, statutes have added requirements that the parties bargain over technological change and that management grant union security clauses. The federal labour code and a few provinces also provide rights of consultation for non-union workers.

Separate legislation exists federally and in eight of ten provinces for employees in the public sector. These statutes normally apply to government employees and occasionally to quasi-government workers, such as teachers or hospital workers. They are patterned after private sector labour relations acts except for two broad areas. The scope of bargaining is restricted by previous civil service personnel practices and broader public policy considerations. Technological change is also often outside bargaining. In a majority of provinces, there are restrictions on the right to strike of at least some public employees. Police and firefighters are the most common category included in such limits, but there is no other common pattern of restrictions. Employee groups without the right to strike have access to a system of compulsory arbitration. While a statute requires arbitration, the parties normally can determine the procedures to be followed and choose the arbitrator.

Although public-sector collective bargaining has been an established feature of Canadian industrial relations since the 1960s, its future was called into question by a series of restrictions on the conduct and results of bargaining introduced in 1982 and 1983. Governments in several jurisdictions sought to combat the prolonged recession by reducing the size of their expenditures. A politically acceptable means was to cut the number and compensation of public employees (at least in real terms). Many governments chose to make these cuts by legislation, rather than through bargaining, leaving public-sector unions with very little to negotiate. It is not yet clear whether these controls on public-sector bargaining will be temporary measures to deal with severe economic problems or permanent features of public-sector labour policy. The federal government and several provinces abandoned their formal control systems, but virtually all jurisdictions have retained either statutory mechanisms to restrict public-sector collective bargaining or policies to restrain compensation there.

The process of industrial relations

The major formal process of Canadian industrial relations is collective bargaining, with union power based on its ability to strike. Joint consultation is sporadic and generally confined to issues such as safety, although in some areas, quality of working life activities consist of consultation on production methods at the level of the work area. Formal systems of worker participation in management are extremely rare. Arbitration of interest disputes is largely confined to the public sector.

Collective bargaining   Collective bargaining in Canada is conducted on a decentralised basis. The most common negotiating unit is a single establishment–single union, followed by multi-establishment–single union. Taken together these categories account for almost 90 per cent of all units and over 80 per cent of all employees. Company-wide bargaining is common only in the federal jurisdiction, where it occurs in railways, airlines and broadcasting. The importance of provincial legislation and practice impedes the formation of wider bargaining units. However, geographic concentration or conscious policies of the parties in industries such as automobiles or meat-packing have resulted in *de facto* company-wide, multi-provincial bargaining units. In response to increased union militancy, employer associations expanded in the 1970s, especially in the construction industry. Several jurisdictions have encouraged this trend by permitting 'accreditation', i.e., giving exclusive bargaining rights to employer associations on behalf of their members.

Despite the decentralised structure of negotiations, bargaining often follows patterns. Although there are no national patterns in bargaining, one or two key industries in each region usually influence provincial negotiations. In larger provinces, such as Ontario and Quebec, heavy industry patterns from steel or automobiles tend to predominate.

The results of bargaining are complex collective bargaining agreements. Few of the terms are the result of the law, and negotiated provisions typically include: pay, union security, hours of work, vacations and holidays, lay-off provisions and miscellaneous fringe benefits. Grievance procedures are a legal requirement and invariably conclude with binding arbitration. In addition, there are often supplementary agreements covering work rules for specific situations or work areas. Seniority provisions are prominent features in almost all collective agreements, covering lay-offs, promotions or transfers, with varying weight given to length of service or ability.

In the workplace, agreements regulate behaviour rather closely. Negotiated work rules are numerous and many parties are litigious, so rights arbitrations are frequent and legalistic. In turn, this emphasis on precise written contracts often permeates labour–management relationships.

Another outcome of collective bargaining is labour stoppages, the most controversial single feature of Canadian industrial relations. In the decade 1974–83, in four key industries Canada lost more working days due to industrial disputes than any other country in this book (see Table A.19). There have been frequent allegations, never really proven, that the nation's economic growth has been seriously hindered by labour unrest. These concerns were especially notable because of the generally low levels of conflict in other aspects of Canadian society.

Historically, strike levels have moved in cycles. There was a wave of unrest early in the twentieth century, another around World War I, a third beginning in the late 1930s and a fourth in the 1970s. As recently as the 1960s, many observers assumed that the strike would 'wither away' in Canada, as was argued in the US. Events of the following decade disproved that hypothesis, as Table 4.3 demonstrates.

By international standards, the two salient characteristics of Canadian strikes are their length and the concentration of time lost in a few disputes. Involvement is medium to low (10 to 12 per cent of union members annually), and the size of strikes is not especially large (350–450 workers per strike, on average). The largest 5 or 6 strikes typically account for 35 per cent of all time lost. In recent years, the average duration of strikes has been about 15 days. These characteristics have not been explained fully, but may be due to the existence of major companies, such as General Motors or International Nickel, and large international unions taking strikes at individual produc-

Table 4.3. **Strikes and lockouts in Canada, selected years**

Year	Number	Workers involved	Days lost	Average length	% of working time
1971-65	355	109,625	1,520,108	14.4	0.11
1966-70	572	291,109	5,709,420	19.6	0.35
1971-75	856	473,795	7,309,102	15.4	0.38
1976-80	1105	618,743	7,824,402	12.6	0.35
1981	1048	338,548	8,878,490	26.2	0.37
1982	677	444,302	5,795,420	13.0	0.25
1983	645	329,309	4,443,960	13.5	0.19
1984	576	184,929	3,890,480	21.0	0.18

Source: Labour Canada, *Strikes and Lockouts in Canada*, various issues.

tion units incapable of inflicting major economic loss on the parent organisations.

Mediation has long been a common feature of Canadian collective bargaining. Two models currently exist. A tripartite board may be appointed and given authority to report publicly on a dispute. Alternatively, single mediators function without the power to issue a report. In most jurisdictions, participation in mediation is a precondition for a legal strike. Although elements of compulsion have diminished, over half of all collective agreements are achieved with some type of third-party intervention.

Outside of the public sector, compulsory arbitration of interest disputes is rare. However, special legislation to end particular disputes is not uncommon in public sector or essential service disputes. Back-to-work laws are extremely unpopular with the labour movement and have contributed to the politicisation of labour relations in some areas. In the public sector, interest arbitration is common. Arbitrators are usually chosen on an *ad hoc* basis from among judges, lawyers or academics. The process is legalistic without the use of sophisticated economic data. When collective bargaining first appeared in the public sector, there were concerns that compulsory arbitration would cause bargaining to atrophy. Experience of the 1970s demonstrated that collective bargaining and compulsory arbitration can coexist successfully, though the availability of arbitration does reduce the incidence of negotiated settlements.

Issues of current and future importance

For most observers, the most important issue in Canadian industrial relations has been time lost due to strikes. In 1982 and 1983, the incidence of strikes fell sharply as the economy suffered a severe recession and unemployment rose. Based on the history of labour unrest in Canada, it is reasonable to expect strike levels to rise again when the economy recovers. Despite public concern about strikes, there have been few efforts to deal with their underlying causes or even to understand them better. Certainly, the fragmented structure of bargaining is one factor that contributes to the pattern of strikes. Yet the causes of fragmentation lie in the nation's governmental structure and politics. Provincial governments resist virtually any effort to limit their powers and the paramount importance of Quebec separatism on the national political agenda has restrained any impulses of the federal government to extend its authority over economic issues. Employees have preferred to seek political solutions rather than work actively to improve industrial relations.

During the 1970s changes in the world economy affected Canada's regions quite differently. Energy-using and manufacturing areas in Ontario, Quebec and the eastern provinces suffered, while the western half of the country generally benefited as energy-producing and resource-rich areas. The recession of the early 1980s tended to reverse this pattern. Naturally, these changes affected industrial relations, but the system lacked any national institutions for dealing with them. Labour, management and government were all divided by regional, economic, political and language lines. As the economy recovers, there are no indications that these divisions will diminish. In fact, they seem to be increasing.

The federal government has attempted to deal with labour unrest in a variety of ways. During the 1970s there were a number of initiatives directed at establishing tripartite systems of consultation as practised in Western Europe. None of these initiatives had any lasting success. Subsequently, the emphasis shifted to greater protection for unorganised workers against economic uncertainty by using many of the techniques of the formal system of industrial relations.

A notable example is protection of individuals who are not union members against unjust dismissal. Two provinces and the federal jurisdiction now grant such rights, including appeal to an impartial tribunal. The administration and results of these systems seem to resemble the unionised sector, although individual grievors are at a relative disadvantage compared to persons who have workplace/union support.

On a collective level, the federal government requires employers planning to terminate 50 or more employees to establish a joint planning committee, half of whom are elected by the employees, to attempt to eliminate the need for redundancies or to minimise the impact of redundancies for individuals. Impasses within the committees are resolved by arbitration. In one province, employers are required to form joint committees to administer safety and health programmes. Although the federal legislation was enacted only in 1982, proposals for joint employee–management committees have been made with respect to adult training programmes, pension fund administration, and the implementation of technological change in office settings.

Experience with these institutions is still limited, so it is difficult to predict their impact or extension. They represent a sharp departure from the North American traditions of government limiting its role in the workplace, to the promulgation of minimum standards and a sharp distinction between the unionised and non-union sectors. The joint committees resemble German works councils more than any indigenous bodies. The labour movement officially has opposed the extension of rights it negotiates to the unorganised, but has not been particularly vocal on the subject. The labour movement's views point to two possible consequences of these initiatives. The new protections may, as unions fear, discourage employees from joining unions. Alternatively, unorganised workers, having experienced collective action or unionlike protections, may choose the broader range of rights currently possible only with a collective agreement.

Constitutional protections   Another issue arises from the Charter of Rights proclaimed as part of the new Canadian Constitution in 1982. Previously, an Act of the British Parliament in 1867 had established the structure of Canadian government, and Canada had relied on the British tradition of an unwritten constitution and the supremacy of Parliament to protect individual and collective rights. Several provisions of the new Charter with potential implications for industrial relations were included without much debate. Thus, their impact will not become clear until complaints are reviewed by the courts. These rights include: freedom of association, freedom of speech, the right to pursue a livelihood in any province and protection against discrimination on the basis of age, sex and race. It is almost inevitable that the courts will apply some of the Charter's protections to industrial relations.

Several issues appear likely to arise. Restrictions on the scope of bargaining and the right to strike that governments impose on their own employees may be challenged as a violation of freedom of association. Union security provisions, almost universal in Canadian collective agreements, may be subject to attack on the grounds that freedom of association also implies protection of the right of non-association. Employer communications during a union organising campaign may fall under the protection of freedom of speech, thereby strengthening management's hand in anti-union campaigns. Many collective agreements require an employer to hire members from a particular local union before turning to 'outsiders'.

Whatever the outcome of these or other issues arising from the Charter, an almost inevitable result will be increased litigation and the remaking of certain long-standing policies entrenched in labour law and the parties' practices.

Political role of the labour movement Although many Canadian unions and union leaders are active in partisan politics, the labour movement has been unable to define a political role for itself. Officially, the CLC supports the NDP, but two problems beset the parties in this alliance. Federally, the NDP has been unsuccessful in raising its share of the popular vote (and legislative seats) beyond about 20 per cent. The CLC is thus left to deal with governments whose election it has opposed. The tensions created by this situation have hampered efforts to establish mechanisms for consultation on economic policies. Secondly, the labour movement has been unable to deliver large blocs of votes to the NDP, though financial contributions and the diversion of staff to the Party are invaluable. As a consequence, when the NDP has governed provincially, it has not been a 'labour' party in the British or Australian modes.

The practical result of these problems is that the CLC has vacillated between wholehearted commitment to the NDP and a more independent posture as workers' lobbyists before governments of any party. To further complicate the situation, most public-sector unions avoid political endorsements and the CFL is strongly apolitical. The founders of the NDP had the British Labour Party as a model, but were unsuccessful in achieving their goal. The American tradition of labour acting as an independent political force has adherents in Canada, despite limited relevance in a parliamentary political system. It thus appears that the labour movement will continue to search for an effective political role.

Conclusions

Industrial relations seldom has been a major issue in Canadian life, but the system is caught up in the central concerns of the nation—the division of powers between provinces and the national government, the relative importance of the public and private sectors, relations with the US and other trading partners, and generally unsatisfactory economic performance. The outcomes of each of these issues will be in doubt for the remainder of the 1980s. While industrial relations will contribute to the resolution of these issues, the future direction of the system is likely to be determined by broader trends in Canadian life. But decisions on economic policy, changes in industrial structure and a new Constitution will ensure that flux and unrest in the Canadian industrial relations system remain high in the future.

Abbreviations

CFL   Canadian Federation of Labour
CLC   Canadian Labour Congress
CNTU   Confederation of National Trade Unions
GDP   gross domestic product
NDP   New Democratic Party

A chronology of Canadian labour–management relations

1825	Strike by carpenters in Lachine, Quebec for higher wages.
1825–60	Numerous isolated local unions developed.
1867	Confederation—Canada became an independent nation.
1872	Unions exempted from criminal and civil liabilities imposed by British law.
1873	Local trade assemblies formed Canadian Labour Union, first national labour central.
1886	Trades and Labour Congress (TLC) formed by 'international' craft unions.
1902	'Berlin Declaration', TLC shunned unions not affiliated to international unions.
1906	Canadian chapter of Industrial Workers of the World founded.
1907	Canadian Industrial Dispute Investigation Act—first national labour legislation, emphasised conciliation.
1919	Winnipeg General Strike—most complete general strike in North American history.
1921	Canadian and Catholic Confederation of Labour formed, Quebec federation of Catholic unions.
1925	British courts ruled that the Canadian Constitution put most labour legislation within provincial jurisdiction.
1927	All-Canadian Congress of Labour founded.
1935	Following the National Labor Relations (Wagner) Act in the US, there were demands for similar Canadian legislation.
1937	Auto workers strike at General Motors, Oshawa, Ont., established industrial unionism in Canada.
1939	TLC expelled Canadian affiliates of US Congress of Industrial Organizations (CIO).
1940	CIO affiliates joined All-Canadian Congress of Labour to form the Canadian Congress of Labour (CCL).
1943	Order-in-Council P.C. 1003 guaranteed labour's right to organise (combining principles of US Wagner Act with compulsory conciliation).
1949	Miners in Asbestos, Quebec, struck in defiance of law, setting off 'Quiet Revolution' in Quebec.

1956	Merger of TLC and CCL to form the Canadian Labour Congress (CLC).
1960	Canadian and Catholic Confederation of Labour severed ties with the Catholic church to become the Confederation of National Trade Unions.
1967	Federal government gave its employees bargaining rights; other jurisdictions followed suit.
1975	Federal government imposed first peacetime wage and price controls.
1982	Federal government enacted Charter of Rights; construction unions withdrew from CLC to form Canadian Federation of Labour.

References

Abella, I.M. (1973) *Nationalism, Communism and Canadian Labour* Toronto: University of Toronto Press
—— ed. (1974) *On Strike: Six Key Labour Struggles in Canada, 1919–1949* Toronto: James Lorimer
Anderson, J. and Gunderson, M. (1982) *Union–Management Relations in Canada* Toronto: Addison-Wesley
Arthurs, H.W., Carter, D.D. and Glasbeek, H.J. (1981) *Labour Law and Industrial Relations in Canada* Toronto: Butterworths
Brown, D.J.M. and Beatty, D.M. (1983) *Canadian Labour Arbitration* 2nd edn, Agincourt, Ont.: Canada Law Book
Craig, A.W.J. (1983) *The System of Industrial Relations in Canada* Scarborough, Ont.: Prentice-Hall
Finkelman, J. and Goldenberg, S. (1983) *Collective Bargaining in the Public Service: The Federal Experience in Canada* 2 vols, Montreal: The Institute for Research on Public Policy
Jamieson, S. (1973) *Industrial Relations in Canada* Toronto: Macmillan
Maslove, A.M. and Swimmer, G. (1980) *Wage Controls in Canada, 1975–1978: A Study of Public Decision Making* Montreal: The Institute for Research on Public Policy
Morton, D. and Copp, T. (1980) *Working People: An Illustrated History of Canadian Labour* Ottawa: Derreau & Greenberg
Rose, J.B. (1980) *Public Policy, Bargaining Structure and the Construction Industry* Toronto: Butterworths
Thompson, M. and Swimmer, G. eds (1984) *Conflict or Compromise: The Future of Public Sector Industrial Relations* Montreal: Institute for Research on Public Policy
Weiler, J.M. ed. (1981) *Interest Arbitration: Measuring Justice in Employment* Toronto: Carswell
Weiler, P. (1980) *Reconcilable Differences* Toronto: Carswell
Woods, H.D. (1973) *Labour Policy in Canada* Toronto: Macmillan
Woods, H.D., Carruthers, A.W.R., Crispo, J.H.G. and Dion, G. (1969) *Canadian Industrial Relations* Ottawa: Information Canada

5 | Australian industrial relations

RUSSELL LANSBURY AND EDWARD
DAVIS

Like Canada, Australia was once colonised by the British, has a
wealth of mineral and energy resources and is sparsely populated.
Australia's population is about 16 million people and its GDP is
US $154 billion. This country has developed almost as predominant
a services sector as the USA and Canada. Thus, out of its civilian
employment of 6.5 million people, by 1984, 66 per cent of them were
employed in services, with 28 per cent in industry and the remaining
6 per cent in the once-dominant agricultural sector.

Having peaked at nearly 10 per cent in 1983, the unemployment
rate in Australia had declined to less than 8 per cent by early 1986.
The rate of increase of consumer prices fell from an average of 9 per
cent for the whole period 1979–84, to 2.6 per cent for 1984, but it
subsequently rose again (see Appendix). Data on pay increases and
industrial disputes also showed a decline. Unlike the other three
English-speaking countries in this book, Australia had a Labor
government in the mid-1980s. The Federal Parliament remains the
formal and symbolic focus of its political democracy, but the
Australian executive and legislature are also particularly important,
as are the state governments.

The context of Australian industrial relations

Australia was founded in 1901. When the former colonial governments agreed to establish the Commonwealth of Australia, they
insisted that the new federal government should have only a limited
jurisdiction over industrial relations. Thus, under the Constitution

of the Commonwealth of Australia (1901), federal government was empowered to make laws only with respect to 'conciliation and arbitration for the prevention and settlement of disputes extending beyond the limits of any one State' (Section 51, para. 35).

Employers were initially hostile to the Commonwealth Court of Conciliation and Arbitration, established under the Conciliation and Arbitration Act (1904), since it forced them to recognise trade unions registered under the Act and empowered these unions to make claims on behalf of all employees within an industry. Having earlier rejected the notion of compulsory arbitration, the unions changed their stand after some disastrous defeats during the strikes of the 1890s. Under the 1904 Act they could force employers to Court even if they were unwilling to negotiate, and once the Court made an award (that is, ruled on pay or other terms of employment), its provisions were legally enforceable. Despite their initial opposition to the system, the employers soon found that they could use arbitration procedures to their advantage and generally supported the system.

The establishment of systems of conciliation and arbitration at the federal and state levels marked an important departure from the British-style industrial relations which had characterised Australia before the 1890s. That British traditions played a large part in Australian industrial relations was unsurprising. British law and British notions of unionism were major imports in the nineteenth century, when the foundations of Australia's contemporary industrial relations system were established. Many Australian unions maintained close links with their counterparts in Britain. Indeed the (then) Australian Amalgamated Engineering Union (AEU) did not become independent of the British AEU until 1968.

The economic and political environment   Industrial relations in Australia are influenced by the nature of its mixed economy. There is a heavy concentration of power in a small number of large enterprises: a handful of firms dominate the economy and structural monopoly and oligopoly are taken for granted. The largest 200 enterprises employ about half of the labour force and account for 60 per cent of fixed capital expenditure. Approximately half of these firms are at least one quarter foreign-owned. Governments at the federal, state and local levels employ approximately one-quarter of the total labour force and have an important impact on industrial relations practices.

Since Federation, conservative political parties have dominated the federal government and made little attempt to develop comprehensive economic planning either of a compulsory or indicative nature. During their brief and intermittent periods in office, Labor governments have made few substantial radical changes in the economic management of the nation, although they have been more sympathetic than their conservative counterparts to union interests. Once in government, all political parties have pursued protectionist policies. This has resulted in the creation of a manufacturing sector which has produced goods for a small domestic market behind high tariff barriers. In recent years, however, these barriers have not prevented the decline of manufacturing employment which has resulted from a combination of structural and technological changes in the Australian economy. During the decade 1973–83, the proportion of the Australian labour force employed in manufacturing declined from 24 per cent to 18 per cent.

The tariff policy was originally designed to insulate the Australian economy from cheap imported goods and provide employment for an expanding labour force. It also enabled wages to be determined by tribunals more on social and equity grounds than in accordance with productivity and market forces. Many protected industries, anticipating the chill winds of unrestricted competition, have tenaciously lobbied governments to retain significant tariff levels. The move of the Whitlam Labor government (1972–75) to reduce tariffs by 25 per cent 'at a single stroke', was strongly criticised by Australian unions as having led to increased levels of unemployment, especially in industries vulnerable to overseas competition.

The Hawke Labor government, which assumed office in 1983, has sought to 'phase in' tariff reductions and encourage competition. Although nominally supporting the new industry policy of the Hawke government in principle, the union movement has been wary of any possible job losses. Until recent years, few unions undertook much analysis of longer-term economic issues and even the central confederation, the Australian Council of Trade Unions (ACTU), has only a small research staff. Thus, for much of the time, the unions have tended to react to government economic policy in an *ad hoc* manner rather than seek to develop independent alternative strategies (Martin, 1980). In the early 1980s, however, there was a change in this tendency, as we shall see later in this chapter.

The legal framework   The system of arbitration includes both federal and state industrial tribunals. Until 1956, the Commonwealth Court of Conciliation and Arbitration carried out both arbitral and judicial functions. Since then, the industrial division of the Federal Court has administered the judicial provisions of the Act while the Conciliation and Arbitration Commission has carried out non-judicial functions. These institutional changes occurred as the result of the 'Boilermakers' Case' (1956) in which the High Court ruled that, under the doctrine of 'separation of powers' laid down in the Commonwealth Constitution, both arbitral and judicial functions could not be carried out by the same tribunal. This requirement does not apply to the state industrial tribunals which administer awards at the state level, covering approximately half the workforce. Federal awards which cover the rest of the workforce tend to set the pattern for all other tribunals, so that a high degree of uniformity has emerged despite the multiplicity of tribunals. Although the Conciliation and Arbitration Commission is empowered to intervene only in disputes extending to more than one state, most important cases fulfil this requirement or can be made to do so. Either party to a dispute may refer a case to the Commission, or it may intervene of its own accord 'in the public interest'. Thus, the powers of the federal tribunal have become much more extensive than originally intended and, from time to time, some states have expressed concern at the continuing drift of control to the federal level.

Under the Australian Conciliation and Arbitration Act, all federal unions are required to register with the arbitration authorities (represented by the Industrial Registrar) in order to gain access to the tribunal and to enjoy full corporate status under the law. Registration requirements also operate for large employers and employers' associations, but registration is more significant for unions since it establishes the conditions for union security, and it has also stimulated union growth. The Act prescribes that a union will not be registered if there is already one in existence to which employees can 'conveniently belong'. While this has helped to reduce inter-union disputes, it has also inhibited the development of new unions and helped preserve some whose principal industry had declined.

The major parties

Trade unions   The establishment of the arbitration system at the turn of the century encouraged the rapid growth of unions and employers' associations. By 1921, approximately 50 per cent of the Australian labour force was unionised. Union density has fluctuated; during the depression of the early 1930s it dropped to little over 40 per cent. The 1940s witnessed a steady increase in density and a peak of 65 per cent was achieved in 1953. Although it declined after this, in 1984, it was still as high as 57 per cent of non-agricultural employees (see Table A.7).

The typical Australian union is small by international standards but varies considerably in size from fewer than 50 members to more than 150 000. Around 30 of Australia's 330 unions enrol 30 000 or more members and this represents approximately 65 per cent of total union membership. As in Britain, unionism originally developed on a craft basis but with the growth of manufacturing, general and industrial unions became more common. The fastest growing area of unionism in recent years has been the service sector, especially in government-related employment, although the density of white-collar unionism is still less than in traditional blue-collar fields (Lansbury, 1980). The basic unit of organisation for the Australian union is the branch, which may cover an entire state or a large district within a state. Plant-level or workplace organisation tends to be informal, but shop-floor committees and shop steward organisations have developed more rapidly in recent years, especially in the Amalgamated Metal Workers' Union which used to be the AEU (Davis, 1980).

The main confederation for both manual and non-manual unions is the Australian Council of Trade Unions (ACTU). It was formed in 1927 and currently has approximately 162 unions covering around 90 per cent of all trade unionists. The ACTU has expanded considerably in recent years following its merger with two other confederations which formerly represented white-collar unions. The Australian Council of Salaried and Professional Associations (ACSPA) joined the ACTU in 1979 and the Council of Australian Government Employee Organisations (CAGEO) followed in 1981. The ACTU has a few formal controls over its affiliates although these formal controls are rarely exercised in practice. The ACTU has considerable influence over its affiliates, however, particularly when conciliating in inter-union disputes. Further, its President tends to be regarded as the union movement's leading representative on major public issues. Officers of the ACTU also play key roles in the presentation of the unions' case before the Conciliation and Arbitration Commission and in the conduct of important industrial disputes. Trades and Labor Councils are also significant in industrial relations at the state level. Although the state Trades and Labor Councils are formally branches of the ACTU, they generally have a much longer history than the ACTU and display some independence in the way they conduct their affairs.

Employers' associations The early growth of trade unions in Australia encouraged the development of employers' associations and led them to place greater emphasis on industrial relations functions than their counterparts in some other countries. Numerous employers' associations have a direct role or interest in industrial relations (Plowman, 1980). However, there is great variation in the size and complexity of employers' associations from small, single-industry bodies to large organisations which attempt to cover all employers within a particular state. In 1977, the Confederation of Australian Industry (CAI) was established as a single national employers' body, almost 50 years after the formation of the ACTU. In 1983, a group of large employers established the Business Council of Australia (BCA) partly as a result of their dissatisfaction with the ability of the CAI to service the needs of its large and diverse membership.

Government The role of government in Australian industrial relations is complicated by the Constitution, which restricts the federal government's industrial powers. The federal government has generally been forced to rely on the High Court's interpretation of the Constitution in order to extend its influence in the industrial arena. The Court's interpretations of the federal government's powers in industrial relations, however, have varied over the years from being liberal to conservative. This has given rise to inconsistencies and uncertainties and has unnecessarily restricted the powers of the Conciliation and Arbitration Commission. The Hawke Labor government has pledged that 'if it is found that these (industrial) powers do not provide a sufficient basis for the provision of a modern, equitable and flexible industrial relations system in accordance with Labor's policies, [the] government will seek appropriate amendments to the Constitution' (Australian Labor Party, 1982). The historical experience of referenda to change the Constitution indicates that the electorate has been extremely reluctant to grant the government increased powers. The existence of a bicameral legislature, in which the Senate has the power to review, amend or reject Bills proposed by the House of Representatives, also provides a restraint on the powers of the federal government when it does not have a majority in the Senate, as has most frequently been the case.

The lack of power to act in industrial relations, particularly in regard to pay policy, has frustrated governments of all political persuasions. During the period of the Fraser Liberal–National Party government (1975–83) there were occasional strong exchanges between the federal government and the Conciliation and Arbitration Commission. For instance, in 1977 the Fraser government argued strenuously that its economic policy would be seriously prejudiced unless the Commission's decisions on wage adjustments were framed in accordance with government wishes. The Commission responded that it was 'not an arm of the Government's economic policy [but] an independent body ... required under the Act to act according to equity, good conscience and the substantial merits of the case' (Isaac, 1977:22).

Local, state and federal governments are also major employers in their own right, employing approximately 25 per cent of the labour force. Their policies as employers are therefore significant. The Whitlam Labor government sought to establish pace-setting conditions for its employees and strove to encourage the extension of union coverage. The election of the Fraser government in 1975 brought considerable change. The conditions of public servants began to fall behind those prevailing in the private sector, and legislation was introduced which strengthened the ability of government as employer to lay off or dismiss workers if it chose. A further measure was the cancellation of the system whereby members' dues in the two largest public sector unions had been deducted from members' wages and forwarded to their unions. The Hawke Labor government repealed those sections of the Fraser legislation regarded as least palatable by the unions and restored the automatic payroll deduction of union dues.

The processes of Australian industrial relations

Compulsory arbitration Interest in Australian industrial relations, on the part of external observers, has tended to focus on the system of conciliation and arbitration. The Australian system of arbitration is compulsory in two senses. First, it requires the parties to submit to a compulsory procedure for presenting their grievances and arguments. Second, the award of the tribunal is binding on the parties. Awards specify minimum standards of pay and conditions which an employer must meet or else face legal penalties.

Parallel systems of conciliation and compulsory arbitration also exist at the state level. Although federal awards have precedence over state awards, the state systems of industrial relations are still very important. Problems arising from overlapping jurisdictions of the state and federal tribunals have been a long-term source of concern to reformers but changes have been difficult to achieve. As one state Premier has observed: for a country with a small population 'it is absurd for us to accept seven separate systems of industrial regulation as unchangeable or sacrosanct' (Wran, 1980). For the purposes of this chapter, however, the focus is on the federal system.

Direct negotiation It is necessary to distinguish between the formal provisions of the arbitration system and the way it works in practice. There is a considerable amount of direct negotiation between the parties. Agreements directly negotiated by unions may co-exist with or take the place of arbitrated awards. They may deal comprehensively with the terms and conditions of work in particular workplaces or supplement existing agreements. It is difficult to be precise about the relative importance of direct negotiations compared with arbitration at any particular time since bargaining often occurs within the process of arbitration.

In a survey of 60 major unions, conducted in the mid-1970s, Niland (1976) reported that three-quarters of the respondents claimed to be using direct negotiation or bargaining procedures in dispute resolution. Some 30 per cent were negotiating solely within the conciliation and arbitration framework, 20 per cent were operating completely outside the system, while 50 per cent were using a mixed approach. These findings provided support for an earlier study by Yerbury and Isaac which reported a substantial increase in the relative importance of directly negotiated agreements at both the federal and state levels. Yerbury and Isaac noted the emergence of a 'peculiar hybrid of quasi-collective bargaining' which, they argued, could well become the dominant feature of industrial relations in Australia (Yerbury and Isaac, 1971).

The introduction of wage indexation in 1975, involving the adjustment of pay by an amount determined by the Conciliation and Arbitration Commission, necessarily centralised the focus of Australian industrial relations. In 1981, however, the Commission abandoned indexation and there were predictions that collective bargaining on an industry or enterprise basis would fill the gap. This was not to be. By the end of 1982, the Fraser Coalition government had imposed a twelve-month wages freeze on its own employees and successfully argued before the Commission for a freeze on private sector wages. The Commission proposed to review this policy after a six-month period. Moves towards the further decentralisation of industrial relations decision-making were therefore thwarted. The trend towards centralisation became more pronounced with the reintroduction of wage indexation in late 1983. A number of factors played their part, including the experience of relatively high unemployment and high inflation which encouraged unions to rely on arbitration tribunals rather than their own bargaining power to defend members' wages and conditions.

Evaluating the system

The settlement of industrial disputes   Any attempt to evaluate the Australian system of industrial relations requires an assessment of the performance of the Conciliation and Arbitration Commission against its original objective 'to prevent and settle disputes'. One of the principal motivations behind the introduction of compulsory arbitration was to render strikes unnecessary. The 'rule of law' provided under arbitration was supposed to displace the 'barbarous expedient of strike action'. For many years, the Conciliation and Arbitration Act contained a provision making strike activity illegal and subject to penalties. Although this provision was removed in 1930, subsequent legislation limited the right to strike. Another 'sanction' used by the tribunals at various times has been to deregister a union which strikes in defiance of a tribunal order to return to work. In practice, however, union deregistration is difficult and those few unions affected have usually been re-registered after making a suitable apology.

One of the main effects of compulsory arbitration has been to shorten the duration of strikes whilst increasing their frequency. Although international comparisons of strike statistics are notoriously difficult (see chapter 1 and Appendix), Australian experience is illuminating. It has consistently been among those countries with a relatively high number of days lost per 1000 people employed. For instance in a study by Creigh and Makeham (1982) of twenty OECD countries, Australia came sixth in terms of the annual average number of working days lost per 1000 employees between 1970 and 1979. The five countries with a higher strike propensity were Italy, Iceland, Canada, the Irish Republic and Spain. Close behind Australia were the UK and the USA.

Although the incidence of week-long strikes increased during the 1970s in Australia, the average strike still lasts for only one or two days (Bentley, 1980). Compulsory arbitration may have increased the number of short-lived strikes 'which are more in the nature of protests against unacceptable arbitration awards and unattended grievances at the shop level' (Isaac, 1968:27). Strikes also appear mainly to involve single issues. Niland's analysis revealed that, as usually categorised, only about one in ten involved more than one issue. Furthermore, in line with Isaac's argument, the majority involved grievances arising out of agreements or awards (Niland, 1976).

Wages policy　Another unintended consequence of the compulsory arbitration system has been the emergence of centralised pay determination. This has been achieved by the progressive dominance of the federal Commission over key wage issues despite a number of constitutional limitations. The Commonwealth Court of Conciliation and Arbitration (as the Commission was originally known) initially became involved in fixing a minimum wage in cases brought before it by the unions. The original ruling by the Court in 1907 described the basic wage as intended to meet 'the normal needs of an average employee, regarded as a human being living in a civilised community'. The basic wage was set at a level sufficient to cover the minimum needs of a single income family unit of five and became the accepted wage for unskilled work. In the 1920s there developed a superstructure of differentials (margins) for skills, based largely on historical differentials in the metal and engineering trades. The Court thus began to regulate wages and differentials through its decisions on the 'basic wage' and 'margins' at the annual national wage case. In 1967, the Commission ended the system of basic wage and margins in favour of a 'total' award. A national minimum wage, representing the lowest wage permissible for a standard work week by any employee, was introduced simultaneously.

The politics of wage indexation   During the early 1970s, the Commission sought to adjust the relative structure of award wages in different industries and to reduce the scope of over-award increases by attempting to bring pay awards more closely into line with actual wages. But by 1973–74, the contribution of national wage cases to total wage increases had declined to approximately 20 per cent as unions bargained directly with employers for large over-award payments.

The influence of the Commission over wage policy reached its nadir in 1974, when 'collective bargaining had become the dominant force in wage increases, its leading settlements being virtually extended to the whole economy within a short time by arrangements and tribunal awards' (Isaac, 1977:14). Faced with the dual problem of rapidly rising inflation and unemployment the Labor government moved to restore the authority of the Commission (Lansbury, 1978). In 1974, both the federal government and the ACTU sought the introduction of automatic cost of living adjustments to wages, against the opposition of non-Labor state governments and private employers. In 1975, the Commission granted full percentage indexation. It also issued guidelines on the principles and procedures of the wage-fixing system under which it believed that indexation should operate. Under these guidelines, no wage increase could be granted without the permission of the Commission (Yerbury, 1980[a]). In December 1975, the new Fraser Coalition government opposed full indexation mainly on the grounds of the depressed state of the economy. It also argued that the unions had failed to comply with the Commission's indexation guidelines. Between 1975 and 1981, partial rather than full indexation became the norm; the system was then jettisoned by the Commission in 1981. A round of direct negotiations followed, similar in style to the collective bargaining round of 1974. It was followed by a sharp recession and the 'wage pause' initiated by the Fraser government, and implemented by the federal tribunal.

The return of a Labor government in 1983, under Prime Minister Hawke, brought the return of the Commission to the 'centre stage' of pay policy. The prices and incomes policy agreed between the Labor party and the ACTU called for a return to 'centralised wage fixation with guidelines based on wage adjustments for price movements and, at longer intervals, for movements in national productivity' (Lansbury, 1985:224). This approach was reflected by the Commission in September 1983, which reintroduced a system of wage indexation. Among the principles announced by the federal tribunal was the requirement that each union agree to forego any 'extra claims' in return for receiving indexation. However, the ability of the Commission, the ACTU and the federal government to discipline unions which seek extra claims is limited and underlines the degree to which the Australian industrial relations system relies upon consensus and informal rules rather than a formal legalistic framework.

Current and future issues

Prices and incomes policy In 1983 a federal election was called ostensibly over the unwillingness of some unions to abide by the 'wage pause' policy of the Fraser government. A draft prices and incomes policy agreed by the Australian Labor Party (ALP) and the ACTU was immediately debated at a special conference of the ACTU's affiliates and overwhelmingly endorsed (Davis, 1984). The policy, known as the Accord, played a major role in the election. Its strength was two-fold. First, it gave the Labor Party an instrument in the fight to reduce unemployment and inflation not available to its conservative opponents. Since the economic policies of the conservative government had had little success, this was of considerable importance. Second, the Accord held out the promise of better industrial relations precisely because of the close links between the Labor Party and the union movement. Much was made of the need for 'consensus' and 'national reconciliation and reconstruction' during the election campaign; the Accord was held up as a symbol of what might be achieved by a government prepared to work with rather than against the union movement.

If the Labor Party's stake in the Accord was considerable, so was that of the union movement. For unions, the Accord presented the means to oust conservative government and replace it with a government committed to economic and industrial policies which unions, through the ACTU, had shaped and moulded. Furthermore, the Accord was perceived as an opportunity for unions to be involved in a broad range of decision-making, stretching from macroeconomic to workplace and encompassing such matters as immigration, social security, occupational health and safety, education, health and employment in the federal public sector.

Following the Labor Party's electoral victory in 1983, a National Economic Summit was convened. The Summit, held in the federal parliament, comprised federal and state government representatives, the full ACTU Executive, representatives from major employer confederations, eighteen 'captains' of industry and representatives from several other organisations. In terms of public relations it was a major success, demonstrating that Australia was rebuilding a national consensus. The outcome of the Summit was the substantial endorsement of the Accord by all parties. Employers too were committed to government economic and industrial relations policy.

In the aftermath of the Summit, there has been a return to centralised pay determination and full wage indexation (Advisory Committee on Prices and Incomes, 1984). Unions, almost without exception, have publicly committed themselves to 'no extra claims' with regard to wages and this has been reflected in a fall in industrial disputes. In the twelve months ending December 1983, there were 249 working days lost per 1000 employees. This represents the lowest comparable period loss since 1967 (Australian Bureau of Statistics, 1984). A Prices Surveillance Authority has also been established. Initially its charter has been to monitor petroleum prices and the charges of organisations such as Telecom and Australia Post. The government has also taken steps to encourage the restraint of non-wage incomes. A number of professional groups (for instance dentists, engineers, and surveyors) have asked the Arbitration Commission to make recommendations on their fees. The ACTU has been closely involved in shaping the federal budgets since 1983. A system of national health care (Medicare) has been established and the government has also repealed much of the industrial relations legislation which had been used against unions under its predecessor. Finally, several tripartite institutions have been set up, such as the Economic Planning Advisory Council and Industry Councils, with substantial union and employer representation.

In view of these innovations, the federal government has argued that it has delivered its side of the Accord. Unions at the 1983 ACTU Congress debated the Accord at length and reaffirmed their commitment (Davis, 1983). Whilst many unions would prefer to see the government taking more action to reduce unemployment and to initiate substantial reform to the system of taxation, there is general satisfaction with the Accord. Unions recognise that the great majority of their members have fared better in material terms than they would have in the absence of the Accord. Further, unions appreciate the considerable amount of information on economic, industrial and social welfare matters which they receive under the Labor government and the opportunity to influence decisions in these spheres. For such reasons, the 1985 ACTU Congress also reaffirmed union commitment to the Accord.

Technological change   Until the mid-1970s, new technologies generated little debate among industrial relations specialists. While significant changes were implemented in specific industries, relatively little dislocation was reported. An exception was the Australian waterfront. The introduction of containerisation among other measures sharply reduced demand for waterfront labour. In direct reflection of this, the size of the union covering waterside workers declined from approximately 23 000 in 1961 to 7000 in 1983 (Deery, 1983). The majority of Australian unions were not so disrupted.

In the mid-1970s many unions became increasingly preoccupied with the issue of technological change. Its sheer speed and breadth of application, shaped in large measure by the versatility of micro-processors, were perceived as major threats to the employment and style of work of union members. An example of the magnitude of change is described in a pamphlet produced by the Printing and Kindred Industries Union:

> To produce a single page of text in a large broadsheet newspaper it might take a hand compositor 22 hours; a machine compositor 5.5 hours; a teletypesetting casting unit 1.3 hours and an electronically controlled photocomposing machine 15 seconds! (Printing and Kindred Industries Union, 1979:9).

An additional critical consideration for unions generally was the steady increase in unemployment in the second half of the 1970s. Members displaced by technological change often could not find other work (Lansbury and Davis, 1984). Most affected were workers displaced from the manufacturing sector; many were unable to find employment in the large and previously receptive services sector. The employer view, however, was that technological change should be implemented without delay to increase competitiveness. Techno-logical change was thus represented as the way ahead. Employers seldom heeded union reservations and claims for involvement in the decision-making process.

The difference of viewpoint between employers and unions was noted in a major report: *Technological Change in Australia* (1980). A Committee of Inquiry, established by the Fraser government in the late 1970s, recommended that Australian industry should press ahead with the implementation of new technology. The Committee was confident that this would create new employment opportunities. But in addition, it argued that employees should be properly informed and consulted, and that social security be made available to those adversely affected. Unions drew little comfort from the report which in their view failed to substantiate its optimism that techno-logical change would improve employment prospects. Further, the underlying theme of the report appeared to be that technological change should be seen as neutral and accepted without reservation. To many unions, technological change is the product of managerial decision-making, designed to serve managerial interests and, in particular, strengthen managerial control. Unions therefore claimed the right to oppose those new technologies believed to be antagonistic to the interests of their members.

The change of federal government in 1983 left its mark. The Accord committed the government to

... support the establishment of rights for employees,
through their unions, to be notified and consulted by employers
about the proposed introduction of technological change
(ALP–ACTU, 1983:8).

Therefore the government supported the ACTU in a lengthy case
before the Conciliation and Arbitration Commission. Under the
terms of the *Termination, Change and Redundancy* decision of
August 1984 employers were required to consult their employees and
unions before introducing major changes to production methods or
to company structure. In addition, where redundancies were con-
templated, the length of notice was increased. Account was taken
of length of service so that for instance, four weeks notice were
granted to any employee of five years service or more. Severance pay
was also increased and was determined on a similar basis. Unions
welcomed this decision which was incorporated into industrial awards
throughout Australia in 1985. Employers were less enthusiastic, see-
ing the decision as increasing costs and impinging on managerial
prerogative.

Industrial democracy   The history of Australian unions illustrates a
sustained interest in influencing managerial decisions on wages and a
narrow band of working conditions. To that extent, workers and their
unions have long sought involvement in at least some critical
decisions. The system of conciliation and arbitration has been one of
the forces that have impeded the further extension of workers'
involvement. The Commission has argued that managers have the
right to manage, and that in consequence the Commission should not
interfere (Isaac, 1980). Furthermore, the process of conciliation and
arbitration takes place at some remove from the workplace, is often
highly detailed (which leaves less scope for workplace decision-
making) and generally involves only a small proportion of the
workers concerned. These factors have necessarily constrained the
effective participation of workers and their unions in the major
decisions that affect life at work. Such 'effective participation' is
treated here as synonomous with industrial democracy.

In the early 1970s, under the influence of two reforming Labor
governments (the federal Whitlam government and the South Australian Dunstan government), industrial democracy attracted considerable attention. There was much discussion of the need to extend
decision-making rights to workers, establish joint councils and committees in the workplace, and place worker representatives on
management boards. In addition it was argued that jobs should be
redesigned to facilitate the more direct control of workers over their
worklife.

A number of employers indicated their support for reform, cherishing the hope that change would reduce problems such as absenteeism and poor quality work and encourage improved productivity. For their part unions wished to see the rights of their members extended and gave their blessing, through the ACTU, to both representative and participative schemes which led to an increase in workers' decision-making power. They made it clear that they strongly opposed plans which failed to provide for the sharing of gains flowing from the implementation of industrial democracy.

Under the 1975–83 conservative federal government and mounting levels of unemployment, the pressure for industrial democracy ebbed away. Unions became increasingly concerned with the defence of members' jobs and wages, and employers found themselves under less pressure to display a commitment to industrial democracy. In addition, the discipline of unemployment rather than the attractions of participation schemes could be expected to reduce problems such as absenteeism and high labour turnover.

The change of federal government in 1983 was again important. The Accord emphasised the need for government, employer and union involvement in macroeconomic and social decision-making. On this basis the government has claimed that it has implemented industrial democracy at the national level and set an example to private-sector employers. The Accord, as noted, argued for workers' involvement in decision-making on the introduction of technological change. More generally, it stressed that 'consultation is a key factor in bringing about change in industry ... (at) industry, company and workplace level' (ALP–ACTU, 1983:9).

There have been several further developments. First, the government has published guidelines on information-sharing which are declared to be a precondition for meaningful participation. Second, the federal and several state governments have taken steps to legislate for improved occupational health and safety. A crucial role is envisaged for joint union–management workplace committees with rights to relevant information, powers to inspect the workplace, and the right to be consulted on all changes in the workplace which affect health and safety. The practice of these rights will result in a considerable increase in workers' involvement in decision-making authority. Third, the federal government has established an Industrial Democracy Unit within the public service and has consulted with public sector unions on a wide range of matters. The government's declared intention is to require each department in its domain 'to develop, maintain and implement an industrial democracy action plan ...' (Advisory Committee on Prices and Incomes, 1984:76).

With regard to the private sector, the Hawke government has

moved cautiously. It has preferred to encourage employers to develop their own approach to industrial democracy rather than impose, by legislation, a particular code of practice. Employers have indicated that they would strongly resist any such imposition. On the other hand, they accept the desirability of increased employee involvement so long as their ultimate decision-making authority remains intact. Put simply, employers have stated that they will support employee participation but will resist threats to managerial prerogative.

If employers are successful, little room is left for the extension of industrial democracy which necessarily entails an increase in workers' decision-making authority. This can only take place at the expense of managerial authority. The extent to which such a shift in workplace power occurs will depend upon a number of factors, including the state of the economy (for instance, lower levels of unemployment will boost union bargaining power), the determination of the government to pursue industrial democracy and the commitment of Australian unions to this goal. The only certainty is that employers will not easily surrender their right to make the key decisions in the workplace.

Reforming the industrial relations system   Soon after assuming office, the Hawke government appointed a Committee of Review into Australian Industrial Relations Law and Systems (chaired by Professor Keith Hancock) to assess the changes necessary to develop a more effective system of industrial relations. After a two-year inquiry, the Hancock Committee delivered its Report which argued strongly for the retention and consolidation of the existing conciliation and arbitration system albeit with certain changes. The centrepiece of the proposed changes was a restructuring of the federal tribunal into two bodies: an Australian Industrial Relations Commission with powers similar to the existing Commission, and a new Australian Labour Court to replace the industrial division of the Federal Court. It was also proposed that the federal and state systems of industrial relations should become more closely integrated. Other recommendations included encouraging union amalgamations by the phasing out of unions with less than 1000 members, the abolition of fines, financial penalties and imprisonment for people involved in strikes and lockouts, and greater emphasis on the process of conciliation in resolving disputes. Further recommendations included a requirement that all awards contain a dispute settling procedure, new steps for dealing with demarcation disputes, and widening the new Commission's powers to deal with all disputes which arose between employers and employees.

The most vocal criticism levelled at the Hancock Report was that it argued for maintaining the framework of the established system and rejected changes which could have led to greater deregulation of the labour market. One concession which the Report did offer, however, was to recommend that employers and unions be allowed to 'opt out' of the formal system if they so wished and to make agreements free from the prescriptions of both federal and state awards. This possibility has always existed under the Act yet has not been utilised by the parties. There remains considerable doubt that, if implemented, the provision to 'opt out' would gain much support while the centralised system persists in its present form.

The High Court has responsibility for interpreting federal government decisions on industrial relations matters in the light of the Constitution. In recent years it has proved a stimulus to reform. In particular, it has supported widening the scope of the federal government's conciliation and arbitration powers and it was applauded for this by the Hancock Committee. More generally, the Hawke government has been cautious in its pursuit of industrial relations reform, perhaps mindful of the experience of the Whitlam federal Labor government. Whitlam had promised to 'reduce government interference' in industrial relations, reconstruct the system of conciliation and arbitration, and facilitate the amalgamation of unions. However, virtually all of the bills introduced into Parliament by the Whitlam government dealing with industrial relations reform were rejected by the Senate which remained dominated by conservative parties (Lansbury, 1975).

The programme of the Hawke government for industrial relations reform is similar in substance to that propounded by the Whitlam government, especially during its final year in office. The dominant concerns are again pay, other incomes, prices, taxation, the 'social wage' and the interaction between labour costs and jobs. There are similarities also in that both governments have striven to strengthen the role of the federal tribunal, despite calls for reassessment of the whole conciliation and arbitration system. However, the Hawke government's approach to the implementation of policy differs in certain respects. For instance, the Hawke government has sought to legitimise its programme of reform by seeking to cultivate public opinion and gain the support of the principal actors through the Hancock Inquiry, before embarking upon legislative change. Yet to be seen is the extent to which the government will move to implement the recommendations of this Committee, and its ability to overcome conservative opposition in the Senate.

Conclusions

The Australian system of industrial relations, as we have seen, has long involved conciliation and arbitration and collective bargaining. The hallmark of the system is the simultaneous operation of these practices, although certainly conciliation and arbitration have appeared the most important. Further, the collective bargaining that has occurred has taken place within the context and availability of conciliation and arbitration.

The number, size and coverage of Australia's unions and employers' associations have been influenced by the requirements of the conciliation and arbitration system. Registration has afforded unions a measure of protection that might not otherwise have been achieved. Many have argued that this has led to a proliferation of unions and employers' associations which has made negotiations even more complex. To some extent this has been offset by the increasingly influential and central role of the Australian Council of Trade Unions. Employers, for their part, have also placed more emphasis on their confederations, the Confederation of Australian Industry and the more recently formed Business Council of Australia.

The third major actor, government, has played a most important part. For much of the chapter, the focus has been on federal government and in that domain it is clear that changes in government have had a marked impact. This is most notable following the election of the Hawke Labor government in 1983. Of great significance for the Hawke government has been the statement of Accord between the Labor Party and the ACTU. The Accord has influenced a range of economic and social policy, and of key significance, it has provided for union involvement in decision-making from macroeconomic to workplace levels. The impact of changes in the political context on Australian industrial relations has been considerable.

Abbreviations

ACSPA	Australian Council of Salaried and Professional Associations
ACTU	Australian Council of Trade Unions
AEU	Amalgamated Engineering Union
ALP	Australian Labor Party
BCA	Business Council of Australia
CAGEO	Council of Australian Government Employee Organisations
CAI	Confederation of Australian Industry
GDP	gross domestic product
OECD	Organisation for Economic Co-operation and Development

Australian industrial relations chronology 1788–1983

1788	European settlers arrived in New South Wales, with separate British colonies established subsequently.
1856	Unions won recognition of the eight-hour day. The Melbourne

	Trades Hall Council (THC) was formed.
1871	Sydney unions created a Trades and Labor Council (TLC); Brisbane and Adelaide unions followed.
1879	First Inter-Colonial Trade Union Conference.
1890–94	The Great Strikes. Following defeat by combined employer and colonial government power, unions founded Labor parties in each colony.
1901	Commonwealth of Australia founded.
1904	Commonwealth Conciliation and Arbitration Court, established under the Commonwealth Conciliation and Arbitration Act, with powers of legal enforcement.
1907	The *Harvester* Case established the principle of the basic wage above which the Court could award a margin for skill.
1916	Widespread union opposition to the Labor government's conscription policy.
1917	NSW general strike, seen as major union defeat.
1921	The All-Australian Trade Union Congress adopted a socialist objective.
1927	Founding of the Australian Council of Trade Unions (ACTU).
1929	The Conservative government defeated in a federal election called over proposed weakening of the Conciliation and Arbitration Court.
1949	A major coal strike, begun around economic demands, saw the federal Labor government take strong action to defeat the Miners' Union.
1950	Penal provisions, known as bans clauses, written into awards, enabled employers to seek an injunction from the court restraining unions from taking industrial action.
1955	The Australian Labor Party split, with breakaway group becoming the Democratic Labor Party.
1956	Following the Boilermakers' Case, the Arbitration Court was disbanded. The Conciliation and Arbitration Commission was set up with arbitral functions, and the Industrial Court with judicial responsibility.
1967	Metal Trades Work Value Case—the determination of a basic wage and margins was discontinued and a 'total wage' was introduced in lieu.
1969	The jailing of a union official for failure to pay fines for contempt of court leading to extensive strike action throughout Australia.
1972	A federal Labor government was elected after 23 years of Liberal Coalition government.
1975	Wage indexation introduced; Labor government dismissed.
1977	The CAI established as a national employers' confederation.
1979	The Australian Council of Salaried and Professional Associations affiliated with the ACTU.
1981	The Council of Australian Government Employee Organisations merged with the ACTU; wage indexation abandoned.

1982   Twelve-month freeze on wages of Commonwealth employees
            imposed by government; six-month freeze on private sector
            workers decided by the Commission.
1983   Hawke Labor government elected. ALP–ACTU Prices and
            Incomes Accord became the lynch-pin of government policy.
            Return to centralised wage fixation and full wage indexation.
1985   The Accord reaffirmed by ACTU Congress. Report by the
            Hancock Committee on Australian Industrial Relations Law
            and Systems.

References

Advisory Committee on Prices and Incomes (1984) *Prices and Incomes Policy*
    Canberra: Australian Government Publishing Service
Australian Bureau of Statistics (1984) *Industrial Disputes, Australia,
    December, 1983* Catalogue No: 6321.0
—— (1985) *Trade Union Statistics, Australia, December, 1984* Catalogue
    No: 6323.0
Australian Labor Party (1982) 'Policy on Industrial Relations' *Annual ALP
    Conference Proceedings*
Australian Labor Party—Australian Council of Trade Unions (1983) *State-
    ment of Accord by ALP and ACTU Regarding Economic Policy* ALP–
    ACTU, 1983
Bentley, P. (1980) 'Recent Strike Behaviour in Australia: Causes and
    Responses' in G.W. Ford, J.M. Hearn and R.D. Lansbury eds *Australian
    Labour Relations: Readings* Melbourne: Macmillan, pp. 21–49
Committee of Inquiry into Technological Change in Australia (1980)
    Technological Change in Australia Canberra: AGPS
Committee of Review into Australian Industrial Relations Law and Systems
    (1985) *Report* Canberra: AGPS
Creigh, S.W. and Makeham, P. (1982) 'Strike Incidence in Industrial
    Countries: An Analysis' *Australian Bulletin of Labour* 8, 3, pp. 139–55
Davis, E.M. (1980) 'Decision-making in the Amalgamated Metal Workers
    and Shipwrights Union' in Ford, Hearn and Lansbury (1980), pp. 124–48
—— (1983) 'The 1983 ACTU Congress: Consensus Rules OK!' *Journal of
    Industrial Relations* 25, 4, pp. 507–16
—— (1984) 'The ALP–ACTU Accord' *National Australia Bank Monthly
    Summary* January, pp. 12–15
Davis, E.M. and Lansbury, R.D. eds (1986) *Democracy and Control in the
    Workplace* Melbourne: Longman Cheshire
Deery, S. (1983) 'The Impact of Technological Change on Union Structure:
    The Waterside Workers Federation' *Journal of Industrial Relations* 25, 4,
    pp. 399–414
Ford, G.W., Hearn, J.M. and Lansbury, R.D. eds (1980) *Australian Labour
    Relations: Readings* Melbourne: Macmillan
Ford, G.W. and Plowman, D. eds (1983) *Australian Unions* Melbourne:
    Macmillan

Isaac, J.E. (1968), *Compulsory Arbitration in Australia* Task Force on Labour Relations, Study No 4, Ottawa: Queen's Printer

—— (1977) *Wage Determination and Economic Policy* The Giblin Memorial Lecture, University of Melbourne

—— (1980) 'The Legal Framework in Australia for Industrial Democracy' in R.D. Lansbury ed. *Democracy in the Workplace* Melbourne: Longman Cheshire, pp. 34–53

Lansbury, R. (1975) 'Promise Against Performance: The Labor Government and Industrial Relations' *Journal of Industrial Relations* 17, 3, pp. 288–95

—— (1978) 'The Return to Arbitration: Recent Trends in Dispute Settlement and Wages Policy in Australia' *International Labour Review* 117, 5 (Sept.–Oct.), pp. 611–24

—— (1980) 'White-collar and Professional Employees in Australia: Reluctant Militants in Retreat' in Ford, Hearn and Lansbury (1980), pp. 100–23

—— (1985) 'The Accord: A New Experiment in Australian Industrial Relations' *Labour and Society* 10, 2, pp. 223–35

Lansbury, R.D. and Davis, E.M. eds (1984) *Technology, Work and Industrial Relations* Melbourne: Longman Cheshire

Lansbury, R.D. and Yerbury, D. (1984) 'Industrial Relations Reform: Challenges Facing a Federal Labor Government' in J. Reeves ed. *Labor Essays* Melbourne: Drummond

Martin, R.M. (1980) *Trade Unions in Australia* Ringwood: Penguin

Murphy, Hon. Justice L. (1983) Address to *Seminar in Changing Industrial Law* Canberra, Australian National University

Niland, J.R. (1976) *Collective Bargaining in the Context of Compulsory Arbitration* Sydney: New South Wales University Press

Plowman, D. (1980) 'Employer Associations: Challenges and Responses' in Ford, Hearn and Lansbury (1980), pp. 248–78

—— (1983a) 'Unions and Incomes Policies: Wage Indexation and Beyond' in Ford and Plowman (1983), pp. 412–34

—— (1983b) 'Union Statistics: Scope and Limitations' in Ford and Plowman (1983), pp. 522–51

Printing and Kindred Industries Union (1979) *New Technology and the Australian Printing Industry* PKIU

Willis, R. (1983) 'Intentions and Aspirations of the Federal Government' *Seminar on Changing Industrial Law* Canberra: Australian National University

Wran, N.K. (1980) Address to the *Annual Convention of the Industrial Relations Society of New South Wales*

Yerbury, D. (1980a) 'Collective Negotiations, Wage Indexation and the Return to Arbitration: Some Institutional and Legal Developments During the Whitlam Era' in Ford, Hearn and Lansbury (1980), pp. 462–503

—— (1980b) 'Industrial Relations Inquiries' *Industrial Relations Reform* Occasional Paper No. 6, Kensington: University of New South Wales, pp. 13–16

Yerbury, D. and Isaac, J.E. (1971) 'Recent Trends in Collective Bargaining in Australia' *International Labour Review* 110 (May), pp. 421–52

III
Continental European countries

6 | Italian industrial relations

CLAUDIO PELLEGRINI

This chapter starts by putting Italian industrial relations into an economic, historical and political context. It describes the various union confederations, employers' organisations and the role of the state. It then continues by considering the different levels and content of collective bargaining and concludes by commenting on the recent controversies about the *scala mobile* (the Italian form of wage indexation) and their consequences on union unity.

Italy had a total population of 57 million people in 1984 with a labour force participation rate of only 60 per cent. This is a lower participation rate than in any of the other countries in the book. One reason for this is that the official participation rate for women is only 41 per cent, which is less than in the other countries (The OECD average for women is 55 per cent, see Table A.2).

In terms of employment in 1984, Italy's agricultural sector (12 per cent) is larger than those of the other countries, even though it has declined from 34 per cent in 1959. Italy has the second-largest industrial sector (35 per cent); only West Germany's is larger (41 per cent). As another Italian characteristic, there is a relatively large clandestine or 'informal' economy, which is unrecorded and untaxed. Some estimate that it amounts to 20 to 30 per cent of Italy's GDP. This characteristic disguises the real rates of GDP, employment participation and unemployment; for example Italy's official GDP in 1984 was US $354 billion; it had a GDP per capita of $6.1 thousand, lower than in any of the other eight countries.

Like most other industrial countries, according to the official statistics, Italy has experienced a substantial rise in its unemployment

121

rate, which more than doubled between 1971 and 1985 from 5.4 per cent to 12.4 per cent (see Table A.5). Half of the unemployed are young people looking for their first job.

There is a major cleavage between the north and south of Italy. The participation rate and pay levels are much lower, while unemployment is much higher in the south than the north. Although the south constitutes 41 per cent of the land and 35 per cent of the population, it contributes only 15 per cent of total industrial employment. Such regional differences have a major influence on collective bargaining.

Another aspect of the economic context is the role played by exports, which represent about 21 per cent of the GDP (about the same percentage as in Britain). However, Italy depends entirely on imported oil. After 1973, the increased oil price and labour costs made it more difficult for firms to maintain their foreign markets. Morever, Italy's average rate of price inflation between 1979 and 1984, was 16 per cent, higher than in any of the other countries. But by 1985 the rate had fallen to about 9 per cent.

Productivity increases in manufacturing have been on average 4.4 per cent between 1979 and 1981; during the recession of 1982 and 1983 they declined to 1.25. In 1984, however, due to the reduction in employment, there was an increase of 7.9 per cent. Wages, however, have not been keeping up with productivity increases (Patriarca, 1985). This has also been the case throughout the entire private sector. In the period 1975–78, 'real wages were increasing on average 4.7 per cent per year and productivity was growing at 1.3 per cent; in the period 1979–84, real wages increased on average 0.1 per cent while productivity growth was 1.7 per cent. If the consequences of fiscal drag are considered, real wages after taxes declined on average 1.4 per cent between 1979 and 1984 (see Table 6.1).

The high level of public deficit is an increasing source of concern. It was nearly 16 per cent of GDP in 1985, almost three times the US level. The deficit is partly due to the increased cost of welfare payments, and to greater public support to the private sector, but it is also related to the inefficiency of the public sector in both manufacturing and services. In 1983, the average take-home pay in Italy was 80 per cent of gross earnings, the average level for the nine countries (see chapter 2, note 2).

Italian politics

After the fall of Fascism and the end of the Second World War, the major political parties that emerged were:

1 the Christian Democratic Party (Democrazia Cristiana, DC) a
   Catholic-oriented inter-class moderate party;

Table 6.1 Italian economic indicators

Year	Consumer price index 1980 = 100 (annual % change)	Wage integration fund (millions of hours)	Index of industrial production 1970 = 100 (annual rate of change)	Real wages (annual rate of change)	Real wages after taxes (annual rate of change)	Productivity: private sector (annual rate of change)
1971	5	199	-.1			2
1972	5.6	174	4.4			4.8
1973	10.3	126	9.7			7.2
1974	19.3	168	4.5			2.7
1975	17.1	349	-9.2	3.1	1.8	-4.3
1976	16.5	286	12.4	6	6	5.4
1977	18.1	255	1.1	7	5.2	1.8
1978	12.4	324	1.9	2.8	1.2	2.4
1979	15.7	299	6.6	1.5	-.8	4.7
1980	21.2	307	5.6	-.6	-1.9	3.7
1981	18.7	577	-2.3	2.2	-.6	-.1
1982	16.3	619	-2.2	-1.0	-2.9	-.4
1983	15	746	-5.2	-1.7	-1.6	-.3
1984	10.6	816	3.1	.2	-.7	2.5

Source: ISTAT aud Banca D'Italia.

2   the Communist Party (Partito Comunista Italiano, PCI) which
    from its revolutionary origin has become a reform-oriented party
    and has played the role of the major political opposition;
3   the Socialist Party (Partito Socialista Italiano, PSI) a social
    democratic party about one third the size of the PCI;
4   other small centre-oriented political parties such as the Liberal
    Party (Partito Liberale Italiano, PLI), the Republican Party
    (Partito Repubblicano Italiano, PRI) and the Social Democratic
    Party (Partito Socialista Democratico Italiano, PSDI).[1]

Between 1945 and 1947, all the anti-fascist parties, including the
PCI, formed a coalition Government of National Unity. In the 1948
Cold War climate, following the electoral success of the DC, the PSI
and the PCI were excluded from government. The DC party, with
about 35 per cent of the vote, has always been in power since then.
Between 1948 and 1964 the governments were based on a coalition
between the DC and other small centre parties; after 1964, the PSI
also entered the coalition.

What are the consequences for industrial relations of this political
context? While in countries such as Australia, Britain, West Germany, Sweden and France, the functioning of the democratic system
is based on the competition between conservative and socialist labour
parties which have been alternatively in power, in Italy the main political opposition, the PCI, has never been in power since the post-war
Government of National Unity. The lack of change between the two
major parties resulted from the Communist Party (in its roots, if not
in its policies) being seen as too far to the left to gain more support or
to form a coalition with other parties. In other words, the PCI was
not considered a legitimate contender for national government. Some
observers have called this situation 'blocked democracy' and it had
negative consequences for the functioning of the political system. The
party that was always in power with little risk of being challenged
became less accountable and less efficient in administration.

In the realm of industrial relations, unlike other European countries a union–government relationship based on accords or social
contracts (as in Australia, Sweden or Britain) is unlikely in Italy.
Firstly because a government based on the major pro-labour party has
never been in power; secondly, even if it were in power, the presence
of competing unions with different political orientations would
prevent the functioning of a union–government accord.

It should be also added that between 1976 and 1979 the PCI
supported the government in Parliament but did not participate in the
Cabinet. This was the only feasible solution, because after the
electoral success of the PCI in 1976, the PSI refused to participate in

governments that did not have support from the PCI. The period of so-called National Solidarity lasted until 1979 (in those years political terrorism was rampant in Italy). Afterwards the PCI, which was losing support, went back to opposition. The government since then has been formed by a coalition between the DC, PSI and all the other centre parties. The President of the Cabinet, however, is no longer DC but has been Spadolini (PRI) in 1981 and 1982, and Craxi (PSI) since then.

The industrial relations parties

In the analysis of industrial relations, it is important to take into consideration some historical background. First, one should consider the late capitalist development of Italy; for instance, in 1901, out of 1000 employees only 238 were in the industrial sector compared to 632 in Britain (Barbadoro, 1973:21). Second, there is a weak democratic tradition (universal voting rights for males over 30 were only given in 1912). Both elements help to explain the strength of the revolutionary and socialist tradition within Italian labour. Another aspect to be considered is the large role played by the organisations of agricultural workers, which explains the importance in the union structure of the local geographical organisations called Chambers of Labour (Camere del Lavoro).

In order to explain the absence of unions based on craft, one should also mention that unionism in Italy took shape at the start of the twentieth century (later than in Britain) and that socialists played a determinant role. At that time, the second international considered industrial unionism the most appropriate form of organisation, because it was the most conducive to worker unity and because it was more suited to the organisation of the large manufacturing plants that were then emerging as the key factor in the industrial sector.

The Fascist period between 1922 and 1944 terminated all the established unions. The corporatist experience has left a legacy, particularly in terms of centralisation of the decision-making process and governmental intervention in industrial relations. This legacy has also reinforced the industrial basis of Italian unionism. For these reasons, after 1944 all the confederations had no doubt about basing their organisation along industrial lines.

A final element to be considered is the Catholic tradition before and after Fascism. Compared with other countries, according to Jemolo (1963:6):

the Italian Catholics were the last to join in organizing the workers, in studying social problems ... There was too long a tradition of agreements between the wealthy classes and the Church.

The situation changed at the turn of the century. The papal encyclical *Rerum Novarum* in 1891 encouraged the formation of Catholic organisations in the industrial sector and competition with the socialist-oriented Chamber of Labour favoured the emergence of Catholic trade unionism. In 1918, the Confederazione Italiana dei Lavoratori was formed. In the same period, Catholics became active in the political arena, from which they had been absent since 1870, when the papal states were annexed by the emerging Italian reign.

The unions The three major organisations are the Confederazione Generale Italiana del Lavoro (CGIL), with about 4.5 million members in 1983, the Confederazione Italiana Sindacati Lavoratori (CISL), with 2.9 million, and Unione Italiana del Lavoro (UIL), with 1.3 million. In the membership are also included retired employees who belong to a separate structure. Without the retirees, the membership for CGIL, CISL and UIL would be 3.2, 2.4 and 1.2 million respectively. Union membership increased dramatically after 1969. In that year the three confederations had 2.6, 1.6, and 0.7 million members respectively. In total, the rate of unionisation jumped from 29 per cent in 1969 to over 50 per cent in the late 1970s, but the rate declined again in the 1980s. The largest organisation, CGIL, is socialist- and communist-oriented; the CISL has a large but not exclusively Catholic component; the UIL has ties with socialist and small centre parties. The relationship between unions and political parties has a long, complex history; here we can highlight only the most important phases and their consequences[2].

In 1944, the representatives of the major political parties that were opposed to the Fascist regime (Communist, Catholic and Socialist) signed an agreement which later led to the formation of CGIL. The three political components that formed the confederation remained together until 1948, when there was a rupture in the coalition government which had included Socialists and Communists. As a consequence there was a split in the CGIL. The Catholic component left the CGIL in 1948 and formed the CISL. In 1950, the Republicans and Social Democrats also left the CGIL and formed the UIL. Socialists remained in the CGIL, but gained strength particularly in the UIL.

During the 1950s, the links between political parties and unions were more direct and the latter had little room for autonomous decisions. During the 1960s, however, inter-union co-operation began to emerge, together with a new political climate (centre–left coalition) and the development of national and plant bargaining, particularly after 1969. Accordingly, the unions became more politically independent. When in 1973 the three union confederations formed the Federazione CGIL–CISL–UIL, it was also decided that their leaders could not hold office in political parties or be members of Parliament (Weitz, 1975). Obviously the political climate has an influence on the three confederations. But it is important to understand that there is a plurality of party allegiances, so compromise is usually necessary between and within each confederation.

Beside the three major confederations in Italy, there are also other unions. In 1950, the Confederazione Italiana Sindacati Nazionali Lavoratori (CISNAL) was founded by the heirs of the Fascist tradition. This confederation, however, has no significant role in Italian industrial relations. In Italy there are also independent union organisations (so-called '*sindacati autonomi*') which are particulary strong in the public sector, education, hospitals and transport. The main organisations are: Confederazione Italiana Sindacati Autonomi Lavoratori (CISAL) present particularly in the municipalities and railways; Confederazione Sindacati Autonomi Lavoratori (CONFSAL), particularly strong in education and public employees; Confederazione Italiana Sindacati Addetti ai Servizi (CISAS) in the services[3].

Managers (*dirigenti*) also have their own organisations. The main one is Confederazione Italiana Dirigenti di Azienda (CIDA) with about 100 000 members, 40 per cent of them in the industrial sector where the unionisation rate among managers was 41 per cent in 1984.

In analysing the union structure inside and outside the workplace, it is important to keep in mind that there are differences between the legal framework, collective bargaining provisions and the *de facto* situation. From 1948 until 1970, the unions were not present as such in the workplace. By agreement with Confindustria there were Internal Commissions (*Commissioni Interne*) which were elected by all the employees, mainly to administer the national agreements. The main competing unions presented candidates for the Commission, but the latter was not formally a union structure as in the case of the French *comité d'entreprise* or the German *Betriebsrat* (see chapters 7 and 8).

During the 1960s, when the economic situation was improving, the unions were enjoying more power and they tried to establish union representatives (*Rappresentanza Sindacale Aziendale*, RSA), a position similar to the *vertrauensmann* in Germany. In 1970, the so-called Workers' Statute was enacted and consequently the workers had the right to establish RSA in the workplace and to have them recognised as such by the unions most representative in the country, or those that had signed national–local contracts applied in the workplace. The leaders of each RSA have the right to a certain amount of working time for union activity, based upon the size of the firm, and are protected from dismissal.

During the early 1970s, new forms of worker representation were emerging based on shop stewards (*delegati*) for each work unit. The shop stewards formed factory councils (*Consiglio di Fabbrica*). Both union and non-union members were eligible to vote and to be elected (Sciarra, 1977). When the three main confederations formed the unitary structure in 1972, they decided to recognise the factory council as the union structure in the workplace and the *delegati* enjoyed the legal protection given to RSA by the Workers' Statute, 1970. Thus at their workplace employees then had only one form of representation, which was also the basis of union organisation and played a major role in collective bargaining at plant level (Regalia et al. 1978).

After the establishment of the Federazione CGIL–CISL–UIL, one problem was to ensure representation of all the major confederations within the factory councils. This difficulty was ameliorated by the growth of all unions after 1970 and by the reduction of the friction between them. It is still possible, however, for a union that does not have members elected in the council to have their representatives as RSA (though this is rarely the case). In 1981, there were 32 021 factory councils with 206 336 shop stewards, representing more than 5 million workers (ETUI, 1985).

Outside the workplace, together with the Federazione CGIL–CISL–UIL, united federations were also formed between the structure of CGIL, CISL and UIL at the (vertical) industrial level and at the (horizontal) geographical level in the cities and regions. When the unitary federations were formed, the goal was to proceed gradually toward a merger. In the transitional period, the statute of the unitary federations simply gave an equal number of seats to each confederation, regardless of its actual membership. Thus none of them risked being engulfed. The merger, however, did not occur. On the contrary, differences between the unions began to emerge in the late 1970s, both because unfavourable economic conditions forced unpopular decisions and because of greater political competition. Decision-making within the unitary structure became cumbersome since majority rule could not be used, and compromise acceptable to all three components had to be found. In 1984, following the change of the national indexation system, the unitary structure collapsed. Since then each confederation has regained autonomy of action. This does not prevent unity on specific issues. At the plant level, however, it is more difficult for unions to cope with the collapse of the Federazione because the workers' councils were based on a unitary structure and hopes of a future merger among the unions. New rules need to be found in order to establish electoral procedures and the structure of worker representation.

The employers The most important employers' organisation for private employers is the Confindustria, which represents associations of the largest firms, in particular in the manufacturing and construction sectors. Firms may join both the regional multi-sector association and the national sector one: the two together form the Confindustria. In 1985 the Confindustria had 106 local associations and about 100 000 local units representing 3 200 000 employees. The local units were distributed geographically in the following way: 57 per cent north, 20 per cent centre and 23 per cent south; the employees had the following distribution: 74 per cent in the north; 15 per cent in the centre and 11 per cent in the south. Some firms do not belong to a local association but only to a national sectoral association, of which there are nearly a hundred.

Confindustria has two main objects: one concerns industrial relations and the other concerns the broader economic, technical and political needs of their members. During the 1970s, Confindustria merged the various metalworking associations into a new organisation, the Italian Metalworking Industry Federation (Federmeccanica), which is exclusively concerned with industrial relations. There was a similar merger in the chemicals sector.

Public sector manufacturing enterprises have their own associations only for the purpose of collective bargaining. The most important is Intersind which since 1958 has represented the Institute for Industrial Reconstruction (IRI), a group consisting of 280 firms and 400 000 employees in 1985. The other public sector employers' association is the Union Association for the Petrochemical Sector (ASAP) with 97 firms and 130 000 employees of the National Institute for Hydrocarbons (ENI) mainly in the chemical and energy sectors.

Private employers also have collective organisations in the commercial sector (Confcommercio) and in agriculture, (Confagricoltura); the latter with 672 000 local units. In the banking and credit sector there is Assicredito with 400 members and 300 000 employees. Small firms are represented by Confapi which in 1980 had 24 318 members and employed 865 000 people; it has eighteen national agreements signed with different unions. Craft shops and small businessmen (*artigiani*) also have their own organisations and several collective agreements with unions on a sectoral basis; the same is true also for the co-operatives.

Within the Confindustria there has been a tense relationship between large industrial groups and other firms. This has hindered the development of a unified strategy towards the unions and governments. In the past, there have also been differences in the employer policies between capital- and labour-intensive industries, with the latter being more concerned with employment costs.

The Confindustria plays an important role in co-ordinating national bargaining in the major industrial sectors, and has a direct role in bargaining with the union confederations on agreements that apply to the entire country. This role has become particularly important because, since 1975, bargaining levels have become more centralised (see later).

In the past, the public sector employers have been innovative and have often been the first to make agreements during bargaining rounds. More recently, the retrenchment in the public sector has imposed severe constraints on their innovative role. However, in the IRI group, an important agreement was signed in 1984 which established joint committees for consultation on a large variety of issues related to strategic decisions and industrial relations policies.

Although in the political arena the Confindustria traditionally had strong ties with the Christian Democratic Party (Martinelli and Treu, 1984:287), relations have been strained due to a shifting balance of power within the Confindustria and within the Christian Democratic Party.

The role of the state   As in Britain before the 1960s, there was relatively little legal intervention in Italian industrial relations. The new Constitution established in 1948 had some provisions regarding the recognition of trade unions and the right to strike, but legislation on this issue was not passed. Traditionally, many matters related to social security and the labour market have been regulated by law. The importance of collective bargaining in determining conditions of employment has always been recognised by the government and in 1959 all the existing agreements were given a legal status (called *erga omnes* provisions) and they constitute a minimum (often improved by further legislation and bargaining) that applies to all (Giugni, 1972).

Legislation has played an increasingly important role since the late 1960s, but labour law does not regulate the bargaining process, the size of the bargaining unit and the right to strike. Besides the earlier-mentioned Workers' Statute, other important laws regulate social security and minimum pay during lay-offs. In many cases, these laws were the result of direct bargaining between unions and government, which was subsequently approved by Parliament and codified by law. In others, they were based on national agreements between employers and unions. Bargained legislation was particularly important during the 1970s, when unions initiated many changes in the social, as well as the political arena. Such a union role reflects the unresponsiveness of the government. The unions became the voice of issues that were emerging in the country and compensated for shortcomings of the political system (Giugni, 1973:37–46). The unions won reforms of the social security arrangements. They also sought reforms related to housing, health services, transport and fiscal policies but in these areas they were less successful.

The government intervenes as a mediator during collective bargaining, particularly on national or industry level agreements (Veneziani, 1972). This mediation role increased during the late 1970s and many settlements were possible only because the employers' costs were subsidised by the state. The government can have a major impact when bargaining with the unions in the public sector, which is large in Italy and includes education, many services (such as health services, transport, telephones) and a significant industrial sector. Altogether, about 28 per cent of all employees are in the public sector (Ferraresi, 1980:134).

Government intervention is also crucial if, and when major industrial corporations face economic difficulties and ask for the prolonged use of Wage Integration Funds (CIG), which guarantee up to 80 per cent of pay during lay-off. The CIG has two main forms: the ordinary one is financed by employers' contributions and used during temporary crises for three-month periods renewable up to one year; the special one is used for more serious crises, is not time-limited and is funded by the state. The CIG has become essential for facilitating technological and structural change. Since 1980, it has been used more and more frequently (see Table 6.1). Another important form of relationship between unions and government is the increased union representation within social security organisations at national and local levels, and in many administrative and advisory bodies (Treu and Roccella, 1979). The unions also participate in local commissions for the allocation of jobs to the unemployed (Commissioni di Collocamento). By legislation, the employer has to communicate vacancies to the commissions which provide the candidates on the basis of seniority on the unemployed list. Highly-skilled workers and top level white-collar employees are excluded from these provisions. The employers have always opposed this limitation in the selection of employees, and except in the larger firms, they have usually been able to avoid the provisions. Recently there also have been changes and now only 50 per cent of the employers' requests have to be based on the unemployed list.

The processes of industrial relations

In Italy there are three major bargaining levels: national, industry and plant or firm. In some sectors, such as agriculture or construction, there is also collective bargaining at a regional level. The three major collective bargaining levels have played different roles over the years and in general they deal with different issues. Italian contract deadlines do not have the same weight in the bargaining process as they do in the USA. Agreements are often signed months after the expiration of the contract and are applied retrospectively when possible, or a lump sum of money is given to employees to compensate for the delays. During the bargaining process, there are also strikes that usually last only a few hours or one day at the most. The number of working days lost in Italy is high compared with most of the other countries in this book (see Appendix). Italy appears to be in an even worse position in relation to the number of workers involved in disputes. However, there was a significant decline between 1983 and 1985.

Strikes are the most widely used form of union action (there is no tradition of product boycotts); strikes are often accompanied by widely attended street demonstrations. As in France (see chapter 7), the Italian unions do not have strike funds. There are no peace clauses in agreements and consequently strikes can be held at any stage, in solidarity with other workers or in opposition to government decisions and for issues not strictly related to wages and working conditions.

National bargaining Agreements at the national level between major employers' associations such as Confindustria and the union confederations played an essential role during the 1950s, became less important between 1965 and 1975 when bargaining increased at the plant and industry levels, but became important again after 1975. The most crucial issue bargained at this level is the indexation agreement (*scala mobile*). Other national agreements relate to hours, holidays, use of the CIG (later transformed into law) and payments in relation to retirement or leaving voluntarily. The bargaining process at this level is strongly centralised and highly politicised. Although unions consult members before and after the agreements, there is little rank and file participation. None the less, bargaining is given wide media coverage as in Australia and Britain.

National bargaining became prominent again after 1975 for three reasons: first, in a period of economic recession there was little scope for bargaining at lower levels where employers' resistance increased; second, in centralised bargaining, the unions could use their influence in the political arena; finally, the employers could benefit from a type of bargaining that inevitably involved governments which, in order to reach a settlement, often mediated and made concessions to them by sharing the cost of settlement (Treu, 1983).

Industry-level bargaining Agreements are signed for various segments of the economy by national unions. In the industrial sector, there are four major contracts: metals, textiles, chemicals and construction. There are three agreements in agriculture and nine in the public sector. Even though there has been a reduction in the number of contracts, one union may be involved in negotiating many agreements. Altogether there are about twenty national unions in each confederation and in the manufacturing sector there are more than 30 agreements with private employers' associations; four with public employers, seven with associations of small firms, and eight with the association of small businessmen.

Industry agreements began to play an important role in the mid-1950s, but in the 1970s, they became very important. Major bargaining rounds have been held about every three years since 1969. As in Australia, the metals agreement often sets a pattern which others follow.

From 1969 to 1976, such industry-level bargaining extended the settlements won in union strongholds to the entire country. This was particularly important, given the differences between the north and the south. In many cases, the agreements specified minimum conditions to be built on according to the bargaining strength at plant level. Industry agreements have been used increasingly by the courts as a standard in disputes, even for employers that had not signed the contracts either directly or through their associations. Industry agreements usually exclude topics that have been regulated by national bargaining (or legislation). The latter has a larger scope and extends to issues such as retirement, insurance and unemployment compensation, unions' and employees' rights.

Industry agreements tend to focus on job classification, job descriptions, hours and overtime, incentive systems, holidays and vacations, discipline, union rights and the disclosure of information to unions. In the metals agreements, for instance, the entire work force is classified into eight classes. Classes 2–5 are shared both by white- and blue-collar workers; consequently the traditional rigid separation between these categories has been reduced.

The unions have generally achieved their goal of narrowing the differentials in pay and fringe benefits between these categories. However, in relation to pay, it is now recognised that this has been carried too far. Inflation and *scala mobile* flat-rate increases reduced the white-collar differentials to 30 per cent over the average for blue-collar workers (Di Gioia and Fontana, 1982:129). In the 1983 bargaining round, the parties agreed on expanding differentials again. None the less, the skilled and professional employees were still dissatisfied. This has become a crucial issue for unions because it has prompted more employers to give personal increases to employees individually, thus undermining the union role in representing the work force collectively.

In the 1980s, there has been a small reduction in the 40-hour standard week in some manufacturing sectors and there is usually a limit of 150 hours overtime per year. Each employee has four weeks of vacation.

In the area of union rights in the workplace, the most important provisions are those related to the direct check-off of dues and allowed time off for union activity. By law each employee can use up to ten hours each year for union meetings during working time, within the plant. The unions usually use part of the paid time in order to employ a shop steward for full-time union activity (these provisions are often improved by sector and plant agreements). Collective bargaining has also been used to influence employers' strategies in terms of investments, plant size, subcontracting and technological change. Information disclosure provisions were negotiated in the late 1970s and were considered a first step toward increased industrial democracy. As in Britain, the results have been disappointing, partly because of employer resistance and partly because of lack of union expertise (Pellegrini, 1983:204).

In the early 1980s, industry-level bargaining was frustrated by the lack of agreements at the higher level (particularly on *scala mobile*). In the bargaining round of 1983, the key issues were related to technological change, training, flexibility on hours of work, increase in workers' job classifications (Giugni, 1984).

Firm and plant collective bargaining   Plant level collective bargaining became important after 1969 as more stewards were recognised in the workplace. In the early 1970s, union breakthroughs in extending the scope of bargaining were first achieved in plant agreements and were later included in sector or national agreements. After 1974 the role of plant bargaining became more limited. A recent study shows that the likelihood of a firm or plant having an agreement increases with its size. In the area of Milan, 70 per cent of plants with more than 150 employees have a plant contract (Cella and Treu, 1982).

During plant bargaining, stewards play a major role in formulating the claim, while the bargaining is usually conducted by full-time union officials. Plant agreements usually last for a fixed term and are renewed after national agreements, but negotiations can be reopened at any stage for issues that become relevant. The content of the agreements differs depending on the size of the plant, the type of product and the method of production.

In general, at the plant level the main issues are supplementary pay increases, the distribution of working hours and overtime, assignment of jobs to the national classes, increasing stewards' facilities, health hazards, canteen costs and food quality. Information rights have, to a certain extent, increased the unions' sympathies for the economic constraints faced by firms, but plant bargaining continues to be confrontational. Such bargaining is the main process used by employees to influence managerial decisions; it often involves workers invoking sanctions. In recent years, there have been more *ad hoc* joint committees formed by stewards and managers for handling issues on a more co-operative basis. In the economic recession, the main controversies were related to lay-offs and other forms of employment reduction or mobility, and with the consequences of technological change.

Current and future issues

A crucial issue has been the national cost of living escalator, *scala mobile*, which guarantees automatic wage increases based upon the price index of a selection of basic goods. The *scala mobile* is regulated by the unions and employers' organisations. Since the Second World War, it has often been modified; in 1969, for instance, differential increases based on gender or geographical difference were eliminated.

A major change was agreed in 1975, with the decision gradually to eliminate differences in the wage escalator based on professional or skill level. After 1977, for every point of increase in the index, all employees were to receive the same increase. The 1975 agreement increased the percentage of wages covered by indexation from 64 per cent in 1974 to 90 per cent in 1977 (Altieri et al. 1983).

The 1975 agreement had many, often unforeseen, consequences. The persistent high level of inflation and the high percentage of wages indexed compressed wage differentials and left little room for wage bargaining. Moreover, the apparently higher levels of pay pushed employees into higher tax brackets. This made it more difficult for the unions to influence the real levels of pay. The unions that defended the indexation system were blamed for the high level of inflation. The government and many employees increasingly demanded that the unions should concede changes in the *scala mobile*. In the early 1980s, the issue was a major industrial relations controversy and bargaining at other levels did not progress because everything depended on the solution of this central problem (Flanagan et al. 1984).

The parties compromised in mid-1983, with the intention of cutting inflation to 13 per cent in that year. To achieve this, unions and employers agreed to reduce indexed pay increases by 15 per cent and to limit the increases in all sector agreements to small, fixed amounts between 1983 and 1985. At plant level there would be no increases for 20 months. The unions agreed to allow tougher management control of absenteeism and more flexible use of working time. The unions also agreed that increases should be differentiated by skill level and that plant bargaining should not deal with issues covered in other bargaining levels, as had been happening since 1969. This agreement also set up an arbitration system to foster the settlement of grievances and to avoid local disputes. For its part, the government agreed to reduce taxes; limit price increases in public utilities to 13 per cent; pay an increasing share of the employers' contribution to the cost of social insurance and to increase welfare subsidies related to family size. The government also promised to improve the operation of the labour market agencies, the CIG, the national health system and pensions.

The agreement was seen by many as a further step towards the centralisation of bargaining and towards the establishment of stable trilateral bargaining between employers, unions and government. However, in 1984, when the three parties met again to evaluate the accord, there was disagreement within the Federazione about the decision of conceding a further reduction of indexation in exchange for concessions on fiscal and other issues. CISL, UIL and the socialist component of CGIL believed that there was the basis for a settlement, while the communists disagreed. According to the latter, during 1983 the workers had made the agreed sacrifices while the government, on the other hand, had not honoured its promises, particularly with regard to prices and taxes. The result was a serious split between the unions and the end of the Federazione. The government decided to use a decree (based upon the accord with CISL and UIL) to put a ceiling on the number of index points that could be paid in 1984. The PCI asked for a referendum on the issue which was held in 1985 and supported the government decision (54 per cent versus 46 per cent).

There are many reasons why it was not possible to repeat the 1983 type of agreement. In 1984, the government faced larger dificits and could no longer use economic incentives to facilitate a settlement. The political situation was also different, because for the first time the Prime Minister was a Socialist. The greater involvement of the Socialist Party in government policies, its effort to show that they were winning the battle against inflation and the increased strife with the PCI had consequences in the industrial relations arena and all unions were affected. The divisions between the unions should not be seen, however, as a mere resurgence of the political parties' influence over them, because their differences were also rooted in their bargaining strategies and goals.

During 1985, the tension among the unions decreased and a new bargaining round proceeded at the national level related to the indexation system, the goals of the reduction of hours and the increase in the level of employment.

It is not easy to foresee future developments in the industrial relations arena, because past trends have been reversed and a new equilibrium has yet to be found. Regarding inter-union relations, after the collapse of the Federazione CGIL–CISL–UIL, each confederation has regained its independence and there will probably be alternate periods of co-operation and dissent according to the topics under discussion and the political climate. It is unlikely, however, that co-operation will be formalised again in a new unitary federation.

Periods of inter-union competition highlight the lack of legislation on bargaining unit size and representation rights, but government regulation in this sensitive area is unlikely. Relations between employers and unions have become less conflictual, especially at plant level, due to union weakness during the recession of 1981–82 and as a consequence of technological and organisational changes. The economic and financial situation has improved for the majority of firms and should result in wage increases related to productivity improvements; but employers' resistance in this area could cause new waves of disputes.

National level bargaining has played the leading role for many years, but in the future, bargaining at plant level will be more important, because it is better suited to deal with issues such as technological change, training and flexible production schedules.

Regarding union representation of technical and professional staff, the trend toward the consolidation of separate organisations (not affiliated with CGIL, CISL and UIL) will increase.

The huge public deficit will force changes in public-sector industrial relations and much-needed productivity improvements should be achieved. Union co-operation with rationalisation in the public sector is made difficult by the fragmentation of employee representation in several competing organisations.

Abbreviations

ASAP	Associazione Sindacale Aziende Petrolchimiche (Employers' Associations of Petrochemical Firms)
Assicredito	Associazione Italiana Credito (Italian Association of Employers in Credit)
CGIL	Confederazione Generale Italiana del Lavoro (Italian General Confederation of Labour)
CIDA	Confederazione Italiana Dirigenti di Azienda (Italian Confederation of Managers)
CIG	Cassa Integrazione Guadagni (Wages Integration Funds)
CISAL	Confederazione Italiana Sindacati Autonomi Lavoratori (Italian Confederation of Unions of Autonomous Workers)
CISAS	Confederazione Italiana Sindacati Addetti ai Servizi (Italian Confederation of Unions in the Service Sector)
CISL	Confederazione Italiana Sindacati Lavoratori (Italian Confederation of Workers' Unions)
CISNAL	Confederazione Italiana Sindacati Nazionali Lavoratori

	(Italian Confederation of National Unions of Workers)
Confagricoltura	Confederazione Generale dell'Agricoltura (General Confederation of [Employers in] Agriculture)
Confapi	Confederazione Italiana della Piccola e media Industria (Italian Confederation of Small and Medium Firms)
Confcommercio	Confederazione Generale del Commercio (General Confederation of [Employers in] Commerce)
Confindustria	Confederazione Generale dell'Industria Italiana (General Confederation of Italian Industry)
CONFSAL	Confederazione Sindacati Autonomi Lavoratori (Confederation of Unions of Autonomous Workers)
DC	Democrazia Cristiana (Christian Democratic Party)
ENI	Ente Nazionale Idrocarburi (National Institute for Hydrocarbons)
Federazione CGIL–CISL–UIL	(Inter-union Federation)
GDP	gross domestic product
IRI	Istituto per la Ricostruzione Industriale (Institute for Industrial Reconstruction)
OECD	Organisation for Economic Co-operation and Development
PCI	Partito Comunista Italiano (Italian Communist Party)
PLI	Partito Liberale Italiano (Italian Liberal Party)
PRI	Partito Repubblicano Italiano (Italian Republican Party)
PSDI	Partito Socialista Democratico Italiano (Italian Social Democratic Party)
PSI	Partito Socialista Italiano (Italian Socialist Party)
RSA	Rappresentanza Sindacale Aziendale (Firm Union Representative)
scala mobile	wage indexation
UIL	Unione Italiana del Lavoro (Italian Union of Labour)

A chronology of Italian industrial relations

1848	First printing workers' associations.
1872	National Printing Union formed.
1891	*Rerum Novarum* papal encyclical.
1892	The Italian Socialist Party (PSI) is founded.
1893	The Italian Federation of Chambers of Labour (Federazione Italiana delle Camere del Lavoro) is formed by the union organisations of 12 northern cities.
1906	The General Confederation of Labour (Confederazione Generale del Lavoro, CGL) is founded, including the Chambers of Labours and national unions.
1907	The Catholic Economic and Social Union is founded (Unione Economico-Sociale dei Cattolici d'Italia).
1918	The above union becomes the Italian Confederation of Labour (Confederazione Italiana dei Lavoratori, CIL).

1922	After the March on Rome, Mussolini becomes Prime Minister.
1922	The CGL holds its last Congress.
1926	Only Fascist unions allowed, which together with the Employers' Confederation formed the National Council of Corporations (Consiglio Nazionale delle Corporazioni) as part of the corporate state.
1943	Fall of Fascism in the south. It remained in power in the north until 1945.
1944	Rome trade union Pact among Communists, Christian Democrats and Socialists provided for the creation of the CGIL.
1945–48	Coalition government of anti-fascist political parties, including Socialists and Communists.
1948	The Christian Democrats (DC) win a parliamentary majority and exclude left-wing parties from government. Catholics leave the CGIL and later form the CISL.
1949	Social Democrats and Republicans also leave the CGIL and later form UIL. Socialists continue to stay in CGIL, which remains the largest confederation.
1962	After a period of economic expansion, trade union weakness and bitter competition, union unity developed in some manufacturing sectors.
1963	The Socialists join the government coalition (until 1974).
1969	Following intense industrial conflict, new unitary forms of workers' representation developed and unions end formal political links.
1970	The so-called Workers' Statute favours and protects unions.
1973	Three major confederations unite into the Federazione CGIL–CISL–UIL.
1974	The Federazione and the employers change the *scala mobile* indexation system. Lower paid workers are particularly favoured.
1977–79	The Communist Party supports the government, but with no direct participation in it.
1983	Tax structure and *scala mobile* changed after two years of controversy. Changes in other areas are also implemented or promised, with the government as mediator.
1984	Negotiations for other national agreements dealing with the indexation system break off. Only CISL and UIL agree with the government offer. The Federazione ends. The government enforces the accord reached with CISL and UIL by decree. The Communist Party promotes a referendum to repeal the degree.
1985	The referendum narrowly supports cuts in wage indexation.

Notes

1 At the election in 1983, the percentage of seats won in Parliament by each party was as following: DC 35.7, PCI 31.4, PSI 11.6, PRI 4.6, PSDI 3.6,

PLI 2.5, MSI–DN (a neo-fascist party) 6.6, other left parties 2.8, others 0.9. As a consequence, the left (PCI, PSI and others) even if it could agree on a common programme, has only 45.8 per cent. The DC with other centre parties has only 46.4 per cent and in order to reach a majority the PSI support is essential. A centre–right coalition is not politically feasible because it would include the MSI–DN support.

2 For a more detailed analysis of unions' political strategies, see Lange P. and Vannicelli M. 'Strategy Under Stress: The Italian Union Movement and the Italian Crisis in Developmental Perspective' in Lange et al. (1982). For a bibliography of studies on Italy see Lange (1977).

3 It is not easy to assess the actual membership of those confederations. In 1984, for the election of the union representative, among 201 717 votes cast in all ministries, the percentage was the following: CISL 30.7, CGIL 24.1, UIL 17.4, CONFSAL 13.6, CISNAL 2.9, CIDA 2.1, others 7.

References

Altieri, G. et al. (1983) *La Vertenza sul Costo del Lavoro e le Relazioni Industriali* Milano: F. Angeli

Barbadoro, I. (1973) *Storia del Sindacalismo Italiano* vol. 2, Firenze: La Nuova Italia

Cella, G.P. and Treu, T. eds (1982) *Le Relazioni Industriali* Bologna: Il Mulino

Di Gioia, A. and Fontana, R. (1982) *La Struttura del Salario* Roma: Editrice Sindacale Italiana

ETUI (1985) *The Trade Union Movement in Italy CGIL–CISL–UIL* Brussels: European Trade Union Institute, Info. 11

Ferraresi, F. (1980) *Burocrazia e politica in Italia* Bologna: Mulino

Flanagan, R.J. et al. (1984) *Unionism, Economic Stabilization and Income Policy: European Experience* Washington DC: Brookings Institution

Giugni, G. (1972) 'Recent Trends in Collective Bargaining in Italy' in International Labor Office *Collective Bargaining in Industrialised Market Economies* Geneva: International Labour Office, pp. 273–94, 1973

―― (1973) *Il Sindacato fra Contratti e Riforme 1969–1973* Bari: De Donato

―― (1984) 'Recent Trends in Collective Bargaining in Italy' *International Labour Review* 123, 5, pp. 599–614

Horowitz, D.L. (1963) *The Italian Labor Movement* Cambridge, Mass.: Harvard University Press

Jemolo, A.C. (1963) *Chiesa e Stato in Italia negli ultimi cento anni* Roma, quoted in Horowitz (1963) p. 96

Kogan, N. (1983) *Political History of Italy: The Postwar Years* New York: Praeger

Lange, P. (1977) *Studies on Italy 1943–1975: Selected Bibliography of American and British Materials in Political Science, Economics, Sociology and Anthropology* Torino: Fondazione Agnelli

Lange, P. et al. (1982) *Unions, Change and Crisis: French and Italian Union Strategy and the Political Economy, 1945–1980* London: George Allen & Unwin

Martinelli, A. and Treu, T. (1984) 'Employers Associations in Italy' in J.P. Windmuller and A. Gladstone *Employers Associations and Industrial Relations: A Comparative Study* Oxford: Clarendon Press pp. 264–92

Merli Brandini, P. (1983) 'Italy: A New Industrial Relations System Moving from Accommodation to Edge of Confrontation' in S. Barkin ed. *Worker Militancy and Its Consequences: The Changing Climate of Western Industrial Relations* New York: Praeger, pp. 81–111

OECD (1985) *Italy* Paris: OECD Economic Surveys, 1984–85 series (Jun.)

Patriarca, S. (1985) *Caratteristiche e Risultati della Politica dei Redditi 1983–84* IRES Materiali n.5/6 (Luglio–Ottobre) Supplemento

Pellegrini, C. (1983) 'Technological Change and Industrial Relations in Italy' *Bulletin of Comparative Labour Relations* 12, pp. 193–209

Regalia, I. et al. (1978) 'Labour Conflicts and Industrial Relations in Italy' in C. Crouch and A. Pizzorno eds *The Resurgence of Class Conflict in Europe* London: Macmillan, pp. 101–58

Sciarra, S. (1977) 'The Rise of the Italian Shop Steward' *Industrial Law Journal* 6, 1 (Mar.), pp. 35–44

Treu, T. (1983) 'Collective Bargaining and Union Participation in Economic Policies: The case of Italy' in C. Crouch and F. Heller eds *Organizational Democracy and Political Processes* New York: Wiley

Treu, T. and Roccella, M. (1979) *Sindacalisti nelle Istituzioni* Roma: Edizioni Lavoro

Veneziani, B. (1972) *La mediazione dei pubblici poteri nei conflitti collettivi di lavoro* Bologna: Il Mulino

Weitz, P. (1975) 'The CGIL and the PCI: From Subordination to Independent Political Force' in D. Blackmer and S. Tarrow eds *Communism in Italy and France* Princeton: Princeton University Press

7 | French industrial relations

JANINE GOETSCHY AND JACQUES ROJOT

France has a population of 55 million (38 per cent of whom are in civilian employment) and a GDP of US $503 billion. It has 59 per cent of its civilian employees in the services sector, 33 per cent in industry and it still has a relatively large agricultural sector, which employs the remaining 8 per cent (cf. less than 3 per cent in Britain). Although France and Britain have a similar size of population and GDP, the annual average increase of the French GDP for the 1978–83 period was 1.5 per cent, compared with 0.8 per cent in Britain.

Between 1979 and 1984, the average annual increase in consumer prices was 11.1 per cent. This rate was higher than in any of the other eight countries except Italy; however, the French rate of inflation had fallen to 4.7 per cent by 1984–85. The average take-home pay in French manufacturing (after annual taxes) is 85 per cent of gross earnings, which is a higher percentage than in the other countries apart from Canada (87 per cent) and Japan (92 per cent): see chapter 2, note 2. Unemployment in France rose from 2.4 per cent in 1970, to 4.1 per cent in 1975, 6.3 per cent in 1980, and 10.3 per cent in 1985 (see Table A.5).

Before the advent of the Fifth Republic in 1958, French politics were more volatile than in most of the other eight countries. In the mid-1980s there are four main political parties in France. The Gaullists and the Republican Independents (which are part of the Union pour la démocratie Française), together with the Centre Right Party are all broadly liberal or conservative, while the Communist Party and the Socialist Party are to the left of centre.

Between 1958 and 1981, France was governed by right of centre

142

governments. The Socialists made a decisive gain in 1981, when a Socialist President was elected: M. Francois Mitterrand. Initially his government was a Socialist–Communist coalition, but the Communists left the coalition in 1984. Although M. Mitterrand's first term as President was not due to finish until 1988, the Socialists were replaced by a right-wing government in 1986, under Prime Minister M. Jacques Chirac. At the time of writing however, the full implications of this change of government are not yet clear.

The industrial relations parties

Industrialisation and urbanisation emerged in France during the mid-nineteenth century, rather later than in Britain. Strikes were not legally permitted until 1864, but even then unions were still illegal (see Chronology at end of chapter). However, many incipient unions were formed in this period, on a local level. There were some parallels with the origins of unions in the English-speaking countries. Craftsmen were the first to organise, but craft unions were soon displaced by industrial unionism. The early unions were often involved in violent clashes with state agencies and employers, which tried to suppress them.

The unions In the 1881 Paris Commune, workers took control of the city for almost two months before they were harshly defeated. Unions began holding clandestine annual conferences in 1876 and were eventually legalised in 1884. Such forms of working class organisation developed particularly during the period of the Third Republic 1871–1910. Labour exchanges (*bourses du travail*) were formed as centres for organising workers' collective action.

Against this background, in the 1980s there are five national union confederations (which are rivals) as summarised in Table 7.1. There is more fragmentation among the unions in France than in any of the other eight countries in this book, with the possible exception of Japan (see chapter 10). The ideological divisions in the international labour movement (see chapter 1) are reflected and exaggerated in France more than in any of the other countries. This is one reason why there is a low union density in France (15–18 per cent). However, French union density data are controversial; there is a large discrepancy between the membership claimed by the unions themselves and evaluations made by employers' organisations.

The CGT (Confédération générale du travail), the oldest French confederation, was established in 1895. With the 1906 Charter of Amiens, the CGT adopted an anarcho-revolutionary programme, wary of political parties and political action. (Interestingly, in the same year, the British unions turned in the opposite direction, by forming their Labour Party.)

The coexistence of Marxists, with anarchist and social-reformist elements led to a major split in the CGT in 1921, with an expulsion of the Marxists, following the split in the Socialist Party after the Russian Revolution. The two wings reunited during the 1936 Popular Front. There was another split in 1939 after the Russo–German pact. Then a further reunification took place during the 'Resistance' and another split in 1948, when the minority group rejected Marxism and established the current FO (see later). Since the 1940s, most of the CGT's leaders have been Communist Party members, both at the top and at the intermediate levels. However, many of the CGT's members remain outside the Communist Party.

Between the late 1970s and the mid-1980s, the CGT membership fell from over two million to about 1.6 million members. It is organised in 40 industry federations, and in 94 geographically-based local unions (*unions départementales*). The four largest federations are in the metal industry, the municipal and health service, building and the chemical industry. The CGT draws its main strength from skilled manual workers. Its membership has changed in four phases since the 1940s. After having reached a peak in 1947, it declined until 1958; it grew between 1959 and 1975, and declined again after the mid-1970s. The CGT has an important technical, managerial and professional staff (*cadre*) section, the UGICT (Union générale des ingénieurs, cadres et techniciens) with about 320 000 members.

The FO (Force ouvrière) claims to be the true heir of the CGT's old policy of political independence and is staunchly anti-communist. By the mid-1980s, the FO claimed to have become the second-largest confederation, with nearly one million members. It sees collective bargaining as the main element of union action, and aims to fulfil a representative role by defending workers' job interests independently of any political party or ideology. It is strongest among white-collar workers, technical and professional groups in the public sector, and has been growing while the CGT has declined. Though it has an image of being a public sector union, it has also been growing in the private sector. By 1979, the FO claimed that as many as 55 per cent of its membership were from the private sector. The FO has a small *cadre* section, the UCI (Union des cadres et ingénieurs), with about 60 000 members.

Confessional unionism began in 1919 with the formation of the CFTC (Confédération française des travailleurs chrétiens). Its main objective was to promote peaceful collaboration between capital and labour, according to the social doctrine of the Catholic Church. The CFTC split in 1964, when the minority group retained the religious orientation and kept the name CFTC. It includes 45 federations and 94 *unions départementales*. Its centres of strength are among miners, Christian school teachers and health workers. Its total membership is supposed to be about 260 000; it has grown slightly since the early 1970s. The CFTC has a tiny *cadre* section, the UGICA (Union générale des ingénieurs et cadres), with about 5000 members.

Following the CFTC's 1964 split, the majority group formally abandoned the Catholic connection and formed the CFDT (Confédération française démocratique du travail). The CFDT used to be the second-largest of the union confederations by a clear margin, but declined in the early 1980s to be a similar size as the FO, with about 0.9 million members. It favours self-management (*autogestion*) and collective bargaining. In 1970, it adopted elements of a socialist–Marxist ideology with elements of Gramsciism. This puts it in competition with the CGT. But after 1979, the CFDT played down its former ideological emphasis. The CFDT includes 25 industry federations and 21 *unions régionales*. It is strongest in the metal industry, health service, oil industry, banking and insurance, and the chemical industry. It is particularly well represented in three regions: the Loire, Bretagne and Alsace, where it benefits from what was its Catholic legacy. Between 1948 (old CFTC) and 1977, its membership nearly doubled. However its membership began to decline in 1978. The CFDT has a small *cadre* section, the UCC (Union confédérale des ingénieurs et cadres), with about 45 000 members. However, UCC membership is restricted to 'senior' *cadres*, so is smaller than most of the other unions' *cadre* sections.

The CGC (Confédération générale des cadres) was formed in 1944. It has 325 000 members who are *cadres* (engineers, executives, salesmen, supervisors and technicians). It is strongest in metal working (42 000), the chemical industry (17 000) and among salesmen (42 000). Its goals focus on issues such as winning more participation for *cadres*, maximising their pay differentials and job security, and protecting their interests in relation to tax and social security. It aims to engage in collective bargaining on behalf of its members and claims not to be party-political. However, since 1981, it has been particularly critical of some socialist policies.

The differences between the various union confederations are summarised in Table 7.1. In brief, the CGT and CFDT have a more radical orientation, whereas the FO, CFTC and CGC are reformist. However, sometimes the FO is more radical than the CGT and CFDT. In general, there is little unity between these confederations. However, from 1969 until the late 1970s, the CGT and CFDT had a 'unity of action' practice, through which these unions had institutional links with political parties. Otherwise, apart from the CGT, none of

Table 7.1   Union confederations

Acronym (date of foundation)	Approximate 1985 membership (millions)	General ideology	Main coverage
CGT (1895)	1.6	Marxist–Leninist communist	Metals, steel, mining, chemicals, docks, glass, electricity
FO (1947)	1.0	Social democratic, anti-communist	Gas, railways, civil service, Paris transport, finance, clothing, civil and electrical engineering
CFTC (1919)	0.26	Catholic	Oil, air traffic control, mining, finance
CFTD (1964)	0.9	Socialist, self-management, some elements of Marxism (Gramsci)	Oil, rubber, metals, textiles, finance
CGC (1944)	0.32	Non-political	*Cadres* in metals, chemicals, sales
FEN (1947)	0.45	Socialist, communist	Employees in public-sector schools, including teachers and administrators

Sources: Various, including *Financial Times*, 26 June 1985.

the older union confederations have close long-term *de facto* ties with particular political parties, though they may forge alliances from time to time. Among many union activists there is a traditional distrust of politicians.

Except for the CGC, unions from all of these five confederations recruit across all industries and trades and across all categories of employees. Thus they compete with each other. However, each of them has a special section for *cadres*, with slightly different recruiting criteria; their membership among *cadres* is illustrated in Table 7.2, which shows that the CGC and CGT are the most important confederations for *cadres*.

All these five confederations are known as 'representative unions'. This is a legal attribute granted on the basis of five criteria and which confers on them some exclusive rights, for instance in collective bargaining, the nomination of candidates in the system of employee representation within the firm (see later), and in terms of representation on numerous government consultative bodies (Verdier, 1982).

There is another important specialist union organisation: the

Table 7.2 Union membership among *cadres*

Acronym	Approximate membership (000s)
CGC	325
UGICT–CGT	320
UCI–FO	60
UCC–CFDT	45
UGICA–CFTC	5

Source: Figures provided by the unions in 1985.

Fédération de l'éducation nationale (FEN), which decided to remain independent at the time of the CGT split. The FEN recruits staff in most types of state educational institutions and has about 450 000 members. Thus, unionism is less fragmented in the education sector than in most other sectors. Measured by membership density in its own sector, the FEN is one of the strongest French unions. However, even within the FEN there are several competing ideological tendencies.

In other sectors there are several other autonomous unions, which often began as breakaways from one of the national union confederations (European Communities, 1983:6). In some firms, there are company unions (for example at Peugeot–Citrôen).

It is difficult to measure union membership in France and the numbers cited here are generally approximate because, by contrast with the other countries discussed, there is little tradition of regularly paying union dues in France and because benefits negotiated apply to all employees, whether or not they are union members. As a legacy of their anarcho-syndicalist roots, French unions have rarely built up bureaucratic organisations on the scale of those in Germany, for instance. In the CGT, in particular, there has traditionally been more emphasis on having an active core of 'militant' organisers, rather than recruiting a stable mass membership (Reynaud, 1975). These militants in the past have tended to see their role as fostering strikes and political action, rather than engaging in collective bargaining with employers, which they saw as class collaboration. Consequently, collective bargaining has not been the main method of industrial relations rule-making, unlike in many other OECD countries; the social partners in France have long preferred legal regulation.

The employers French industry includes a high proportion of small firms. In the post-1945 reconstruction there has been extensive corporate rationalisation involving many mergers, in the face of the increasing international competition within the European Communities. Nevertheless, 46 per cent of the work force is still employed in firms of less than 50 employees. Such small firms are usually family businesses and often have a strong Catholic tradition of paternalism.

In contrast to the plurality of unionism, at national level the employers are more united—in the CNPF (Conseil national du patronat français)—than the various union confederations. The CNPF embraces more than three-quarters of all French enterprises. Unlike its counterparts in the English-speaking countries, the CNPF does engage in collective bargaining, though not on wages, which are regulated at an industry-wide level. The CNPF was established in 1945, although employers were already organised in a range of industry federations from the early nineteenth century, and at national level from 1919 onwards, in a forerunner to the CNPF.

The post-1973 economic crisis stimulated important changes in the employers' strategy. The employers found a renewed justification for the role of management and the legitimacy of their prerogatives and managerial rights of direction over the enterprise. The employers then aimed to convince government, the unions and public opinion that there was a crisis and that businesses were vulnerable. But the employers contended that it was their responsibility to deal with the crisis and to resist international competition.

Management, in the words of the CNPF, should pursue an 'active social policy' at plant level, to complement its negotiations with the unions at other levels. Employers aimed to take more initiatives. They tried to improve training and the development of their human resources, as well as to keep employees better informed. Managers were being encouraged to replace their old 'autocratic' behaviour by a consultative dialogue with all employees. The employers wanted this dialogue to be direct, however, not through unions. Some employers increased the status of supervisory staff by letting them deal directly with grievances at a lower level in the managerial hierarchy than hitherto. This also meant that unions were often by-passed and has tended to further weaken their role (Landier, 1981).

The employers are also aiming to improve the quality of working life, through various means, including quality circles and the individualisation of the employment relationship, in order to reduce the number of issues that are confronted by collective action. Such new policies are being implemented in different ways, depending on the industry, the size of the enterprise and the managers' sensitivity to the CNPF's message.

Besides changing its policies, the CNPF also has a new leader. After a bitter and unusually public fight, a newcomer, M. Gattaz, emerged as the leader of the CNPF. Contrary to a tradition of leaders coming from large businesses or the CNPF's hierarchy, M. Gattaz came from a medium-sized enterprise. Although the CNPF was frequently consulted by the Mitterrand government, the CNPF's views carried less weight in comparison with previous governments. The recession and the wave of new legislation also contributed to considerable discontent among employers, which the CNPF finds it difficult to contain, particularly in small and medium-sized businesses.

The state is also a major employer, with about a quarter of civilian employees working in the public sector. This was expanded considerably after 1981 and is rather more unionised than the private sector. The French public sector embraces a wider range of nationalised industries than is usual in most other Western countries. In addition to the public services, the public sector includes banks, an oil company, railways, electricity, gas, telephones and a car manufacturer (Renault). However, some nationalised corporations such as Renault often behave more like a private-sector firm.

The state   Many observers have noted that state intervention is very important in French industrial relations. This reflects the traditional reluctance of unions and employers to use voluntary collective bargaining (Delamotte, 1983; Sellier, 1984). In periods when the Left has been in the ascendancy, some of the unions have tended to press for new laws; for instance, in 1936 with the Popular Front, in 1945 with the Liberation, in 1968 following the May events, and more recently 1981 with the advent of the Socialist government. Between 1981 and 1983, as we shall see, about a third of the labour law code was revised.

Since the late 1960s, there have been closer links between the law and collective bargaining, so that it became usual for laws to embody the result of previously negotiated agreements or earlier discussions between unions, employers and the state. Furthermore, laws were increasingly seen as a general framework, within which unions and employers should negotiate at lower levels. The state 'no longer plays a mere authoritarian role in industrial relations'; but 'this does not mean that the state's role is now reduced merely to seeking consensus among the social partners' (Reynaud, 1978:119). Rather, it has tried to reform the legal framework of collective bargaining.

The main processes of industrial relations

The successive statutes on collective bargaining (1919, 1936, 1946, 1950, 1971, 1982) reveal a recurrence of typically French labour law prescriptions. These attempt to compensate for the unions' organisational weaknesses and the lack of effective collective bargaining. For example, all employees, whether or not they are unionised, may benefit from the terms of a collective agreement. Furthermore, French labour law reinforces union pluralism and in some ways even favours the minority organisations (such as the CFTC, CGC and formerly the FO). Thus, a collective agreement is valid even if only one representative union has signed it. In practice, this provision has divided the union confederations. The most radical ones (CGT and CFDT) tend to adopt an uncompromising approach during the negotiation process, while the more reformist ones (FO, CFTC, CGC) are usually more willing to compromise and sign agreements. In many instances, however, such a division usually seems to have suited both categories of union. The CGT and CFDT members can then benefit from an agreement, even though their leaders have not compromised themselves by signing it.

Collective bargaining has traditionally taken place at industry level. Both employer and union organisations preferred such bargaining for ideological as well as tactical reasons. This practice also reflects the lack of mutual recognition between unions and employers at plant or company level. Industry agreements cover the maximum number of employees, which is an advantage to the unions when their membership is low. The employers have favoured industry agreements which establish minimal standards for a given industrial sector. Furthermore, this has spared employers from having to recognise unions at plant level.

After 1965 there was a significant development in multi-industry bargaining and in plant-level bargaining: both practices were reinforced by the 1971 amendments to the 1950 Collective Bargaining Act. Innovative multi-industry agreements dealt with such issues as job security, vocational training, the introduction of salaried status for manual workers, unemployment benefits following redundancies, and working conditions. Such national agreements provided a 'framework' which aimed to encourage collective bargaining at lower levels (in a specific industry or firm).

The increasing number of plant-level agreements resulted from the 1968 Statute, which legalised union delegates at plant level and provided them with a collective bargaining function. The plant-level agreements were not generally innovative (Bachy et al., 1974), but rather improved on or adapted higher-level agreements to local conditions. In practice, such domestic bargaining was confined to the large firms.

Following the 1973 energy crisis, plant-level agreements have become less numerous. Multi-industry enabling agreements were less often followed by agreements at lower levels; there were significant difficulties, for instance, in implementing the 1975 multi-industry agreement on working conditions. On the contrary, during this period, there were many successful multi-industry agreements settling detailed and precise conditions, especially about such employment issues as job security and redundancy.

The coming to power of the Left induced a different political and legal context for collective bargaining in the 1980s. The Mitterrand government had two major objectives which impinged on industrial relations (Caire, 1984a). The first was to create more public sector jobs in 1982. This involved a reduction of working hours from 40 to 39 hours a week (with no reduction in pay) and the introduction of a fifth week of holidays. Firms were also urged to sign 'solidarity contracts' with the state, whereby either early retirement schemes or shorter working hours schemes would enable the creation of jobs, especially for the young and the unemployed. In the working hours schemes, the firm would have to pay lower wage-based contributions for newly hired employees. The government further restricted temporary and part-time work. Employers were discouraged from resorting to short-term contracts if this meant avoiding granting indefinite contracts. The pay of temporary employees had to be comparable with that of permanent employees (Pelissier, 1983). The government also substantially increased the statutory minimum wage.

The second major objective of the Mitterrand government was the reform of workplace relations. It was outlined in the 'Report on the Rights of Workers' by the Minister of Labour, M. Jean Auroux. It aimed to provide employees with 'real citizenship within the firm' and to create new opportunities so that 'employees may become actors of change within the enterprise'. The Auroux Report was not completely new; it adopted a gradual rather than a revolutionary approach and partly reflected the 1975 Sudreau Report. Though the Report paid heed to the unions' platforms (especially the CGT's and CFDT's), it followed the government's own industrial relations policy and was thus diversely received by the different union and employer organisations (Goetschy, 1983).

The Auroux Report enumerated the following deficiencies from which the French system of collective bargaining was suffering:

1 Many wage earners were not covered by any collective agreements, whether at industry or plant level (i.e. 11 per cent of wage earners in firms of at least ten employees). Such 'excluded workers' were particularly concentrated among temporary workers, for example, in the distributive trades and in hotels and restaurants.
2 Many agreements lacked job classification structures.
3 There was a large gap between basic minimum wages and actual pay (an average of 30 per cent).
4 Collective agreements were highly fragmented (40 of the 1023

national or regional level collective agreements covered more than half of the total number of wage-earners).

5 Only a quarter of wage-earners were covered by a plant agreement.
6 The low density of unionism and the divisions between unions undermined the 'legitimacy' of agreements.

The 1982 Collective Bargaining Act followed the Auroux Report. The 1982 Act included many prescriptions, most of which aimed to improve the existing system, but some of them were innovative. For instance, in firms which have union sections, employers are obliged to open negotiations every year on pay and on working hours. However, there is no obligation to reach an agreement and the employer has the final say. Unlike in the USA, there is no requirement to bargain 'in good faith'.

Such provisions aim to foster collective bargaining within the firm. The intention is to provide a learning process leading to 'contractual' attitudes, whereby employers will become more aware of their social responsibilities and unions more attentive to economic constraints. Further, it is assumed that agreements would be more likely at this level, where bargainers are less likely to be susceptible to political arguments.

As another innovation, non-signatory unions can veto a plant-level agreement, for example, if an agreement contradicts one reached at a higher level or includes illegal clauses in relation to shorter working hours. Before using a veto, the non-signatory opponents must win more than half of the votes in the works council or employee delegates elections. Granting such veto rights to the largest opposition unions (i.e. CGT and CFDT) is expected to lead to more legitimate agreements. Further, in national industry agreements, the obligation to meet once a year to negotiate wages, and every fifth year for discussing a possible revision of job classification should bring the basic minimum pay rates and other conditions closer to actual practice. Whether at the firm or industry level, the frequency of meetings (a compulsory social dialogue) is expected to strengthen the negotiators' sense of responsibility in negotiations and to make them more representative of their constituents.

The obligation to negotiate at company level has been the most controversial prescription. The critics accuse it of promoting inflation and of undermining higher-level agreements, on the grounds that employers with plant agreements could later build on them. Moreover, as there is no obligation to agree at company level, collective bargaining about some issues could disappear at both levels. Others argue that the inflationary risk is not serious, given that of 288 industrial sectors, only 26 settle actual pay in collective agreements;

the rest fix basic minima. Furthermore, the implementation of the working hours ordinance and the 1982–83 wage policy demonstrated that industry agreements remain of major importance.

Another criticism of the obligation to bargain at company level is that it might lead to disparities between larger firms and the smaller ones, which are exempted. To prevent such a development, the law has been extended so that firms with less than eleven employees can form a group, either on a geographical or sectoral basis, to engage in local collective bargaining. Critics also argue that annual negotiations will increase the number of disputes within companies.

There are several prescriptions which aim to enlarge unions' rights to receive information and to have expert help in the bargaining process. The Act also improves the existing procedures under which the Minister of Labour can extend certain collective agreements to non-signatory firms. These extension procedures are very important, given that the employer may initially refuse to sign an agreement.

Both the Act and some other 1982 ordinances give priority to collective bargaining rather than to the law. The changes are not seen as final. The government is evaluating them before deciding whether the parties have successfully dealt with issues autonomously, or whether it should legislate further. The search for a new balance between state intervention and collective bargaining was the hallmark of its post-1981 strategy of social reform. However, the foundation of this strategy can be traced back to the 1969–71 industrial relations policy of the then right-wing government.

Industrial disputes An alternative way of settling differences is by strike action. The right to strike is guaranteed by the French Constitution, but as with any other right, it is qualified. In the public sector, since 1963, the unions have had to give five days notice before a strike. But there is little legal regulation of strikes in the private sector. The distinction between legal and illegal strikes is drawn by the courts. In the private sector, a strike is legally defined as a stoppage of work. Hence other action such as industrial sabotage, working to rule or a slow-down is unlawful. A lawful strike has to concern 'industrial relations issues'. There is no legal prohibition of spontaneous strikes, despite legal constraints on sit-ins; such action is generally permitted when its primary aim is to seek negotiations, rather than merely to disrupt production. Nevertheless, excessive disruption of production through strikes is illegal and lockouts are generally illegal.

Although there is little legislation on strikes, there are elaborate procedures for the resolution of disputes, including conciliation, mediation and arbitration, but these procedures are rarely used in practice. Conciliation is a procedure which aims to bring the parties together in the hope of reaching a settlement. Since 1955, mediation has been another optional procedure which may take place either after conciliation has failed, or directly on request from one of the parties or from the Minister of Labour. After investigation, the mediator recommends a settlement to the parties. If they do not accept it, they must oppose it within eight days and justify their refusal. Both the refusal and the recommendation are publicised, so that the public can judge the parties' goodwill or insincerity. Mediation was used successfully in 1982 for ending disputes in the car industry. When arbitration is used, the arbitrator's recommendations are compulsory.

Industrial disputes tend to be unpredictable in France, but are usually short-lived. Strikes tend to be short because, as a legacy of the anarcho-syndicalist tradition, French unions have few financial reserves and generally do not grant strike pay. Hence, in the international league table, France loses relatively few working days due to stoppages, compared with Italy and the English-speaking countries (see Appendix). Between 1979–1984, the number of days lost per annum was less than half of the annual average registered between 1969–79. However, both in 1982 and 1984 there were temporary increases in the number of working days lost in France, probably induced by the working-hours Ordinance (in 1982), the disputes in the car industry, and to a lesser extent by the incomes policy. The average length of disputes has increased slightly since 1978. This probably reflects the greater frequency of disputes about redundancies.

Employee representation   At plant level, there is a multiplicity of representative institutions set up in response to particular social and political pressures in different periods: 'employee delegates' (*délégués du personnel*) were instituted by the Popular Front in 1936; 'works committees' (*comités d'entreprise*) in 1945 following the Liberation and 'workplace union branches' (*section syndicale*) in 1968. We can generalise that employee delegates deal with individual employee grievances, works committees deal with workplace consultation, while union branches and stewards represent their union and participate in collective bargaining at the workplace. A legal framework has been provided for all these bodies.

Unlike the shop stewards or workplace delegates in the English-speaking countries who are union representatives, French employee delegates are not union representatives, though in practice most of them are elected from a union slate. Delegates must be elected every year by the total work force in all organisations which employ more than ten people. The 1982 Act stipulates that delegates may also be elected in firms with less than eleven employees, in cases where several firms operate on a common site (such as a building site or a commercial centre), and if there is a total of at least 50 employees. Most of the private sector is thus covered by the Act.

Employee delegates deal with individuals' claims on wages, working conditions, the implementation of labour law and collective agreements; they may also call upon the Labour Inspector in cases where there is disagreement. The number of delegates elected varies according to the size of the firm. The employer must meet them collectively at least once a month. To fulfil their duties, they are allocated fifteen hours paid working time per month.

Delegates are elected by proportional representation. Manual workers and lower clerical staff vote separately from technicians and *cadres*. The detailed election procedures must be agreed between the employer and the unions. There is no exclusion of foreign 'guest workers' from voting or being candidates.

Unlike those of other countries, under these election procedures there is a two-round secret ballot. In the first round, candidates can be nominated only by one of the main union confederations, or by any other affiliated union which is recognised as 'representative' within the firm. If less than half of the electorate votes in the first round, then any employee may stand as a candidate for the second round. In practice, however, a second round is rarely required.

Works committees are supposed to be established in all firms employing at least 50 employees. They use election procedures similar to the ones mentioned above. These committees have little real decision-making power, except in relation to welfare issues. These committees do have the right, however, to be informed and consulted at specified periods on the general management of the business, particularly in relation to the number and organisation of employees, their hours of work and employment conditions.

Each quarter, the employer is required to inform the works committee about the general progress of orders, production and finances. Employers also should provide employment data including details of any short-term contracts and subcontract work; the employer must justify the use of such measures. Once a year, the employer submits a general report in writing to the works committee, covering the business's activities, turnover, losses or profits, the overall production achievement, substantial capital transfers, subcontracting, the allocation of profits, grants from the state or other public authorities and their use, investments, and salaries. To examine the annual accounts, the works committee may choose an expert accountant to assist it. Further, on an *ad hoc* basis, the committee must be informed and consulted on all changes in the economic or legal organisation of the business, in cases such as sales or mergers, for instance. Moreover, under the 28 October 1982 Act, the committee has to be informed and consulted before any large project involving the introduction of new technologies, whenever there may be consequences related to employment, qualifications, pay, training and working conditions; in firms with at least 300 employees, an expert can be involved to study the situation (Rojot, 1983).

The works committee may not only have to give its opinion, but its agreement is required on such issues as arrangements for profit-sharing and changes in individual working hours. The representatives have to maintain confidentiality about the employer's information on production processes and finances when requested by the employer. The works committee is composed of the employee representatives and the employer or his deputy, who chairs the meeting which takes place at least monthly. Each representative union can appoint a union observer to the committee. To fulfil their duties, each employee representative can use 20 paid working hours per month. The works committee can create sub-committees to examine specific problems. Health, Safety and Improvement of Working Conditions Committees are compulsory in firms with at least 50 employees. Firms with at least 300 employees have to set up an employment–training committee. Firms with at least 1000 employees have to set up an economic committee. Many employers initially resisted works committees, but most have gradually come to accept them as having a legitimate role.

Since 1968, there have also been workplace union sections in parallel to the representative bodies. Before 1968, unions had no legal right to establish such sections. In firms of a certain size, sections can have an office and other facilities, and can appoint their own stewards; they can collect dues during working hours, use notice boards, distribute leaflets, and organise monthly meetings (outside working time). The Mitterrand government improved union rights by increasing the number of paid hours allocated to stewards for union duties and allowing them to circulate freely within the work-place. All employee representatives are legally protected against dismissal. Hindering a representative or the various bodies is a criminal offence.

The representative bodies do not form a coherent system, but have grown in an *ad hoc* way. Moreover, with the complex and sometimes imprecise legal framework, there is some confusion of functions among the various bodies, not least because individual representatives frequently fulfil several functions. Often there is a lack of candidates to be appointed as stewards to fill the various elected positions. In the larger firms, stewards often co-ordinate the activities of the works committees and employee delegates. Although this may be accepted by managers in big firms, in smaller firms managers may resent what they see as union interference. In 1982, 73 per cent of the total number of eligible firms actually had a works committee. This percentage had grown substantially since 1968.

A major innovation of the 1982 Act was to set up a *group/combine committee* within large multi-plant companies whose registered office is in France. The function of such committees is to receive, at least once a year, information about the financial and employment situation within the group or combine.

Current and future issues

The weakness of the union movement is a major issue of French industrial relations. Why does the French labour movement formally organise less than 20 per cent of those eligible? We can offer the following explanations. First, closed shops are legally prohibited (though there are *de facto* closed shops in some sectors such as printing and the docks). Second, all wage earners benefit from any improvements won by the unions; after it is signed, a collective agreement applies immediately to all employees, whether unionised or not. Third, no specific welfare benefit accrues to a union member, as may be the case in other countries. Fourth, employers have often opposed any extension of union influence, and there is a continuing paternalistic tradition, particularly in the numerous smaller firms. Fifth, it was only in 1968 that unions obtained the right to establish workplace branches. Sixth, the fragmentation of unions on ideo-logical and political grounds hampers the recruitment and reten-tion of members. However, unions do in fact have more political and industrial influence than their low density implies. Unions play an important role in collective bargaining and in representative elections.

Works committee elections The works committee election results show that, in total, the five representative unions obtain more than 80 per cent of the votes (see Table 7.3). Thus, the unions have a much higher degree of support than might be inferred from their low membership. However, although non-union candidates receive only a low percentage of the votes (18 per cent in 1982), they tend to win a relatively high percentage of seats (37 per cent). This disparity reflects not only peculiarities of the electoral system, but also the large proportion of small firms which are not unionised.

Between 1976 and 1986, the CGT and CFDT lost support whereas the FO gained. Several explanations have been suggested for the decline of both the CGT and CFDT. First, as in many of the other countries, the post-1973 industrial restructuring reduced the labour force in highly unionised sectors such as the steel and shipbuilding

Table 7.3   Results of works committee elections in the private sector

	1982		1972	
	Votes received (%)	Seats obtained (%)	Votes received (%)	Seats obtained (%)
CGT	32	24	44	32
CFDT	23	18	19	14
FO	12	9	8	6.3
CFTC	2.9	3	2.6	2
CGC	7	6	5.6	5
Other unions	4.4	3.2	7	5
Non-unionists	18	3.2	14	36

Source: Liaisons Sociales, 26 March 1984.

industries. Second, the number of part-time and short-term contract workers has increased and they are difficult to unionise. Third, there has been a shift in the economy towards services, which has brought into the labour force more white-collar employees without a union tradition. Finally, the threat of unemployment has worked against unionisation by favouring individual solutions rather than collective ones.

After the Left's 1978 electoral failure and the priority given by these unions to political issues rather than to economistic issues of wages and conditions, CGT and CFDT leaders were demoralised. Furthermore, the CFDT and CGT both initiated a process of self-criticism. The CFDT admitted that it had been too dogmatic and that it was inattentive to workers' daily preoccupations. The CGT was less self-critical and did not question its fundamental strategies or links with the declining Communist Party, which had exacerbated its own decline. Following the Left's 1981 electoral success, an increase in the CGT or CFDT membership might then have been expected (as was the case in 1936 and in 1945); but in the mid-1980s, these unions generally seem to be losing members, although the FO has continued to grow.

Employee participation   The February 1982 Act gives employees the right to stop working if they consider the job to be dangerous, but this law does not allow them to stop their machinery. The August 1982 Act is a further extension, which offers employees the right to influence their work content, its organisation and, more generally, their working conditions. The Act prescribes that employees' views should be expressed 'directly' and should be organised collectively (for example, on the basis of a homogenous work group). In firms with at least 200 employees, the specific implementation of this Act has to be negotiated voluntarily between the employer and unions at company level. After a two-year trial period, the government evaluated the impact of these provisions in an attempt to decide whether to replace them with more detailed legal prescriptions.

A preliminary analysis of 2400 participation agreements signed between February and October 1983 indicated that the law has achieved a positive effect. Of the agreements analysed, 53 per cent allocated between three and six meeting hours per year to direct participation; 93 per cent of them stipulated that meetings should be organised on the basis of regular work groups; and 63 per cent of them granted supervisory staff a leading role in the conduct of the meetings. When they were present in negotiations, most unions had signed such agreements. The incidence of agreements signed by unions, as a percentage of the firms in which they were present in negotiations was: CGT 75 per cent; CFDT 74 per cent: FO 66 per cent; CFTC 85 per cent; CGC 90 per cent.

Austerity plans The attempts by the Mitterrand government to promote collective bargaining, employee participation and other social reforms became entangled with its 'austerity plans'. In June 1982, after a second devaluation of the French currency, the government froze prices and wages until 31 October 1982. This was the first austerity plan. Except for the statutory minimum wage, all wage increases were prohibited in the private as well as in the public sector. This action involved an unprecedented suspension of collective bargaining by the government.

Following the freeze, the government recommended that: the widespread practice of index-linked pay increases should cease (this practice had theoretically been forbidden since 1959), pay increases should not exceed 10 per cent in 1982 and 8 per cent in 1983 and should be linked to productivity increases. Moreover the public sector was controlled tightly, as an example to the private sector. Such measures seriously challenged the union's scope for action.

In April 1983, the second austerity plan attempted to restore the balance of external trade, to contain the deficit of public finances, to reduce the deficit of the social security system and to reduce the level of inflation. The plan aimed to cut wage earners' purchasing power in the short run, but it also involved postponing further reductions in working hours.

Conclusion

By the mid-1980s, French industrial relations were in turmoil. Unemployment was at record high levels for the post-war period and there were growing inequalities in the labour market, which had become increasingly segmented. French unions were weakened in terms of their already scarce financial resources, and by deep ideological divisions. Three of the five confederations (CGT, CFDT, CGC) had lost members, and the loss was not compensated for by the growth of the other two (FO and CFTC). The pre-eminence of the CGT was thus in doubt. The propensity to strike declined after 1978. Union priorities became the maintenance of purchasing power and job security. However, some unions proposed alternative industrial strategies for economic sectors in difficulty, such as steel (Mouriaux, 1983).

Turning to the other two major parties in industrial relations, the employers were increasingly pro-active and adopted new management techniques, some of which served to undermine union consciousness. The role of the government continued to be vital. Although it emphasised a preference for collective bargaining rather than statute law, the Mitterrand government enacted many new laws. This spate of legislation did not induce revolutionary changes. However Mitterrand tried to introduce gradual changes and to revitalise older legal provisions, which had previously been ineffective, Nevertheless, French industrial relations were still less institutionalised and less of a 'system' than those in any of the other eight countries in this book.

Abbreviations

CFDT	Confédération française démocratique du travail (French Democratic Confederation of Labour)
CFTC	Confédération française des travailleurs chrétiens (French Confederation of Christian Workers)
CGC	Confédération générale des cadres (General Confederation of Executive Staffs)
CGT	Confédération générale du travail (General Confederation of Labour)
CNPF	Conseil national du patronat français (National Council of French Employers)
FO	Force ouvrière (Workers' Force); also known as CGT–FO
FEN	Fédération de l'éducation nationale (National Federation of Education)
GDP	gross domestic product
OECD	Organisation for Economic Co-operation and Development
UCC	Union confédérale des ingénieurs et cadres
UCI	Union des cadres et ingénieurs
UGICA	Union générale des ingénieurs et cadres
UGICT	Union générale des ingénieurs, cadres et techniciens

A chronology of French industrial relations

1791	Le Chapelier law forbad strikes and unions, but not employers' associations.
1821	Building industry employers' association established.
1830s–40s	Many illegal combinations of workers and some collective agreements.
1864	Abolition of Le Chapelier law.
1871	Paris Commune.
1884	Unions were entitled to organise on a craft or industry basis, but not at the enterprise or plant level.
1895	Foundation of the CGT.
1906	Anarcho-syndicalist Amiens Charter asserted the CGT's independence of political parties.
1919	The CFTC established following the Pope's 1891 encyclical (see Chronology, chapter 6). First national industrial employers' confederation founded.
1920	Peak of union density (c. 25–30 per cent).
1921	CGT split, following Russian Revolution.
1934	General strike called by the CGT.
1936	Election of the Popular Front coalition of socialists, communists and radicals. Many strikes and sit-ins. Agreements between the employers' association and the reunited CGT heralded major social reforms including the introduction of employee delegates.
1944	The CGC established.
1945	The Liberation government initiated works councils within enterprises.
1946	The CNPF established as the main current employers' association.
1948	Creation of the FO after a split within the CGT.
1950	Law on collective bargaining and the establishment of a minimum wage system.
1958	Multi-industry unemployment insurance agreement introduced the principle of national agreements.
1964	CFDT established as a secular breakaway from CFTC.
1965	Multi-industry four-week holiday agreement.
1966	Works committees' role extended in relation to training and profit sharing.
1968	Events of May precipitated a general strike; workplace union branches permitted.
1970	Multi-industry job security agreement; a multi-industry *mensualisation* agreement granted 'single status' for blue-collar workers.
1971	Amendment to 1950 Act to permit plant-level bargaining.
1974	A multi-industry redundancy agreement, including a continuation of 90 per cent of previous job's pay levels.

1981	Mitterrand's Socialist–Communist coalition formed the government.
1981	39-hour working week Ordinance.
1982	Auroux law enacted; prices and incomes policy initiated; retirement age reduced from 65 to 60.
1983	Major strikes in the car factories.
1984	Abortive multi-industry negotiations to introduce more flexibility in employment protection laws (initiated by CNPF); Communists left 1981 coalition.
1986	Socialist government replaced by a right of centre government.

References

Adam, G. (1983) *Le Pouvoir Syndical en France* Paris: Dunod

Adam, G. and Reynaud, J.D. (1978) *Conflits du Travail et Changement Social* Paris: PUF

Ardagh, J. (1982) *France in the 1980s: The Definitive Book* Harmondsworth: Penguin

Bachy, J.P. et al. (1974) *Représentation et Négociation dans l'Entreprise* Sceaux: CRESST

Balassa, B. (1982) *The First Year of Socialist Government in France* AEI Studies in Economic Policy, London: AEI

Bellecombe, L.G. de (1978) *Workers' Participation in Management in France* Research Series 34, Geneva: International Institute for Labour Studies

Bunel, J. and Saglio, J. (1984) 'Employers Associations in France' in J.P. Windmuller and A. Gladstone eds *Employers Associations and Industrial Relations: A Comparative Study* Oxford: Clarendon

Caire, G. (1984a) 'The French Left and Labour Relations Policies' *Economic and Industrial Democracy* 1, pp. 131–47

—— (1984b) 'Recent Trends in Collective Bargaining in France' *International Labour Review* 123, 6 (Nov.–Dec.), pp. 723–40

Cohen, S.S. and Gourevitch, P.A. (1982) *France in the Troubled World Economy* London: Butterworth

Delamotte, Y. (1983) *Le Droit du Travail en Pratique* Paris: Edition de l'organisation

—— (1985) 'Recent Trends in the Statutory Regulation of Industrial Relations in France' *Labour and Society* 10, 1 (Jan.), pp. 7–26

Dubois, P. (1979) *Sabotage in Industry* Harmondsworth: Penguin

European Communities (1983) *The Trade Union Movement in France* Brussels: EC Trade Union Division of the Directorate-General for Information X/101/83–EN

Eyraud, F. (1983) 'The Principles of Union Action in the Engineering Industries in Great Britain and France: Towards a Neo-institutionalist Analysis of Industrial Relations' *British Journal of Industrial Relations* 21, 3 (Nov.), pp. 358–78

Goetschy, J. (1983) 'A New Future for Industrial Democracy in France' *Economic and Industrial Democracy* 1, pp. 85–103

Hanley, D.L. et al. (1984) *Contemporary France: Politics and Society Since 1945* London: Routledge & Kegan Paul (new edn)

IDE Group (1981) *European Industrial Relations* Oxford: Clarendon Press

Johnson, D. (1982) 'How much has France Changed Under Mitterrand?' *New Society* 18 March, pp. 427–9

Kesselman, M. ed. (1984) *The French Workers' Movement: Economic Crisis and Political Change* London: George Allen & Unwin

Landier, H. (1981) *Demain, Quels Syndicats?* Paris: Librairie Générale Francaise

Lange, P. et al. (1982) *Unions, Change and Crisis: French and Italian Union Strategy and the Political Economy, 1945–1980* London: George Allen & Unwin

Lash, S. (1984) *The Militant Workers: Class and Radicalism in France and America* London: Heinemann

Liaisons Sociales (various issues)

McAllister, R. (1983) 'Trade Unions' in J. Flower ed. *France Today* London: Methuen

McCormick, J., Andrews, W. and Hoffman, S. eds (1981) *The Impact of the Fifth Republic in France* Buffalo: State University of New York

Maurice, M. et al. (1984) 'Rules, Contexts and Actors: Observations Based on a Comparison Between France and Germany' *British Journal of Industrial Relations* 22, 3 (Nov.), pp. 346–63

Meyers, F. (1981) 'France' in A.A. Blum ed. *International Handbook of Industrial Relations: Contemporary Developments and Research* London: Aldwych, pp. 169–208

Moss, B.H. (1980) *The Origins of the French Labor Movement 1830–1914: The Socialism of Skilled Workers* Berkeley: University of California Press

Mouriaux, R. (1983) *Les Syndicats dans la Société Francaise* Paris: Fondation Nationale des Sciences Politiques

Pelissier, J. (1983) 'Travail a Durée Limitée et Droits des Salariés' *Droit Social* 1 (Jan.), pp. 17–26

Rand Smith, W. (1984) 'Dynamics of Plural Unionism in France: The CGT, CFDT and Industrial Conflict' *British Journal of Industrial Relations* 22, 1 (Mar.), pp. 15–33

Reynaud, J.D. (1975) *Les Syndicats en France* Paris: Seuil

—— (1978) *Les Syndicats, les Patrons et l'Etat* Paris: Editions Ouvrières

Rojot, J. (1983) 'Technological Change and Industrial Relations' in G.J. Bamber and R.D. Lansbury eds *Technological Change and Industrial Relations: An International Symposium.* A Special Issue of the *Bulletin of Comparative Labour Relations* 12, pp. 175–93.

Ross, G. (1982) *Workers and Communists in France: From Popular Front to Eurocommunism* Berkeley: University of California Press

Savary, J. (1984) *French Multinationals* London: Frances Pinter

Sellier, F. (1984) *La Confrontation Sociale en France: 1936–1981* Paris: PUF

Shorter, E. and Tilly, C. (1974) *Strikes in France: 1830–1968* London: Cambridge University Press

Sudreau, P. (1975) *La Réforme de l'Entreprise* Paris: Seuil

Verdier, J.M. (1982) 'Les Réformes et le Droit Syndical' *Droit Social* 4 (April), pp. 291-9

Wright, V. ed. (1984) *Continuity and Change in France* London: George Allen & Unwin

8 | Industrial relations in the Federal Republic of Germany

FRIEDRICH FUERSTENBERG

This chapter starts by putting West German industrial relations into context. It discusses the unions' and employers' roles before considering the main processes of industrial relations: collective bargaining and co-determination. The chapter concludes by trying to evaluate the German experiences of industrial democracy and technological change.

The Federal Republic of Germany was founded in 1949 within the western territories of the former German Reich. Almost a quarter of the West German population originally entered the country as refugees. West Germany has a total population of 61 million people; 41 per cent of them are in civilian employment and 8.3 per cent of the labour force are foreign 'guest workers' (1983). Relatively more people are employed in industry (41 per cent) than in any other OECD country. The services sector employs 53 per cent, while less than 6 per cent are in the agricultural sector (see Appendix and *Wirtschaft und Statistik* 1984, 5:403). The most substantial shift has been from the agricultural sector which employed 25 per cent in 1950 (*Statistisches Jahrbuch* 1967:138). These shifts also had a profound impact on the structure of the labour force, as shown in Table 8.1. The female participation rate (49 per cent) is lower in West Germany than in other countries in this book except for Italy (41 per cent). West Germany has a lower birth rate (9.5 per 1000) than any of the other countries, but it is already more densely populated (246 people per square km) than any of the others except Japan (322 people per square km).

The reconstruction of industry after the Second World War has

165

Table 8.1 Status categories of the German labour force

	1950[1]	1961[1]	1970[2]	1983[3]
		(percentages)		
Blue collar	51	49	47	40
White collar (incl. civil service)	21	29	36	47
Independently employed	14	12	10	9
Assisting family member	14	10	7	4
Total	100	100	100	100

Sources: 1 *Statistisches Jahrbuch* (1967:138).
2 *Wirtschaft und Statistik* (1982, 11:735).
3 *Wirtschaft und Statistik* (1984, 5:170).

been termed the 'economic miracle'. West Germany's GDP was US $612 billion by 1985 (higher than the other countries except for the USA and Japan). Its GDP per capita was $10 025, which is about the average for all the nine countries. By 1 January 1986, West Germany's official reserves were almost $44 million special drawing rights (higher than any other OECD country). However, this country has experienced a relatively greater *increase* in unemployment since 1970 than in any of the other countries (1971: 0.6 per cent; 1984: 7.7 per cent). This dramatic rise in unemployment has been seen in some quarters as signalling the end of the economic miracle.

Between 1979 and 1984, the annual average rate of increase in consumer prices was 4.5 per cent, less than in all the other countries except Japan (3.9 per cent). By 1985, the German rate had fallen to 1.8 per cent, the same rate as Japan (see Table A.7).

According to OECD statistics, the level of West German government revenue is about 46 per cent of GDP (1984), which is slightly above the average for all OECD countries. But West Germany has been the only OECD country with constantly decreasing revenue levels of government revenue since 1980. Nevertheless, due to high social insurance contributions, the average take-home pay in German manufacturing industry is only 73 per cent of gross earnings (about the same as in Britain; see chapter 2, note 2).

West German politics have been dominated by three political parties since the Second World War:

1 the Christian Democratic Union (CDU) with its sister party in Bavaria, the Christian Social Union (CSU);
2 the Social Democratic Party of Germany (SPD); and
3 the Free Democratic Party (FDP).

In view of the system of 'personalised proportional representation', it is extremely difficult for one party to win the absolute majority in elections. Only in 1957 did the CDU–CSU succeed in so doing. Otherwise, at the federal level in West Germany, there has always been a coalition government, with the FDP playing an important role in spite of its small share in votes. Before 1966 and since 1982, the CDU–CSU has had the majority in cabinet. From 1969 until 1982 the SPD had the majority, while from 1966 until 1969 there was a Great Coalition between CDU–CSU and SPD.

As they are 'integrative' parties opposing radicalism, both CDU–CSU and SPD have strong factions representing workers' interests. Within the present Federal Diet, 2 per cent of CDU–CSU (and 8.9 per cent of SPD) deputies are *employees* of trade unions or other workers' organisations, while 35 per cent of CDU–CSU and 99 per cent of SPD deputies are trade union members. In 1983, out of 519 members of the Federal Parliament, 317 were affiliated to unions. Following the principle of 'bargaining autonomy', the federal government abstains from direct interference in industrial relations; there is no definite pro- or anti-union policy. Thus, for example, co-determination was first introduced under a government dominated by the CDU–CSU, led by Adenauer.

The industrial relations parties

Industrialisation in Germany began later than in Britain, but then took off relatively quickly in the closing decades of the nineteenth century. Unlike Britain the factory system developed within a society which retained a legacy of paternalism. Notions of a 'vertically-bonded works community' grew in this context (Fox, 1978).

Labour organisations The German labour movement grew out of the 1848 revolution (see Chronology at end of chapter). German unions were mainly occupationally-based with strong ideological affiliations. They were strongly opposed by the state and employers during Germany's Imperial era, but won significant social and political roles in the post-1918 Weimar Republic. However, the unions were all abolished by Hitler under national socialism in 1933. Following this traumatic experience, after the Second World War, the surviving union leaders aimed to establish a more unified union movement, as an important way of fostering democracy. This was also the aim of the Allied occupation forces, especially the British.

At present, there are four major union confederations: the German Trade Union Federation (Deutscher Gewerkschaftsbund—DGB) with 17 affiliated unions (1983: 7 745 000 members), which is the most influential; the Confederation of German Civil Service Officials (Deutscher Beamtenbund—DBB) with 801 000 members

Table 8.2 **Organisation density of West German unions in percentages (1981)**

Employees		Employees				
		Civil service	White-collar	Blue-collar	Total	Women
Employees	total (millions)	2.27	10.16	11.36	23.79	8.92
	% of all employees	9	43	48	100.0	38
Percentage of unions share among organised employees	DGB	50	72	98	83	77
	DBB	44	2.6	0.31	8.6	10
	DAG	—	21	—	5	9
	CGB	5.6	4	3.1	3	3.5
	total %	100.0	100.0	100.0	100.0	100.0
Union density	total %	74	23	49	40	24
(Percentage of union members in the relevant work force)	DGB	37	17	48	33	18
	DBB	33	0.59	0.15	3.4	2.4
	DAG	—	4.9	—	2.1	2.2
	CGB	4.1	0.86	1	1.2	0.84

Source: Institut der Deutschen Wirtschaft, Köln 1982 (figures rounded).

(1983); the German Salaried Employees' Union (Deutsche Angestell-tengewerkschaft—DAG) with 497 000 members (1983); and the Confederation of Christian Trade Unions of Germany (Christlicher Gewerkschaftsbund Deutschlands—CGB), operating in some regions (1981: 295 000 members). The relative density of organisation is shown in Table 8.2.

There is also a much smaller confederation: the Union of Senior Executives (Union der Leitenden Angestellten—ULA). It does not generally identify itself with labour movement and aims to represent senior executives. However, in 1981 it had only 40 000 members and only two of its affiliates were recognised for collective bargaining.

Under its federal structure, the real power within the DGB lies with the single industrial unions. The three largest among them are the Union of Metal Industry Workers (IG Metall) with 2 536 000 members (1983), the Union of Public Service, Transport and Communications Workers (Gewerkschaft Öffentliche Dienste, Transport und Verkehr) with 1 174 000 members (1983) and the Union of Chemical, Paper and Ceramics Industry Workers (IG Chemie-Papier-Keramik) with 635 000 members (1983). They also dominate the tri-annual congress of the DGB. The DGB mainly performs co-ordinating and representative functions for the union movement. It also maintains a major research institute (Wirtschafts und Sozialwissenschaftliches Institut des DGB), which regularly publishes survey results and monographs about the issues of working life.

With the exception of the CGB, West German unions are based upon an ideological pluralism which, of course, leaves scope for internal competition among factions; the social-democratic group is the most influential. Thus far, radical factions have attained influence only at local levels. The internal structure of the unions is characterised by representative democracy. But there is still an important element of direct member participation. With the exception of the union of printing workers, a union may call a strike only after having won a 75 per cent majority in favour, in a secret ballot. On the whole, however, union policy is highly centralised due to the following three factors:

1 collective bargaining is conducted mainly at industry and regional levels;
2 unions pursue policies which embrace wider social issues;
3 industrial relations is highly bureaucratic and legalistic, which has induced the involvement of experts.

It is important to note the generality of the DGB's policies. These aim to safeguard and improve workers' rights, not only at the workplace and enterprise levels, but also at the level of the industry and wider society. Union activity thus transcends the realm of working conditions to embrace, for instance, concern about technological change. The DGB and its member unions own one of the largest West German banks, the largest building corporation and a major insurance company. The unions also participate actively in adult education activities through their well-equipped training centres.

Union policy is 'co-operative' insofar as the unions receive information and are consulted about all major areas of social and economic policy. This extends to practically all public policy relating to the quality of life of the working population and their dependants. Though the unions are technically neutral in party politics, their political presence is obvious. Thus, the West German unions are not only powerful partners in collective bargaining, but they also exert great influence on political and social life. Their structural power gained from institutionalised participation (see below), was augmented in the 1970s by an increase in unionisation, due to favourable labour market conditions and the politicisation of younger employees. (Density of the DGB unions increased from 30 to 37 per cent.)

Unlike the position in most of the other countries, the economic recession of the early 1980s did not immediately precipitate a decline in union density.

The employers   There is considerable industrial concentration in the economy. In 1980, more than 39 per cent of those in employment worked in establishments with more than 1000 employees (compared with less than one per cent who worked in establishments with less than 20 employees).

Unlike the English-speaking countries, for instance, in West Germany corporations have a two-tier board structure. It is the lower, managing board (*Vorstand*) which runs the firm, designs long-term policy and which implements most decisions. However, the bigger decisions are formally endorsed by the upper, supervisory board (*Aufsichtsrat*) which controls managerial performance. The supervisory board appoints the top managers, but generally meets only four times per year, so cannot interfere directly in management (as discussed later).

Employers' associations began for defensive purposes as a response to the growth of unions in the second half of the nineteenth century (Bunn, 1984). Neither unions nor employers' associations were allowed under the Third Reich period. After 1945, the employers' associations re-emerged, following the unions. Employers' interests were organised centrally in parallel to those of the unions. The Confederation of German Employers' Associations (Bundesvereinigung Deutscher Arbeitgeberverbande—BDA) represents 46 national branch federations and 12 regional federations, comprising about 80 per cent of all enterprises (1977). The Confederation has 21 committees and working groups, which provide expert opinions and prepare political platforms. For this purpose, the employers' federations also operate jointly two research institutes (Institut der Deutschen Wirtschaft and Institut für Angewandte Arbeitswissenschaft).

Neither the BDA nor DGB participate directly in collective bargaining, but they co-ordinate and provide information. The member organisations, however, are the real centres of employers' power. They have substantial 'strike protection funds' and are the partners of unions in collective bargaining, except where there is company bargaining (e.g. at VW, which is an unusual case). Unlike their equivalent associations in the English-speaking countries, the German employers sometimes organise lockouts of workers, as in a major metalworkers' dispute in 1963 (Owen Smith, 1981:199). In common with most other countries, the employers are ideologically conservative and act as an employers' voice to the state.

In spite of the large variety of enterprises, differing in size, production and market situation, the employers try to maintain solidarity during industry-wide negotiations. However, there is some flexibility provided by the system of enterprise- or plant-centred negotiations between works councils and management. These negotiations implement and augment collective agreements at industry level (see below).

There are different organisations in the public sector. At municipal level, the Federation of Local Government Employers' Associations (Vereinigung der kommunalen Arbeitgeberverbande—VKA), and at state government level, the German State Government Employers' Association (Tarifgemeinschaft der Deutschen Laender—TDL) have operated since 1949. At national level, since 1960 the Federal Minister of Interior has been 'the employer' in negotiations.

The role of government West Germany has an extensive framework of labour law. The Federal Constitution (1949) grants the freedom of association and right to organise. Employer–employee relations are generally regulated by statutory law. There is a division of labour between local courts, regional appeal courts and a federal labour court.

There is extensive legislation, for example, on labour standards, hours of work, sick pay, protection against summary dismissals and establishing employment rights for young workers, women and disabled people, as well as expectant or nursing mothers. In addition there are health and safety laws, which are implemented by Industrial Injuries Insurance Institutes (self-governing public corporations under state supervision). Labour and management are equally represented on the decision-making bodies of these institutions. Under the Occupational Safety Act (1974) there are about 80 000 industrial safety officers, supported by about 25 000 safety representatives at plant level, nominated by the employer in accordance with the works council. In recent years, special attention has been given to improve both the quantity and quality of workplace medical practitioners.

A comprehensive social security system has developed since the first introduction of social insurance in the 1880s. It is administered by self-governing agencies with either bipartite or tripartite boards. There is a Federal Institute for Labour at Nuremberg which administers the Federal Employment Service, the Unemployment Insurance Fund as well as Unemployment Assistance and Family Allowances. It also operates a large research institute on all matters of labour market policy.

There is a high level and coverage of vocational training in West Germany. In 1982, 60 per cent of all employees had completed a three year period of such training and/or vocational school attendance after having finished full-time education. Further, 6.6 per cent had completed technical college training, 2.7 per cent had graduated from professional schools and 5.9 per cent were university graduates.[1] Moreover there is a continuing trend towards higher qualifications in the upper grades of the labour force.

The attempt to create a form of 'concerted action' aiming at a kind of national incomes policy has failed, due to disagreement about the goals (cf. Clark et al., 1980). On the other hand, the main strategies of employers and unions cannot succeed without taking government action into consideration (e.g. in the case of policy options for or against generating state-financed additional employment). Government policy on industrial relations, however, is not to interfere, thus respecting the principle of bargaining autonomy (*Tarifautonomie*), limiting state influence to setting a normative framework and publishing basic pay data, especially on socio-economic targets, and on trends in planning the federal budget, etc.

The main processes

Governmental interference in collective bargaining is rare. There is no governmental mediation, as the parties concerned provide their own voluntary conciliation system. Nevertheless, in major disputes the government usually becomes involved, informally.

Collective bargaining   West German industrial relations has a dual structure. At workplace and plant levels there is no direct bargaining between unions and employers. Instead, works councils and employers negotiate on a statutory basis. It is at industry-wide and regional level (and less often at enterprise levels) that unions and the employers' federations enter into negotiations, which usually result in collective agreements. Out of more than 38 000 registered collective agreements in 1979, 36 per cent were enterprise agreements (which are different from the plant agreements between work councils and management). The Collective Bargaining Law (1952) grants legal enforcement of agreements only to union members. However, most agreements apply to all employees in the particular sector of the economy. Distinctions between unionised and non-unionised workers are not allowed in collective agreements (following a Federal Labour Court decision in 1967).

There is a distinction between framework agreements, which have a relatively long duration, and 'ordinary agreements' which usually last for a year and regulate major conditions of work (pay, working time, leave of absence etc.). Some of the ordinary agreements are concluded between one employer and the relevant union (enterprise agreements), as for example in the case of VW. As can be seen from Table 8.3, a wide range of special provisions may become the subject of collective agreements.

Table 8.3 Some contents of collective agreements

	1963	1978
Total of valid registered collective agreements	12 647	36 705
Enterprise agreements	4 495	13 216
Framework agreements	2 044	3 685
Enterprise master agreements	930	1 822
	1974	**1978**
Fringe benefits		
holiday pay	79%	93%
annual bonus	60%	76%
profit/capital sharing	77%	92%
Social security		
job security	32%	52%
wage guarantees	40%	62%
protection in case of rationalisation	45%	48%
additional unemployment compensation		21%
sickness pay	30%	42%

Source: Boedler and Kaiser (1979:26).

Procedures in collective bargaining are highly formalised and even ritualised, as illustrated in the following example of a typical set of IG Metall negotiations:

1 The claim is discussed at plant level by the members and officers and then screened by negotiation committees which make recommendations about the form and extent of the claim to the union board. Four weeks before termination of the collective agreement, the union informs the employers about the claim.
2 A negotiating committee is established. Bargaining starts two weeks before the expiry date of the current collective agreement.
3 There is a peace obligation which continues to apply for four weeks after the expiry date. After this period, the workers may initiate demonstrations and other sanctions.
4 A new collective agreement is negotiated, or in case of a failure to agree, one or both parties may declare a breakdown of the negotiations, then the union negotiating committee may propose a strike ballot.

Under stage 4, after a failure to agree, the parties may jointly appeal to a conciliation board within two working days; after another working day this may be done by either party, unilaterally; the other would then have to join after two more working days. Then the independent chairman of the conciliation board (usually a well-known retired politician or public servant) has to be nominated without delay. The board must convene within three working days and present a proposal within five working days. After six more working days, the parties in dispute have to decide whether or not to accept this proposal.

Unlike the position in Britain or Australia, for instance, such procedures are usually followed strictly. Moreover, there are relatively few stoppages (see Appendix), in spite of the lack of legislation concerning strikes or lockouts. However, there are many legal constraints on industrial action, partly deriving from court decisions. Thus, legal strikes are strictly limited to industrial relations topics. It is generally illegal to call a strike about a political issue.

However, there have been some major disputes. There were stoppages in 1984, both in the printing and the metal industries. In the latter, for example, the union wanted a cut in the basic working week from 40 to 35 hours, with no loss of pay. This was part of the union's strategy to counter high levels of unemployment. But the employers insisted that such a cut would render German goods less competitive in international markets. Therefore, as an alternative, the employers proposed to introduce more flexible working hours. The government did not support the union's campaign, though it proposed to introduce early retirement provisions from the age of 58.

The outcome of this bitter dispute was a compromise. The average basic week would become 38.5 hours in 1985, but this could vary between 37 and 40 hours for different groups of workers in a plant. Such variations were to be negotiated at plant level. This represents a decentralisation of collective bargaining and increases the role of works councillors. The 1984 dispute revealed a new set of union tactics, called 'the new flexibility'. These tactics included local strikes, for example, in component-making firms, which in effect would stop production in much of the car-manufacturing industry, without having called a general industry-wide stoppage.

Although for Germany this was an uncharacteristically bitter dispute, there is still a widespread consensus that stoppages should be a last resort and only about fundamental issues.

Co-determination   There is a long tradition of attempts to introduce industrial democracy in Germany. Works councils were first established by law in 1916, in industries which were important for the economy in the First World War. They became obligatory under the Works Councils Act of 1920.

Since the Second World War, union influence at the enterprise level has been enlarged by the various laws on co-determination, in particular:

1 the Works Constitution Act (1952–1972) enlarged the legal rights of works councils in private enterprises;
2 the Co-Determination Act (1951) established full parity co-determination within the supervisory boards of the coal and steel industries, and a labour director as full member of the managing board;
3 the Co-Determination Act (1976) established countervailing parity in supervisory boards of limited liability companies with more than 2000 employees; and
4 the Personnel Representation Act of 1974, provided for the election of staff councils in public services and enterprises.

The pattern of co-determination rights after 1978 is summarised in Table 8.4. The main instrument for implementing co-determination is the works council, elected by all employees of a firm, regardless of their union affiliation, and operating on a defined legal basis. However, works councillors usually co-operate closely with union officers or hold union office themselves. Works councils cannot call a strike,

Table 8.4 The pattern of co-determination rights

Form of co-determination	Sector	No. of employees covered (millions)
Full parity co-determination in supervisory boards and a labour director in management board; works councils	Coal and steel industries	0.6
Counterbalancing parity in supervisory boards; works councils	Large companies with more than 2000 employees	4.1
One third of seats for employee representatives in supervisory boards; works councils	Smaller and medium-sized companies	0.9
Works councils	Other private enterprises with more than five employees	9.4
Personnel councils	Public service	3.6
No institutionalised workers' participation	Private enterprises with less than five employees	3.0

Source: *Sueddeutsche Zeitung*, 27 February 1979.

but they have the right to sue management in a case of alleged breach of contractual rights. In such rare cases, the issue is referred to an Arbitration Tribunal.

Works councils have many rights to information, consultation and co-determination. The 1972 Works Constitution Act, for example, allows works councils to regulate: works discipline, daily working hours and breaks, temporary short time or overtime work, the fixing of job piece rates, pay systems, suggestion schemes, holiday schedules, any monitoring of employee performance, safety regulations, welfare services in the establishment, and the administration of works housing for employees.

Works councils can also co-determine any changes to the pace of work or the working environment. In such cases, works councils may demand ergonomic data. They can also co-determine the process of personnel selection and occupational training. In the event of any major operational changes in the enterprise, the employer and the works council shall negotiate over the change and, in the case of any economic disadvantages for employees, agree on adequate lay-off and compensation arrangements.

A representative system of co-determination always poses the problem of adequately representing all the different interests in a constituency. Works councils do reflect the relative strength of blue-collar and white-collar interests. Some groups tend to be proportionately under-represented, however—e.g. younger workers, the unskilled, women and foreign 'guest workers'—but there is a trend towards increasing the proportion of the last two categories.

The relations between works councils and the unions are usually close. In most enterprises, union officers participate in works council meetings from time to time. They regularly address works assemblies. Communication between works councils and unions varies according to the degree of unionisation of the employees.

Labour directors were first established in the coal and steel (*Montan*) industries in 1951. They are appointed in the same way as other members of the managing board, but they cannot be appointed against the wishes of the employees' representatives on the supervisory board, who usually initiate such an appointment. Usually these directors are highly qualified and experienced union members (but not officials). Labour directors have a special concern with personnel and social policy, but also participate fully in the shaping of general company policy, which has to be jointly agreed by the members of the managing board. Thus a dual allegiance is established: the labour director is responsible both for effective management and for effective representation of the workers' points of view.

Labour directors in other industries are not institutionally linked with unions and have clearly defined managerial functions. Therefore, there is no question of a dual or conflicting loyalty. In dealing with co-determination in supervisory boards, two types of legal provisions have to be considered. In the case of a minority representation, members elected by the work force cannot determine decisions, against the will of shareholders' representatives. Such situations are typical outside the coal and steel industry, for companies with more than 500 employees, where one third of the supervisory boards have to be employee representatives, nominated by the works councils.

Parity of workers' representation has been achieved only in the coal and steel industries. There, since 1951, representatives of capital have been nominated by the shareholders' meeting, while the 'labour' ones have been nominated by works councils and unions. The parties choose a chairman by co-opting a 'neutral' person. In 1976, this system was extended to all German companies with more than 2000 employees. There are, however, two major differences between the 1951 and 1976 laws. Outside coal and steel, at least one employee representative is nominated by the *leitende Angestellte* (senior executives). Furthermore, in impasse situations, the chairman (nominated by the shareholders) has a casting vote.

From the employers' point of view there are five problems with the 1976 Co-Determination Act: the contradiction between parity and the property principle, the endangered autonomy of collective bargaining, the representation of middle managerial employees below the senior executive level, the election procedures for nominating workers' representatives for the supervisory board and the position of the labour director.

By contrast, the unions see other problems, especially the evasion tactics of some firms. By reorganising, altering the capital composition and changing the legal form of the enterprise, in 1978 alone about 30 companies tried to avoid extended co-determination in supervisory boards. Some other companies tried to change their statutes. Unions were also concerned about their secrecy and the lack of information, and about procedures which gave advantages to shareholders' representatives, such as the double vote for the chairmen in committees with a non-parity composition. In spite of such problems for unions, co-determination at supervisory board levels has generally led to a gradual modification of entrepreneurial goals, towards more socio-economic goals.

Current and future issues

Co-determination fosters a strategy of 'co-operative unionism', for several reasons. The unions were re-established after the Second

World War as integrative associations, representing jointly the interests of workers with different political and ideological affiliation. The resulting concentration on social and economic issues and the independence from political parties marks a decisive difference when compared with industrial relations in France or Italy, for example. Traditionally, German unions never considered themselves merely as labour market institutions or 'business unions', unlike those in North America. The German unions always aimed at settling larger issues in the wider society. There are still minorities of radicals and 'reformers' who have different orientations, but the conceptionalisation and realisation of reforms is possible only by getting involved in decision-making processes. In the course of implementing the different co-determination laws, thousands of new functions and positions for union officials have been created, thus establishing a network of influence which cannot easily be abandoned. They have also acquired much knowledge which has increased union concern with new types of problems. Gradually the unions have developed an infrastructure matching their claim for co-determination and enabling them to deal with the employers on many more issues than traditionally defined by the scope of collective bargaining.

The relative success of co-determination was possible only because the employers and the managers became convinced that such a system provided an efficient way of managing the employment relationship. The relatively low number of stoppages (see Appendix) reflects the alternative means for settling disputes. Works councils provide an efficient grievance machinery within the plants. Co-determination in supervisory boards is a form of conflict management; it provides for discussion of all major issues and possible problems for the work force, before final decisions are taken. Consultation and negotiation starts before the two sides become entrenched. The unions have an involvement at the early stages of social, technological and economic change. Strikes as an ultimate means for pressing workers' claims become necessary only in rare cases of fundamental dissent. As a consequence, however, bureaucratic procedures and oligarchic structures develop. These may exclude the shop floor from direct participation. Thus the co-determination institutions at a higher level may lose touch with the rank and file.

Those who plead for more militancy and direct, mandatory democracy in industrial relations usually regret the strong union involvement in managerial affairs. But, putting ideological considerations aside, the growth of a segmented internal labour market in large companies calls for new union strategies. Co-determination is a pragmatic approach towards influencing working conditions. The effects of investment policy, for instance, on the organisation of work, qualifications and skills cannot be influenced by traditional bargaining techniques. Instead, the whole process of making investment decisions and implementing them by technological, economic and possibly social planning needs to be accompanied by continuous communication and consultation in order to avoid outcomes detrimental to workers' interests. It is precisely this communication and consultation structure, combined with the opportunities for greater influence, that co-determination provides. Its greater efficiency, however, is offset by complaints about the lack of direct participation. Thus, the demand for more self-determination at workplace level is an inherent dynamic factor in West German industrial relations.

Technological change　　In the 1980s, the German economy was faced with structural changes. Their impact upon industrial relations can be illustrated by the current changes in technology. The union strategies focus upon protection against an increase of work load and stress, against deskilling and on the reduction of working time as a protection against loss of jobs. There has not yet been a general policy of job creation by reducing working time. Hence, the possible consequence, an equivalent reduction of workers' income, is still an unsettled issue, despite the 1984 metal industry dispute (see earlier discussion).

Demands for government action usually focus on employment stabilisation, the improvement of job security, and the maintenance of skills and qualifications. Unions are demanding a greater conceptual linkage between the government's labour market and educational policies on the one hand and its measures to improve the economic structure on the other hand. They advocate a streamlining of all policies directed towards influencing technological change. The research programme for the 'humanisation of work life' administered by the Federal Ministry for Research and Technology, is supported in principle by all unions. However, as a prerequisite for this support, the unions want to be involved in the design of research projects, through their representatives in advisory boards and works council participation in their implementation at plant levels. Thus far, there have been many such action research projects, though they have mainly been pilot studies. There is still a need to foster a wider application of results.

Employers and their associations also assume some social responsibility for technological change. The great challenge for them is to develop and utilise new technology in order to foster productivity and competitiveness, whilst also providing a more humane form of job

Table 8.5   State regulations on humane work design

State Regulation	Year	Contents
Safety of Machines Act	1963	Obliges all users of machines and equipment to ensure that all safety instructions and technical rules are observed.
Works Constitution Act	1972	Regulates co-operation between works council (i.e. shop committee) and management; contains special information rights and participation of workers concerning job design (workplaces, processes, technologies, environment).
Work Security Act	1973	Regulates the employment of security staff (medical and engineering) and the application of scientific findings in humanisation of work.
Workplace Decree	1975	Contains minimum requirements for the work environment (noise, lighting, climate etc.)
Decree on Toxic Substances	1975	Sets maximum workplace concentrations of toxic substances to be observed.

Source: Projekttraeger Humanisierung des Arbeitslebens (1981:20f).

design. It is not easy for employers to find workable compromises between social, economic and technological considerations. Nevertheless, there is considerable scope for them to discuss such matters with unions and works councils. There are numerous cases of management, union and works council participation in the humanisation of work programmes.

Government strategies to improve industrial relations in view of technological change primarily focus upon adjusting the legal framework (Recent state regulations are listed in Table 8.5). As a result, the socio-economic environment for introducing technological change has been profoundly restructured. In particular, the 1972 Works Constitution Act provides considerable information, consultation and co-determination on plant-wide industrial relations issues due to technological change (see Figure 8.1).

However, these are necessary but not sufficient requirements for coping successfully with the problem of innovative applications of technology, while maintaining consensus between the industrial relations parties. Perhaps the most important factor is job security. By 1986, unemployment had risen to about 8 per cent—the highest level since the 1930s. Between 1980 and 1990 the labour force will

Figure 8.1   Regulation of issues associated with technological change within the Works Constitution Act (1972)

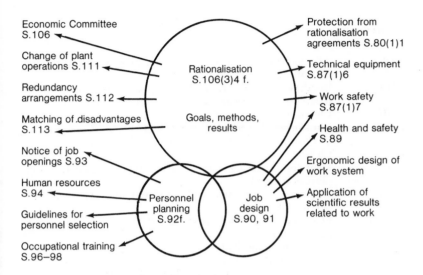

Source: Adapted from Wiesner (1979:46).

increase by 1.9 million people. Most West Germans seem to accept that new technology is not generally destroying jobs; rather, its impact on employment depends on how it is introduced and on the market conditions. However, there is currently a fierce debate about whether the employment consequences of technological change are positive or negative.

Conclusion

Unions and employers are demanding government initiatives, but they are arguing from different points of view. It is not yet possible to see a compromise between the competing arguments. However, the prospect of maintaining the post-1949 innovations in industrial relations depends on the continuation of a basic consensus between the parties concerned. Until the mid-1970s, sustained economic growth induced consensus. It may be questioned whether this can continue to guide industrial relations into the 1990s. Perhaps joint efforts for the social assessment of technology will become increasingly important for evaluating particular changes. The growing number of collective agreements containing provisions related to the introduction of new technology demonstrates at least some continuing flexibility in the West German model of industrial relations.

Abbreviations

ADGB	Allgemeiner Deutscher Gewerkschaftsbund (General Federation of German Trade Unions)
BDA	Bundesvereinigung Deutscher Arbeitgeberverbande (Confederation of German Employers' Associations)
CDU	Christian Democratic Union
CGB	Christlicher Gewerkschaftsbund Deutschlands (Confederation of Christian Trade Unions of Germany)
CSU	Christian Social Union
DAG	Deutsche Angestelltengewerkschaft (German Salaried Employees' Union)
DBB	Deutscher Beamtenbund (Confederation of German Civil Service Officials)
DGB	Deutscher Gewerkschaftsbund (German Trade Union Federation)
FDP	Free Democratic Party
GDP	gross domestic product
IG Chemie-Papier-Keramik	Union of Chemical, Paper and Ceramics Industry Workers
IG Metall	Union of Metal Industry Workers
OECD	Organisation for Economic Co-operation and Development
SPD	Social Democratic Party of Germany
TDL	Tarifgemeinschaft der Deutschen Laender (German State Government Employers' Association)
ULA	Union der Leitenden Angestellten (Union of Senior Executives)
VKA	Vereinigung der kommunalen Arbeitgeberverbande (Federation of Local Government Employers' Associations)

A chronology of West German industrial relations

1832	Secret association of German craftsmen in France, Switzerland and Britain.
1844	Silesian weavers' revolt.
1846	Gesellenverein (journeymen's association) founded.
1848	Year of revolutions.
1848–54	General German Workers' Fraternity, comprising 31 workers' associations and three workers' committees.
1848–53	Association of cigar-producing workers.
1849–53	Printers' association formed.

1863	Foundation of the General German Workers' Association.
1865–67	First national associations of cigar workers, printers and tailors.
1869	Foundation of Social Democratic Workers' Party.
1869	Prussian Trades Law grants freedom of coalition.
1873	First collective agreement (in the printing trade).
1878–90	Anti-socialist legislation.
1891	First industrial union: German Metal Workers' Association.
1892	First trades union congress.
1894	Foundation of first large Christian trade union (coal miners).
1899	Congress of Free Trade Unions recommends collective agreements.
1904	Main employers' association founded.
1905	First long strike by the German miners' union.
1913	Association of German Employers' Federations established. 3 million union members; 10 885 collective agreements cover 1.4 million employees.
1914–18	First World War.
1916	Law to enforce works committees in all production establishments with more than fifty workers.
1918	Law on Collective Agreements.
1918–24	Central Working Commission of employers and workers in manufacturing industries and trades.
1919	Foundation of General German Trades Union Federation (ADGB).
1920	General Strike against rightist riot (Kapp–Putsch).
1920	Works Councils Act.
1921	Foundation of Akademie der Arbeit (Academy for Labour Studies).
1927	Law on Labour Courts.
1928	Law on Collective Agreements.
1928	Thirteenth ADGB Congress discuss co-determination.
1933	Unions abolished by National Socialist government.
1939–45	Second World War.
1945	Decision to found the DGB.
1949	Founding congress of DGB.
1951	Co-determination Act for coal and steel industries.
1952	Works Constitution Act.
1955	Personnel Representation Act (for employees in the public sector).
1963	Foundation of Christian Trade Union Movement.
1963	Lockout of metal workers.
1967	'Concerted action' begins.
1972	New Works Constitution Act.
1974	New Personnel Representation Act.
1976	Co-determination Act for firms with more than 2000 employees.
1978–79	Steel strike: dispute about shorter working week.
1984	Metal workers' dispute about a shorter working week.

Note

1 These data are derived from the microcensus, published in *Wirtschaft und Statistik* (1984, 2:108); 28.9 per cent of these interviewed gave no response, most of them had no such training.

References

Boedler, H. and Kaiser, H. (1979) 'Dreissig Jahre Tarifregister' *Bundesarbeitsblatt* p. 26

Budde, A. et al. (1982) 'Corporate Goals, Managerial Objectives and Orgainsational Structures in British and West German Companies' *Organisation Studies* 3, 1, pp. 1–32

Bunn, R.F. (1984) 'Employers Associations in the Federal Republic of Germany' in J.P. Windmuller and A. Gladstone eds *Employers Associations and Industrial Relations: A Comparative Study* Oxford: Clarendon, pp. 169–201

Clark, J. et al. (1980) *Trade Unions, National Politics and Economic Management: A Comparative Study of the TUC and DGB* London: Anglo-German Foundation

Federal Republic of Germany (1978) *Co-determination in the Federal Republic of Germany* (translations of the Acts of 1952, 1972 and 1976) Bonn: The Federal Minister of Labour and Social Affairs

Fox, A. (1978) 'Corporatism and Industrial Democracy: The Social Origins of Present Forms and Methods in Britain and Germany' *Industrial Democracy: International Views* University of Warwick: Industrial Relations Research Unit of the Social Science Research Council, pp. 3–60

Fuerstenberg, F. (1978) *Workers' Participation in Management in the Federal Republic of Germany* Geneva: International Institute for Labour Studies

—— (1983) 'Technological Change and Industrial Relations in West Germany' *Bulletin of Comparative Labour Relations* 12, pp. 121–37

—— (1984) 'Recent Trends in Collective Bargaining in the Federal Republic of Germany' *International Labour Review* 123, 5, pp. 615–30

—— (1985) 'The Regulation of Working Time in the Federal Republic of Germany' *Labour and Society* 10, 2, pp. 133–50

Fuerstenberg, F. and Steininger, S. (1984) *Qualification Aspects of Robotisation: Report of an Empirical Study for the OECD* Bochum: Ruhr Universität Bochum (mimeo)

Gunter, H. and Leminsky, G. (1978) 'The Federal Republic of Germany' in J.T. Dunlop and W. Galenson eds *Labor in the Twentieth Century* New York: Academic Press

Hartmann, G. et al. (1983) 'Computerised Machine Tools, Manpower Consequences and Skill Utilization: A Study of British and West German Manufacturing Firms' *British Journal of Industrial Relations* 21, 2, pp. 221–31

Hartmann, H. and Conrad, W. (1981) 'Industrial Relations in West Germany' in P.B. Doeringer et al. eds *Industrial Relations in Interna-*

tional Perspective: Essays on Research and Policy London: Macmillan, pp. 218–45

Hassencamp, A. and Bieneck, H.J. (1983) 'Technical and Organisational Changes and Design of Working Conditions in the Federal Republic of Germany' *Labour and Society* 8, (Jan.–Mar.), pp. 39–56

Hutton, S.P. and Lawrence, P.A. (1981) *German Engineers: The Anatomy of a Profession* Oxford: Clarendon

Institut der Deutschen Wirtschaft (1982) *Zahlen zur Wirtschaftlichen Entwicklung der Bundesrepublik Deutschland* Köln: Deutscher Instituts-Verlag

Keller, B.K. (1981) 'Determinants of the Wage Rate in the Public Sector: The Case of Civil Servants in the Federal Republic of Germany' *British Journal of Industrial Relations* 19, 3 (Nov.), pp. 345–60

Kissler, L. and Sattel, U. (1982) 'Humanization of Work and Social Interests: Description and Critical Assessment of the State-sponsored Program of Humanization in the Federal Republic of Germany' *Economic and Industrial Democracy* 3, pp. 221–61

Lapping, A. (1983) *Working Time in Britain and West Germany* London: Anglo-German Foundation

Lawrence, P. (1980) *Managers and Management in West Germany* London: Croom Helm

Maitland, I. (1983) *The Causes of Industrial Disorder: A Comparison of a British and a German Factory* London: Routledge & Kegan Paul

Marsh, A. et al. (1981) *Workplace Relations in the Engineering Industry in the UK and the Federal Republic of Germany* London: Anglo-German Foundation

Miller, D. (1978) 'Trade Union Workplace Representation in the Federal Republic of Germany' *British Journal of Industrial Relations* 16, 3 (Nov.), pp. 335–54

Moses, J.A. (1982) *Trade Unionism in Germany from Bismarck to Hitler* vol. 1: 1869–1918; vol. 2: 1919–1933; Totowa, NJ: Barnes & Noble

Owen Smith, E. (1981) 'West Germany' in E. Owen Smith ed. *Trade Unions in the Developed Economies* London: Croom Helm

Projekttraeger Humanisierung des Arbeitslebens (1981) *Das Programm zur Humanisierung des Arbeitslebens* Frankfurt & New York: Campus

Reichel, H. (1971) 'Recent Trends in Collective Bargaining in the Federal Republic of Germany' *International Labour Review* 104, 6, pp. 253–71

Seglow, P. et al. (1982) *Rail Unions in Britain and West Germany* London: Policy Studies Institute–Anglo-German Foundation

Sengenberger, W. (1984) 'West German Employment Policy Restoring Worker Competition' *Industrial Relations* 23, 3 (Fall), pp. 323–44

Sorge, A. and Warner, H. (1981) 'Culture, Management and Manufacturing Organisation: A Study of British and German Firms' *Management International Review* 21, pp. 35–48

Sorge, A. et al. (1983) *Microelectronics and Manpower in Manufacturing: Applications of Computer Numerical Control in Great Britain and West Germany* Berlin: International Institute of Management; Aldershot: Gower

Statistisches Jahrbuch (1967) Stuttgart & Mainz: Kohlhammer

Streeck, W. (1984) *Industrial Relations in West Germany: A Case Study of the Car Industry* London: Heinemann

Sueddeutsche Zeitung (1979) 27 February edition

Wiesner, H. ed. (1983) *Bismarck to Bullock* London: Anglo-German Foundation

Wiesner, H. (1979) *Rationalisierung* Köln: Bund-Verlag

Willey, R.J. (1974) 'Trade Unions and Political Parties in the Federal Republic of Germany' *Industrial and Labor Relations Review* 28, pp. 38–59

Wirtschaft und Statistik (1982 ff.) Statistische Monatszahlen, Stuttgart & Mainz: Kohlhammer

9 | Swedish industrial relations

OLLE HAMMARSTRÖM

Sweden became an industrial society later than most of the other countries in this book. At the turn of the century, Sweden was a poor agrarian society with high emigration. In common with Australia, Sweden still has only 30 per cent of its civilians employed in industry (a lower percentage than any of the other countries in this book, except Canada). Five per cent are still in the agricultural sector, while 65 per cent are now in the services sector.

Swedish industrial relations have long fascinated foreign observers. With a total population of 8.3 million and with 4.3 million civilian employees, Sweden is the smallest of the countries in this book. However, 77 per cent of its women are in the labour force, which is the highest female participation rate of any OECD country. In comparison with the other countries, Sweden tends to lose fewer working days in stoppages (apart from Japan and West Germany) and has the lowest unemployment rate (about the same as Japan).

There are five main political parties in Sweden. The percentage of the popular vote which they each received in the 1985 elections is given in brackets. Three of them are non-socialist parties: the Moderate/Conservative Party (21%); the Centre/Agrarian Party (12%); and the Peoples/Liberal Party (14%). These parties formed the government by coalition between 1976 and 1982. The small Communist Party (5%) has never formed the government, but it has sometimes been an ally to the much more important Social Democratic Party (45%), which has formed the government for 47 years in the 53 year period 1932–85, including a continuous period of 44 years between 1932 and 1976. During this period, Sweden became known as a country of high taxes and a developed welfare state. In 1984, the average *take-home* pay in Swedish manufacturing industry was only 66 per cent of *gross earnings* (after tax and social security contributions, but excluding family benefits), which was a lower percentage than in any of the other countries (see chapter 2, note 2). In the period 1979–84, the average annual rate of increase in consumer prices in Sweden was about 10 per cent, higher than any of the other countries except for France (11 per cent) and Italy (16 per cent) (see Table A.7).

Context of industrial relations

Following its relatively late industrialisation, Sweden also became unionised relatively late compared with other countries. The trade union movement started to develop during the 1880s. At first, the Social Democratic Party, which was established in 1889, functioned as a union confederation, but then the Swedish Trade Union Confederation (LO) was formed in 1898. The employer organisations developed as a response to the growth of the unions. The Swedish Employers' Confederation (SAF) was established in 1902.

The Swedish union movement began with craft unions. By 1910 the concept of industry unions was dominant. Several factors explain this development. Craft training was poorly developed at the time when the first unions were formed. Furthermore, industrialisation occurred to a large extent in the form of '*bruk*' or one company towns or villages, where it was natural to form one union against the one employer.

The right to organise and bargain collectively had no legal basis at first and was strongly contested by the employers. The first industrial disputes were combined struggles for the right to organise and for higher pay in the 1870s. These struggles intensified around the turn of the century, for example, in the lockout in the engineering industry in 1905.

These conflicts led to the recognition of union rights in the so-called 'December compromise' of 1906. In an agreement with LO, the SAF acknowledged the unions' right to organise and bargain collectively. For its part, the LO accepted that all collective agreements were to include a clause giving the employer 'the full right to hire and fire and to organise production'. The agreement was seen as a major step forward by the union side. The right to organise had been achieved, even though employers' rights were then generally seen as natural. This was the first example of a major agreement reached by the central organisations on behalf of their affiliated unions and employer associations.

However, the 'December compromise' was not fully recognised

by all employers. Therefore, some of them continued to implement anti-union policies. The first nation-wide dispute was in 1909. The legendary 'great strike' started as a lockout by employers, as an attempt to weaken the unions. The dispute ended with the workers returning to work, without an agreement. It was a heavy defeat for the unions whose membership declined from 162 000 members in 1908 to 85 000 members in 1910.

Industrial relations legislation developed slowly. It was reactive rather than promoting reform. In 1906 an Act on voluntary mediation was passed and a small mediation office was established. From 1910–20, employers and conservative politicians tried on several occasions to introduce legislation that would restrict unions' rights to strike. These attempts were blocked by socialist and liberal interests. As strikes continued to be seen as a major social problem, Acts on Collective Bargaining and the Labour Court were passed in 1928 despite union opposition. These Acts were the first legal recognition of union rights.

After the election of the first Social Democratic government in 1932, the situation changed. The unions adopted a new strategy as they no longer saw the government as a natural ally of the employers. The new relation between capital and labour led to the 'Saltsjöbaden Agreement' of 1938, which laid the foundation for labour–management co-operation and consultation. The spirit of co-operation was further developed during the Second World War, even though Sweden was neutral.

During the pre-war years, the Social Democratic government largely followed a Keynesian economic policy, which used budget deficits to fight unemployment. After the war, a modified version of Keynesian policy was developed. In 1951, the LO Congress adopted a policy based on the so-called 'Rehn–Meidner model', named after two prominent LO economists who proposed a new approach to economic policy. The LO took the view that trade unions should take into account the government's economic policy when formulating their wage demands. In exchange for union support, the government agreed to pursue a policy of full employment. Economic growth was secured by union commitment to rationalisation and technical development. This government also gave support to an 'active labour market policy' which encouraged both geographical and skill mobility for displaced workers.

In adopting this programme, the unions assumed partial responsibility for the national economic performance, thereby changing their policy from the early 1930s. Industrial conflict, then, was partly transferred to the political arena with the state taking an active part in income redistribution through taxation and social security legislation.

The period from 1950 to the end of the 1960s was one of stability in the labour market. Steady economic growth, particularly through the 1960s, meant that wage disputes could be settled without great difficulties. Unions accepted management's right to 'hire and fire' and to rationalise the production process as a precondition for economic growth. Those workers who were made redundant were absorbed within the expanding sectors of the economy. This transition process was facilitated by the government's active labour market policy. The main emphasis of union demands during this period was for improved social security. Major reforms in the old age pension system were introduced in 1958 along with other social benefits.

During this period, the LO's policy of 'solidaristic' wage policy was also developed. The policy had two ingredients. One was 'equal pay for equal jobs' regardless of industry or company. That meant that company profit levels were not the main target for negotiations. Subsequently, poor economic performers were forced out of business, while the profits in the most successful companies were not challenged by the unions. The other dimension of the 'solidaristic' wage policy was the narrowing of the gap between the lower-paid and the higher-paid workers. The gap was attacked by both a progressive taxation system and by pay contracts which gave extra wage increases to low income earners.

The harmonious pattern of industrial relations that emerged in Sweden during the 1950s and 1960s was facilitated by steady economic growth. The industrial development of Sweden was primarily based on natural resources: iron, timber, and hydro-electrical power. In addition, some important innovations facilitated the start of some major industries such as AGA (light houses), SKF (ball bearings), Kema Nobel (explosives), Ericsson (telephones), and Alfa-Laval (separators). Sweden became the home base for multinationals, rather than merely a host country. The number of people employed by Swedish multinationals outside of Sweden is at least five times as many as the number of Swedes working in foreign-owned multinationals. Industrial relations in Sweden has thus developed on a national basis without any strong influence from other countries.

Sweden is as heavily dependent on international trade as Britain. Around 20 per cent of Sweden's gross national product is exported. Approximately half of the production of the engineering industry, which is dominant in the Swedish economy, is exported. The figures are even higher for such other sectors as the iron, steel, and wood industries. The strong dependence on international competition has also been a factor that has inclined Swedish unions in the private sector to accept productivity improvements. Both technical as well as administrative rationalisation has traditionally been accepted, and often welcomed by Swedish unions.

The main participants in industrial relations

The unions Unlike the position in Australia, the establishment of a union in Sweden does not require any registration or acceptance by government authorities or courts. Any group of employees is free to form its own union and will be automatically covered by industrial relations legislation. The more advanced union rights are, however, reserved for unions holding contracts. The most significant of these rights is access to company information and the right to initiate bargaining on any major changes before they take place. There are relatively few newly-organised unions in Sweden, primarily because the existing unions serve their members effectively and they protect their area of interest from competing unions. There are few significant cases of new unions being established.

There are three main union confederations: the LO (The Swedish Trade Union Confederation) and TCO (Central Organisation of Salaried Employees) dominate the blue and white-collar sectors respectively. A third confederation, SACO SR consists of professional unions representing employees who generally have had an academic training.

The LO was formed in 1898. The 21 affiliated unions have a total membership of around two million. This means that the LO covers more than 90 per cent of blue-collar employees—a very high density by international standards. The majority of affiliated unions are organised on an industrial basis with one union in each company or site. The largest unions are the Swedish Municipal Workers' Union (620 000 members), and the Swedish Metal Workers' Union (450 000 members). The LO represents its affiliated unions in the areas of social and economic policy. It also bargains collectively on behalf of all members in the private sector. In the public sector, however, the two major unions bargain directly, without the direct involvement of the LO.

The TCO was formed in 1944 by the merger of two organisations, one covering private-sector employees and the other covering public-sector employees. The 20 unions affiliated to the TCO have about one million members. TCO does not take part in collective bargaining, but is active in training and represents its unions in negotiations with the government on general economic and social policies. The largest member unions are the Swedish Union of Clerical and Technical Employees in Industry (SIF), and Swedish Union of Local Government Officers (SKTF). The four largest member unions, which are also 'vertical' industry unions, comprise three-quarters of total TCO membership. The other member unions are organised on an occupational basis. For the purpose of collective bargaining, the TCO-affiliated unions are organised into three bargaining cartels: PTK for the private sector, KTK for the local and regional government sector, and TCO–S for the national government sector. PTK also includes unions outside TCO which are affiliated to SACO SR.

SACO SR is the smallest of the three confederations. The 26 member unions of SACO SR have around 225 000 members. The unions are organised primarily on the basis of common academic background. The largest unions are those which organise teachers in secondary education and graduate engineers. SACO SR has bargaining cartels for the state and local government sector. In the private sector most SACO SR unions are affiliated to PTK.

The links between LO and the Social Democratic Party (SAP) are stronger than those in most other countries. The LO's financial support to the party is of prime importance, particularly in election campaigns. A significant part of the local electoral work is also carried out by union activists. The strong links between the LO and SAP are also demonstrated through the controversial system of collective membership. Many local branches of unions are collectively affiliated to the Social Democratic Party. The close relationship is also reflected in the Party's leadership and in the government. During the long period of Social Democratic government, approximately half the cabinet was recruited from the union leadership.

Most employees in Sweden are members of unions (see Appendix, Table A.17), including more than 95 per cent of blue-collar employees and some 75 per cent of white-collar employees. This is an exceptionally high density of unionisation by international standards and is explained by several factors. One important reason is that the unemployment benefit system is organised by the unions. Most workers regard it as natural to belong to a union for protection against possible unemployment. Other benefits offered by the unions also help them in recruiting members. However, perhaps the most important reason is the degree of union influence achieved during the long period of Social Democratic government. The close relationship between the government and the LO has helped the unions to establish themselves as a significant force in this society. Thus, for most Swedes, it is almost automatic to join a union when they enter the labour market. In contrast to the LO's affiliation with the Social Democratic Party, TCO and SACO SR have no formal political affiliation.

Employer organisations   Employers in Sweden are as well organised as the employees. There are four employer confederations: one for the private sector and three for the public sector. The Swedish Employers' Confederation (SAF) organises employers in the private sector. SAF acts for 40 000 affiliated companies organised in 36 sectoral associations. The SAF-affiliated companies employ some 1.3

million people. For the national government authorities there is the National Agency for Government Employers (SAV) and for the local government sector there are two organisations. The municipalities collaborate through the Swedish Association of Local Authorities and the county councils through the Federation of County Councils. These organisations act on behalf of 278 municipalities and 23 county councils. The public sector has approximately 1.5 million employees of whom more than half a million are national government employees.

Characteristics of the social partners Swedish unions and employers' organisations (the 'social partners') are large and well-funded by international standards, in view of their high density of membership and their relatively high level of subscriptions. Union subscriptions are normally in the range of one to two per cent of gross earnings. In addition to subscriptions, the social partners also enjoy some government funding, particularly for training. The unions accumulate funds to meet the costs of industrial disputes. The size of funds vary, but the best-funded unions can compensate their members for two or three weeks on full pay. The employers' associations also accumulate such funds, but claim to be less well-funded than the unions in this respect.

Another feature of Swedish unions is the high degree of centralisation in decision-making. Decisions about strikes and accepting collective agreements are normally taken by central bodies such as the executive committees. Even in cases where centralisation in decision-making is not formally regulated in the statutes, members usually follow the recommendations of their leaders. Although Swedish unions are centralised, this does not mean that they are weak or inactive at the local level. On the contrary, in comparison with unions in other countries, the level of local activity is high. Wherever there are ten or more members, it is usual that a local branch of the union will be formed. Approximately 10 per cent of union members hold an elected position in their union organisation and 15–20 per cent of the membership have some form of union training each year. Participation in union meetings, however, is usually low. It is common to find only 5–10 per cent attendance at regular meetings. Attendance of 50 per cent or more is common only for annual meetings or when decisions are to be taken on collective agreements or strike action.

The role of the government The Swedish state is a large employer. Usually there is a Government Minister for Wages, who is ultimately responsible for the state's employment policies, which are implemented by at least two agencies. Pay negotiations are handled by the National Agency for Government Employers (SAV). The permanent head of the Ministry of Wages usually chairs the SAV board. However, the government is not directly involved in wage negotiations for state employees.

The private sector has been the traditional pacesetter in Swedish pay negotiations. It is also widely accepted that the production costs and productivity of the export sector is of prime importance in pay determination. However, there are cases where the public sector takes the lead and reaches agreements ahead of the private sector. In non-pay issues it has been common for SAV to break new ground, ahead of the private sector. One example is the area of industrial democracy (discussed later in this chapter).

The government exerts its main influence on industrial relations through its political role. Traditionally, industrial relations has been left to the employers and unions. However, during the 1970s, new laws were introduced which affected industrial relations. These deal with issues such as industrial democracy, the work environment, security of employment, and union rights. These laws generally limit the rights of employers and strengthen those of employees and their unions.

The main processes of industrial relations

Every union has its own statutes, including rules about how to enter into collective agreements. It is common practice that the right to conclude agreements is entrusted to a union's executive committee. A union may give its mandate to a central union council or a bargaining cartel to bargain on its behalf. Central agreements have been the general practice since the late 1950s. A central agreement is normally a recommendation that has to be endorsed by each participating union before it is binding.

Such central agreements include a peace obligation, whereby the employers agree to increase economic rewards, in exchange for a guaranteed period of labour peace. Once an agreement is ratified, the detailed applications are worked out through industry-wide and local agreements. Any disputes must be referred to the central level, rather than settled by industrial action.

Central agreements usually include several pay components. It is common to have a general pay increase (either in percentage or absolute terms) as well as specific increases directed towards special groups such as low-income earners, women, shift-workers, tradesmen, etc. Agreements may also include guarantee clauses which permit an adjustment of pay according to changes in the consumer price index or agreements reached by other unions. This means that the central agreements are supplemented by industry, plant or company level agreements before the individual wage increases are finally determined. Central agreements are generally used to cover a period of one to three years. During this period, there may also be local bargaining. Where piece-rate pay systems are in use, there may be a great deal of local bargaining. Separate increases in pay apart from the central agreement is called 'wage drift'. During the late 1970s and early 1980s, wage drift accounted for at least 50 per cent of negotiated wage increases. This arrangement for central agreements between LO and SAF broke down in 1983–84.

In addition to the pay agreement, there are other central agreements. They cover such subjects as working hours, the working environment, joint consultation and equal opportunities for women. Central agreements may also be supplemented by local agreements which specify how the rules are to be applied in particular situations. Collective agreements sometimes replace or supplement the law in regard to non-pay issues.

Local bargaining Although the structure of local bargaining differs markedly from one workplace to another, we will describe the process in a typical medium-sized private-sector company with 300–400 employees:

> The employees are organised in three local union 'clubs'. All manual workers belong to an LO-affiliated union. The first-line supervisors belong to SALF and the rest of the white-collar employees belong to SIF. SALF and SIF co-operate in the bargaining cartel PTK. The local unions are represented on the company board with one LO and one PTK representative, and their deputies also attend. There is a work environment committee with a majority of union representatives. The economic performance of the company is regularly discussed in the economic committee, where the LO and PTK representatives meet with management. There are regular meetings every month in which management reports about production and investment plans, among other things. The unions indicate if they wish to take an issue further, in which case separate negotiations about that issue are organised. The unions initiate negotiations about grievances, as requested by the members. Most of the contacts between management and unions are informal. Formal labour–management contacts are limited to four or five board meetings, three or four meetings of the work environment committee and four to six cases of collective bargaining, beside the pay negotiations.

Union–management relations in the public sector are not very different. However, some differences should be mentioned. There are usually more unions among salaried employees, as professional unions are more strongly represented in the public sector, where there tends to be larger concentrations of employees. Another difference is the greater degree of formalisation in union–management contacts. For example, there are often formal negotiations by mail. The employer fulfils the 'primary duty of negotiation before deciding on a change of the operation' by sending a written proposition in the form of 'draft minutes' which describe the proposition. The union representatives confirm that they accept by signing the minutes. A formal document confirming the agreement is completed, but no meeting is ever held. This greater formality in the public sector can, in part, be seen as a reflection of the more bureaucratic traditions in the public sector, but can also be explained by the large size of most public sector organisations.

Dispute settlement   The Swedish government plays only a limited role in settling industrial disputes. The Swedes differentiate interest disputes and rights disputes (see chapter 1). In the case of interest disputes, parties have the right to engage in industrial action after giving proper notice (usually one week). A small state agency provides mediation. However, the mediator has only an advisory role, and there is no formal obligation for the parties to accept the mediator's proposal or to with-hold industrial action if requested by the mediator. In most years there are 30 or 40 cases of mediation. Parliament may legislate to seek an end to an industrial dispute, but such action is very unusual.

In the case of rights disputes, there should be no industrial action. Disputes about the interpretation of laws or agreements must be referred to the National Labour Court or, in some cases, to regional lower courts. Verdicts of the lower courts may be appealed to the Labour Court, which is the final arbiter for all labour disputes. The Labour Court hears around 250 cases per year, including individual grievances.

The right to engage in industrial action includes lockouts as well as strikes. In addition, there are milder forms of industrial action such as bans on overtime and new recruitment, as well as 'black bans' on certain jobs. However, industrial action is only allowed when contracts have either expired or been properly terminated. Industrial action undertaken during a contract period is prohibited by law. Actions in support for other unions (secondary conflicts) are, however, always allowed. If a union engages in a strike, either at the local or central level, the employer may sue the union for damages. To avoid responsibility for an illegal strike, union officials must actively discourage their members from taking part. Only in this way can they avoid being fined or sued for damages. Individual union members who take part in unlawful industrial action can also be fined by the Labour Court. However, fines are limited to a maximum of SKr200.

Issues of current and future importance

During the 1960s when Sweden experienced a period of high economic growth and continuous industrial peace, the concept of the 'Swedish model' became well known to the world. The model can be briefly described as having relatively few well-organised and strong employers' associations and unions. The unions have positive attitudes to rationalisation and rely upon the government to pursue an active labour market policy in order to absorb technological and structural unemployment. The Swedish model is normally traced from 1938 when LO and SAF reached the first so-called Basic Agreement which regulates the procedures of collective bargaining and matters of co-operation. Under the Basic Agreement, decisions about what to produce and how to organise production are managerial prerogatives. Pay and conditions are subject to bargaining, with the right to take industrial action when the contracts are to be renewed.

The first Basic Agreement was reached after a long period of sustained conflict. Throughout the 1920s and 1930s Sweden had one of the highest levels of industrial disputes in Europe. Then, there were strong demands for legislation that would restrict the rights to strike, to hold lockouts, and engage in free collective bargaining.

The 'Swedish model' worked well until the early 1970s, and then came under increased strain. The unions' radical demands for economic and industrial democracy met with strong employer resistance. The political and economic scene changed when 44 years of Social Democratic government came to an end in 1976. At that time, Sweden was engulfed in economic crises. The employers felt it was both politically possible and economically necessary to fight back. The demands for 'economic democracy', in the form of Wage Earner Funds, were strongly opposed by the three non-socialist political parties and by the SAF, which played a highly visible role in the election campaign of 1982.

In 1980 there was the biggest ever industrial dispute in Sweden. A strike was met by an employer lockout of 80 per cent of the work force. The dispute was settled after two weeks on the basis of a mediated proposal. Some commentators claimed that this conflict symbolised the end of the 'Swedish model' and its spirit of co-operation. This dispute certainly marked the end of an era of relatively peaceful central collective bargaining. However, the Swedish model had never precluded the possibility of industrial disputes. The 1980 dispute can be attributed partly to the role of the government in the pay determination process. Throughout the 1970s, government had sought to influence this process in various ways. Public statements on what was acceptable were issued and adjustments to the taxation system were frequently used. Furthermore, the government's intervention in the 1980 pay round was ill-timed. The pay settlements in 1981 and 1983, however, were made without disputes. During 1983 and 1984 agreements were reached, in the main, without the assistance of mediators.

An important new element in Swedish industrial relations is the move towards decentralised bargaining. Following the failure of their 1980 lockout, the private employers realised that such tactics would no longer be effective in opposing union power, so they have aimed to break up the centralised bargaining arrangement and return to industry-wide bargaining. The first step was taken in 1983 when the influential Engineering Employers' Confederation managed to reach agreements with its counterpart unions, outside of the central round of negotiations. The 1983 experience has led LO to declare that centralised bargaining is no longer possible and industry-wide bargaining was introduced throughout the private sector in 1984.

Industrial democracy   Industrial democracy is a broad term which refers to the influence of employees on their working lives or, more precisely, 'what and how they produce'. The debate in Sweden has concentrated on two areas: first, work organisation and the individual's influence over his or her job; second, union influence over top management decisions via collective bargaining and through representation on company boards.

As in most countries, industrial democracy has been part of the debate on the radical Left in Sweden for many years. Towards the end of the 1960s, demands for increased employee influence were raised in the unions. The debate has been influenced by the effects of technological change in the workplace, the growing awareness of work environment issues, health hazards and the wave of radical political ideas that swept through Europe. Some union demands were heeded in the political arena and a number of reforms were introduced.

In a simplified form, the union strategy on industrial democracy can be described as follows. Mobilisation of interested members and union activists was achieved by focussing on problems of health and safety at work. This created a political climate in which new laws and regulations in support of industrial democracy could be introduced, which culminated in a revision of the industrial relations legislation, in an Act on Co-determination at Work (MBL). These laws were supplemented by financial support for training and research which, to a large extent, was channelled through the unions.

The MBL has become the legal framework for industrial democracy in Sweden. The MBL prescribes that management should be a joint effort by capital and labour—i.e., managers and union representatives. Both sides should have equal rights to information, which means that unions should be able to obtain all the relevant information available in the company. Further, the MBL stipulates that management has to consult the unions before any decision on major changes in the company is taken (such changes range from reorganisation to the introduction of new technology). Although management is not obliged to reach agreement, it has to allow time for unions to investigate the matters for decision and negotiate at either local or central level before it implements decisions. MBL also gives the unions priority rights in interpreting agreements in some cases. They also have rights of veto over the hiring of subcontractors if they suspect that their use might violate laws or agreements. By law, two local union-based directors (and two deputies) can belong to the board of most private companies which employ at least 25 people. This right is commonly used in large and medium-sized companies but less commonly used in small companies.

The introduction of MBL and other laws which constituted the legal base for reform of working life has been very controversial. The employers strongly opposed most of the laws and predicted that reforms would lead to inefficiency, higher costs and inhibit the decision-making process. The employers also argued that this legislation would be preferable if it promoted individual employee involvement, rather than union activity. On the union side, there were high expectations that the reforms would lead to an improved work environment, greater job satisfaction, better control for individuals over their daily life at work and a stronger say for the local unions in the development of the enterprises in which their members work.

The outcome of the reforms so far has proved both sides wrong. The effects have been limited. Problems that were expected by the employers have, by and large, not materialised. Management has continued to operate without undue difficulties and few negative effects have been recorded. From the unions' perspective, there is a general feeling of disappointment about the reforms. No significant change in the power situation on the job has taken place. While the reforms are seen as a definite step forward, the step is too short and much too slow for most union activists.

It is generally accepted that MBL has led to improved provision of information by management to the local unions. Consultation with the unions before deciding on changes has become standard procedure. It is also reported that the operation of the board has improved in some companies as the result of participation by union representatives at this level.

There are many possible explanations as to why the reforms did not have more lasting significance. One key factor is the economic situation. When the MBL was formulated, the thinking of policy-makers was still dominated by the economic expansion of the 1960s. The assumption was that the economy was still expanding and that management involved deciding about new investments, recruitment and similar issues. However, by the time the reforms were introduced in 1977, the situation had changed and Sweden was in the grip of world-wide economic crisis. Instead of discussions about new investments, the unions found themselves involved in negotiations about plant closures, retrenchments and shortening of the working week. The new 'influence' and 'co-determination' tended not to involve positive plans about the expansion of enterprises, but controversial decisions about how to survive in a recession. Within the public sector, negotiations were focussed on cuts in government spending and their effects. Thus, the relationships between management and unions became increasingly strained.

In spite of these strains, in 1982, SAF made a new basic agreement with LO and the Federation of Salaried Employees (PTK). This agreement was an attempt to implement MBL in the private sector, by setting up a joint Development Council, which would promote efficiency and participation in individual firms. Significantly, this agreement provided for considerable adaption depending on local circumstances, for instance, in relation to technological change.

Technological change   During much of the 1970s, industrial democracy was a focal point of debate. During the 1980s, however, the call for industrial democracy has gradually receded and been replaced by a debate on 'new technology', concerning the use of microprocessors in all shapes and forms. In common with their counterparts in other advanced industrial societies, Swedish employers support the introduction of new technology on the grounds of economic necessity. To stay competitive, they argue, there is no choice but to make use of new technology. Although such changes may have negative effects on the level of employment, in the short run, failure to keep abreast of technological developments will mean failure in the long run.

Swedish unions have traditionally sympathised with economic rationalisation and technological development. The success of several large Swedish multinational enterprises in the engineering industry, such as Volvo, Saab–Scania, and Ericsson, has had considerable influence on the thinking of the unions. One debate within the union movement has been whether computer technology represents 'traditional' technological change or should be regarded as a new and different phenomena which requires a different strategy. By and large, Swedish unions have favoured the former approach. Computer technology may have far-reaching consequences for the nature and level of employment. However, Swedish unions feel that their traditional policies and practices can be applied to most forms of new technology.

Union strategy on computer technology has been developed in three broad phases. The first phase can be described as 'fact finding'. This involves obtaining basic information about the technology. What systems are being marketed, sold and installed? What are the consequences of these installations? In the first phase, unions have been hesitant observers rather than adopting a highly active role.

The second phase of union strategy has involved the negotiation of 'technology agreements'. The emphasis of this phase has been on putting demands to employers. It is argued that unions should not get involved in detailed negotiations about what equipment to buy and how to install it. The unions' role should be to make demands on the management in terms of desired outcomes. Typical union aims are to regulate the number of jobs or to obtain agreements on no lay-offs. They may also seek to regulate noise levels, ergonomic standards and exposure times in front of VDUs. Computer technology has been regarded as a 'black box'. Unions should not get involved in the content of the box but get guarantees of the uses, through collective agreements. They should say 'no' to the installation of computer technology unless specific criteria are met.

The 'technology agreement' strategy has resulted in several 'technology policies' at both central and local levels and on some collective agreements. However, the success of these agreements has been limited. In many cases, management has expressed sympathy for the union demands, but found no means of meeting them. Economic realities have forced unions to accept new technology even when their criteria has not been met. This experience has led the unions to the third phase: the trade union alternative to computer technology.

The third phase has involved unions becoming active in research and development. This strategy is derived from the insight that unions cannot exert sufficient influence on those who are designing and marketing computer technology by putting pressure on the buyer (that is, the management). To ensure that new technology is in compliance with their demands, unions must deal directly with the producers (of hardware and software) and seek to influence the product development process. This is a very recent stage of development and so far, there is only limited experience. By 1984 there were four projects in which unions were involved in research and development. The most advanced attempt was one where the Nordic printing unions collaborated with researchers to develop software systems for newspaper production.

Economic democracy—wage earner funds Economic democracy has been a dominant issue in the Swedish political debate since the 1971 decision of the LO Congress to investigate this matter. The concept has included two ideas: profit sharing and collective ownership. The arguments in favour of these developments have been both economic- and power-related. Employees should get a share of the profits, but part of the wealth which is generated should be reinvested in Swedish industry through a system of collective ownership. The LO saw eco- nomic democracy as a necessary complement to the 'solidaristic' wage policy, whereby wages are not related to the profits in an individual company, but the economy as a whole. The argument in favour of expanding workers' power through wage earner funds was put for- ward in view of the limitations of industrial democracy. Employees would exert influence, it was argued, if they were part-owners of their firms, through the funds.

The first radical proposal for wage earner funds, the Meidner Plan, was submitted in 1975. It aimed, in the long run, to make the unions the majority shareholders in all major industries in Sweden. It was based on a compulsory issuing of new shares based on company pro- fits. These shares would then be transferred to funds controlled by the unions.

The plan met unprecedented opposition from the employers. The Social Democratic Party was largely positive in its support, but had some reservations. The Liberal–Centre political parties acknowl- edged the need for such reforms, but favoured individual rather than collective arrangements.

The wage earner fund proposal was discussed at length by the LO and the Social Democratic Party but they had difficulties finding a proposition that was radical enough to satisfy the LO, yet practical enough to be politically feasible. The whole issue became a political burden to the Social Democratic Party and it lost the elections in 1976 and 1979 partly on this issue. However, it managed to win the election in 1982, despite controversy surrounding the wage earner fund issue. Following the long and intensive counter campaign by the employers, the three non-socialist parties did not promote their own separate propositions. Instead, they all focussed their campaign on criticising the LO–Social Democratic Party proposals. The employer campaign totally polarised the debate so that those who were not openly against the idea were accused of supporting it. The labour movement made several different proposals but the coalition of employers and the non-socialist parties used the same argument against all.

Although the issue had become a political burden, the Social Democratic Party was elected in 1982 on a policy which committed it to implement a form of wage earners' funds. In October 1983, the opponents of these funds mounted an unprecedented protest demonstration in Stockholm, when more than 100 000 members of the business community marched on Parliament. Nevertheless, in November 1983, the new government introduced a diluted version of the original proposal, which includes the establishment of five regional funds which will receive money in two ways: firstly, through an increase of 0.5 per cent of the pension fee, payable by employers; secondly, through a profit-sharing system whereby 20 per cent of profits exceeding a set proportion ('excess profits') are paid into the funds. The five regional funds can use the money for investments in shares. They are required to give a dividend of 3 per cent, plus any increase in the consumer price index, which is to be paid into the national pension funds. Each of the regional funds will be administered by a separate board appointed by the government after consultation with the unions. The parliamentary decision on the funds includes a provision that contributions will be paid up to 1990 but not thereafter. The LO wants the system to be extended into the 1990s. However, the opposition parties have declared that, should they get elected to government, they will terminate the funds and stop the whole system.

The five regional funds began operation during the latter half of 1984. Following a general boycott by the employers, no established business leaders accepted nomination to the fund boards. In the absence of such representatives, the boards were comprised of politicians, leaders of public sector organisations, union representatives and academics. The range of interests represented on the fund boards are not as wide as intended by the supporters of the fund concept, but each region has been able to assemble a board.

The recruitment of staff for the funds has been widely debated. As a consequence of the employers' boycott, it was expected that no top professional people from banking or stockbroking would be prepared to work for the funds. There have also been propositions from banks offering to undertake all administrative work and provide expert advice for the funds. Such an arrangement would make it possible for the funds to continue without any secretariat. However, four of the five funds have decided to hire their own experts. In spite of all the difficulties, the funds have managed to recruit executive directors with proven competence in the field. The West Fund has decided not to hire an executive director but to rely on the advice of bankers in their investment decisions.

The first investments made by the funds were shares in established Swedish industries listed on the Stockholm Stock Exchange. The engineering industry has been the main area of interest. It is also clear that the funds are attempting to buy into industries in their own region. There are some examples of companies issuing shares direct to a fund, but the majority of placements have been on the open market.

The initial impression is that the five wage earners' funds will operate in the same manner as insurance companies and pension funds. So far, there are few signs of them precipitating a 'fundamental change of the economic system in the direction of state socialism' as had been predicted by earlier opponents of the funds.

Conclusions

Industrial relations in Sweden has passed through three stages. The first stage was from the beginning of the union movement in the 1890s up to the mid-1930s. During this period the labour movement was established. The relationship between capital and labour was antagonistic and there was a high level of industrial disputes. The government was either passive or supported the owners of capital.

The second stage lasted for most of the 44 years of Social Democratic government from the mid-1930s to the early 1970s. The 'Swedish model' was established during this period with a 'solidaristic' wage policy, an active manpower policy and labour–management co-operation. An economic policy reliant on economic growth subsumed many of the pay-related problems for the unions and paved the way for a pattern of labour–management relations with few industrial disputes.

A third stage began in the early 1970s. More radical union ambitions, the election of a non-socialist government in 1976, severe economic problems and a militant strategy on the employer side represented a significant change. The 1980 dispute symbolised these new developments. Wage earner funds were introduced, but were not really seen as a victory by the unions. The wage earner fund system became a political burden for the labour movement and does not yet constitute a basic change in Sweden's economic system. The employers tried to exploit the situation as far as they could. Their prime objective was to de-regulate Sweden and allow for more market influence. Fragmentation of the bargaining structures, more flexible working time arrangements, profit sharing, and payment by results systems became examples of initiatives advanced by their associations.

Labour–management relations include a network of formal and informal systems which do not generally change rapidly. It is therefore too early to predict future directions of industrial relations in Sweden. The union movement is still strong. Membership has not declined as in many other countries, while both public acceptance and support remains high. Nonetheless, there is also a new radical Right in Sweden, which has to some extent been inspired by the policies of the new Right in the early 1980s in the USA and Britain. Perhaps such moves in Sweden represent something of a reaction to what some employers saw as an unacceptably high degree of union power throughout Swedish society.

If economic crises continue and if non-socialist governments become more prevalent in Sweden through the 1980s and 1990s, it is likely that labour–management relations in Sweden will move in a 'continental European' direction. This would be likely to lead to fragmented bargaining structures, greater government intervention, and a consequent weakening of the unions. The other possibility is that the 'Swedish model' will survive and develop. This depends on a fairly consistent governing role for the Social Democratic Party and economic policies which continue to tip the labour market balance in favour of the workers and unions.

Abbreviations

KTK	Local and regional government sector bargaining cartel of TCO
LO	Swedish Trade Union Confederation
MBL	Act on Co-determination at Work
OECD	Organisation for Economic Co-operation and Development
PTK	Federation of Salaried Employees; private sector bargaining cartel of TCO
SACO SR	Confederation of professional unions representing employees with academic training
SAF	Swedish Employers' Confederation
SALF	Swedish Supervisors' Union
SAP	Social Democratic Party
SAV	National Agency for Government Employers
SIF	Swedish Union of Clerical and Technical Employees in Industry
SKTF	Swedish Union of Local Government Officers
TCO	Central Organisation of Salaried Employees
TCO–S	National government sector bargaining cartel of TCO

A chronology of Swedish industrial relations

1898	LO founded.
1902	SAF founded.
1906	December Compromise Agreement.
1909	General strike of 1909 followed by a severe decline in union membership.
1928	Establishment of Labour Court, and a Collective Bargaining Act.

1936	Law regulates unfair dismissal for union activity, and the social partners' rights to negotiate.
1938	SAF–LO Basic Agreement at Saltsjöbaden, which set a co-operative 'spirit' for labour relations.
1944	TCO founded.
1946	SAF–LO–TCO Works Councils Agreement, revised in 1966 and ended in 1977 by MBL.
1956	Beginning of LO–SAF central bargaining.
1971	LO and TCO adopt policies for industrial democracy.
1972	LO–SAF Rationalisation Agreement on productivity, job satisfaction, and job security.
1973	Initial law on board representation for local unions.
1974	Law makes it difficult to dismiss employees, and for companies to hire workers on probation without union approval. Law gives local union representatives time off for union work with pay.
1975	The wage earner funds debate begins. Law to give employees educational leave.
1976	Non-socialist coalition government replaces the Social Democratic Party.
1977	Co-determination at Work Act (MBL) implemented.
1980	Lockout–strike throughout most of the private sector
1981	LO and Social Democratic Party congresses approve principles for wage earner funds.
1982	Social Democratic Party re-elected. SAF–LO–PTK Agreement on Efficiency and Participation.
1983	Wage earner funds implemented. Industry-wide bargaining replaces the 1956–83 centralised pattern.

References

Abrahamsson, B. (1980) *The Rights of Labor* New York: Sage

Albrecht, S. and Deutsch, S. (1982) 'The Challenge of Economic Democracy: The Case of Sweden' Conference paper, International Sociological Association

Asplund, C. (1981) *Redesigning Jobs: Western European Experiences* Brussels: European Trade Union Institute

Evans, J. (1982) *Negotiating Technological Change* Brussels: European Trade Union Institute

Forsebäck, L. (1980) *Industrial Relations and Employment in Sweden* Stockholm: Swedish Institute

Fry, J.A. (1979) *Industrial Democracy and Labour Market Policy in Sweden* Oxford: Pergamon

Gardell, B. and Svensson, L. (1980) *Co-determination and Autonomy: A Trade Union Strategy for Democracy at the Work Place* Ann Arbor: Institute for Social Research

Gunzburg, D. (1978) *Industrial Democracy Approaches in Sweden: An Australian View* Melbourne: Productivity Promotion Council of Australia

Hammarström, O. (1978a) *Negotiations for Co-determination* Stockholm: Swedish Working Life Centre

—— (1978b) *On National Strategies for Industrial Democracy: Some Reflections on Ten Years of Industrial Democracy Development in Sweden* Stockhom: Swedish Working Life Centre

—— (1982) 'Industrial Relations in Europe 1970–82' *International Issues in Industrial Relations* Sydney: Industrial Relations Society of Australia

Hammarström, O. and Hammarström, R. (1977) *Industrial Democracy in Sweden*, Parts 1 and 2, Adelaide: Unit for Industrial Democracy

Hammarström, O. and Piolet, F. (1980) *Evaluation of the Main Trends in Work Organisation within the Context of Economic, Social and Technological Changes* Brussels: European Communities

Himmelstrand, U. (1981) *Beyond Welfare Capitalism* London: Heinemann

Holzhausen, J. (1981) *Employee Representation on Company Boards* The Hague: ILO Industrial Relations Seminar

Industrial Relations Services (1983) 'Sweden: Employee Investment Funds' *European Industrial Relations Review* 119, (Dec.), pp. 22–3

Korpi, W. (1978) *The Working Class in Welfare Capitalism: Work, Unions and Politics in Sweden* London: Routledge & Kegan Paul

Meidner, R. (1983) *Strategy for Full Employment* Stockholm: PSI Symposium

Neel, A.C. et al. (1981) *Law and the Weaker Party: An Anglo-Swedish Comparative Study, vol. 1, The Swedish Experience* Oxfordshire: Professional Books

Sandberg, T., Molin, R. and Rudenstam, N.G. (1978) *The Swedish Industrial Relations System in an Economic, Social and Political Setting* Research Report 1978/1 Uppsala: Department of Business Administration

Schmidt, F. (1976) *The Democratisation of Working Life in Sweden: A Survey of Agreements, Legislation, Experimental Activities, Research and Development* Stockholm: TCO

—— (1977) *Law and Industrial Relations in Sweden* Stockholm: Almqvist & Wiksell International

IV
Japan

10 | Japanese industrial relations

YASUO KUWAHARA

This chapter starts by putting Japanese industrial relations into context, sketches some historical background, then discusses the roles
of unions and employers and the Japanese approach to collective
bargaining. The current issues discussed include: job security, small
and medium-sized enterprises and technological change.

In terms of GDP (US $1308 billion) and population (120 million
people), Japan has the second-largest economy of the nine countries
discussed in this book (the USA is the largest). Japan's rate of
economic growth is higher than any of the other countries, with an
annual average increase in GDP of 4.1 per cent between 1978 and
1983 (the crude average for the nine countries was 1.7 per cent).
In this period, Japanese exports of goods grew more rapidly than in
any other country (6.3 per cent per annum). It is a dominant force in
world trade in such sectors as cars, motor cycles, electronics and office
machinery.

Japan's civilian employees include 49 per cent of its population. It
still has relatively more people employed in agriculture (8.9 per cent)
than any of the other countries in this book, except Italy (12 per cent).
Japanese industry employs 35 per cent of civilian employees, and 56
per cent work in the services sector.

Japan is in many respects the most distinctive of the nine countries.
On average, the Japanese enjoy the longest life span, work for more
hours and lose relatively less working days in industrial disputes.

Japan's GDP per capita was US $10 457 in 1984, which was for the
first time just above the average of the nine countries (see Table A.6).
Japan's average annual increase in consumer prices during the 1979–

84 period (3.9 per cent) was less than in any of the other eight countries. Japanese government revenue (30 per cent of GDP) is less than in any of the other eight countries. (To some extent this reflects Japan's relatively low expenditure on national defence.) The average Japanese take-home pay is 90 per cent of gross earnings, which is a higher percentage than in any of the other countries (see chapter 2, note 2).

Since the end of the Second World War, with the exception of a short period just after the war, Japanese politics appear to have been dominated by what is now called the Liberal Democratic Party (LDP), which is a conservative party. The opposition parties have exerted influence from time to time. However, none of them has obtained enough power to hold office in national politics. Depending on their dominant ideology, unions are associated with various opposition parties such as the Japan Socialist Party (JSP), Democratic Socialist Party (DSP), and the Japan Communist Party (JCP). Successful candidates of the opposition parties may be either recommended and supported by a union, or those who have been associated with unions in the past. (The alignment of the main union confederations is discussed later.)

The Japanese model of industrial relations

The growing international interest in Japanese management and industrial relations has been perplexing to the Japanese themselves, since throughout the twentieth century Japan has tried to follow models derived from the West, for example, Britain, the USA and Germany, in successive periods. Before the 1973 oil crisis, they tended to see such countries as so much more advanced, that various management techniques and technologies were imported from them.

In the 1970s, Japan unexpectedly entered the leading group of major industrial countries. Attention to the Japanese industrial relations 'model' has emerged in this setting and is thus closely related to its economic performance, compared with other industrialised countries. Japan has been the envy of some countries due to its relatively healthy economy, as shown by the indicators mentioned earlier. To what extent does its superior macro-economic performance determine the system of industrial relations or vice versa? Many people in other countries, both developed and developing, want to 'import' the Japanese model, but which of its aspects are transferable to other countries?

To begin to answer such questions, we need some historical background. Japan's feudal era ended with the Meiji Restoration of 1868 (see Chronology at end of chapter). Hitherto, Japan had little contact with Western countries. Industrialisation began in the following decade—a hundred years later than in Britain. Japan's early factories in major industries were begun by the state, but in 1880 it sold most of them to a few selected families. These were the origin of what later became the powerful *zaibatsu* groups of holding companies, which were based on commercial banks.

Although some unions began in this period, the familial basis of industrialisation continued well into the twentieth century. Many factories had their own dormitories, especially in textiles. The *oyakata* (master workmen) were subcontractors, like the early British foremen. By contrast, however, the *oyakata* relationship was more akin to father and child, rather than the British masters and men relation (see chapter 2). This was an important element in the growth of Japanese corporate paternalism which still influences contemporary management–labour relations.

Following the First World War, there was an acute shortage of skilled workers. Firms wanted to recruit directly. Hence many large firms intervened in the *oyakata's* prerogative to recruit. Consequently, many *oyakata* helped to form unions, to defend their own positions.

The employers responded by offering the *oyakata* guarantees of managerial status and *shushin koyo* (permanent or lifetime employment). From the incorporation of the *oyakata*, developed another feature of the modern Japanese model: *nenko joretsu* (the seniority pay and promotion system). These innovations were an attempt to reduce the high rates of labour turnover. By linking pay to length of service (e.g. rather than skill), employees have a strong incentive to stay with one employer.[1]

As the paternalist tradition developed in the 1920s and 1930s, the unions did not exert much sustained influence. Unions were dissolved between 1938 and 1943 and the various employers' associations were absorbed into the mobilisation for war production.

After Japan's unconditional surrender in 1945, the General Headquarters of the Allied Powers (GHQ) tried to reshape the organisation of work and industrial relations, as part of the post-war reconstruction. Thus, the main elements of the present model were established after the war, under American influence.

The unions The Japanese labour movement developed rapidly, aided by the democratisation programme of GHQ. Although much of Japan's industrial base was destroyed during the war, only four months after its end, union membership had reached pre-war levels and by 1949 there were 6.6 million union members—a density of 56 per cent. There were, none the less, some setbacks for the unions.

For instance, their plans to hold a general strike in 1947 were countermanded by GHQ. However, the unions continued to grow and recorded a peak membership of 12.6 million members in 1965, a density of 36 per cent.

After this peak, both membership and density stagnated. Membership density fell to a low of 29 per cent in 1984. What was responsible for this decline? One of the main causes has been the change in industrial structure, especially the shift towards the service sector. During the decade after the 1973 oil crisis, there was substantial rationalisation in the manufacturing sector, which is highly unionised. Although there has been an increase in the number of employees in the service sector, the average sizes of firms in terms of employment tend to be relatively small, which makes it difficult and costly for unions to organise (Figure 10.1).

Although the level of unemployment in Japan is less than that of

Figure 10.1 Trend of union members by industry

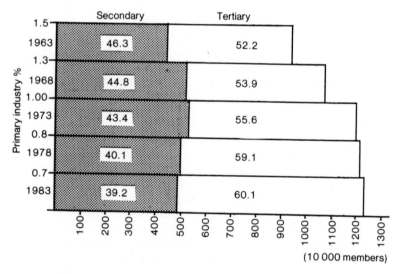

Notes: a Industries are classified as follows:
        Primary—agriculture, fishery, and mining
        Secondary—construction, and manufacturing
        Tertiary—wholesale, retail, finance and insurance, real estate, transportation and communications, utilities, services, and civil service
      b Unclassifiable industries are excluded; see Table A.4 for the OECD classification.
Source: Shimizu (1984).

most Western countries (e.g. 2.9 per cent in early 1986), unemployment has more than doubled since 1973 (see Appendix Table A.5). Against this background, many companies have adopted a tougher stance towards unions, claiming public support for such policies. Employees have become more concerned about the competitive position of the companies for which they work. This reflects their expectation of 'lifetime employment' and seniority-based wages; such practices were apparently consolidated after the Second World War. Permanent manual and non-manual staff are employed not for specific categories of professions or occupations, but as company employees. Companies prefer to employ new school leavers rather than experienced workers who have been trained in other firms. Their induction programme is designed to enable them to adapt to new workplaces. These employees are usually expected to stay in the same companies until retirement age. An increasing number of companies are raising the retirement age from 55 to 60 years old, in accordance with the lengthening average life span of the Japanese.[2] Many workers remain in work, even after reaching their mandatory retirement. They find other jobs in subsidiaries or smaller enterprises or start small business by investing their retirement allowances and other financial resources.

Young recruits start at lower pay, based on their educational qualifications. Their pay increases in proportion to the length of their service in the firm. Promotion is largely based on length of service, which is supposed to correlate with the employee's level of skill developed within the organisation. Therefore, it is disadvantageous for workers to change employers and for employers to lay off employees who have accumulated specific skills, required in that particular company. This type of worker is typically found in the so-called primary labour market (e.g. permanent employees working for big organisations).

Most unions in Japan are not organised by occupation or by job, but by enterprise or establishment. An enterprise union consists solely of regular employees of a single firm, regardless of their occupational status. These employees are expected to stay in the same company until their mandatory retirement age, unless they are made redundant or leave voluntarily. This core of genuinely regular employees constitutes only about a third of all employees.[3] Many of the other employees work in smaller businesses or on a temporary or part-time basis and are often excluded from unions. Therefore, union density among female workers (who constitute the majority of part-time workers) was 23 per cent, compared with 33 per cent for male workers (Shimizu, 1984).

Many employees who have been promoted to supervisory and/or managerial positions were previously union members and some were even union leaders. These enterprise unions include non-manual staff and manual workers of the same enterprise (i.e. blue-collar and white-collar workers). Consequently, a worker leaving the company would lose union membership automatically. It is generally believed that the advantage of enterprise unionism is that it reflects the situation in each enterprise at the level of the firm, rather than any broader craft or political issue.

On the other hand, there are disadvantages from a union's point of view: as newly employed workers automatically acquire union membership, union dues being 'checked off' from their pay automatically, their 'union consciousness' is less than their 'enterprise consciousness'.

In spite of its name, an enterprise union does not only function for the benefit of the enterprise. It has legal protection against an employer's interference into its affairs as well as against other unfair labour practices. Unionism is strongest in the primary labour market. In 1983 about 85 per cent of enterprise union members worked in firms which employed more than 100 employees (Figure 10.2).

Many such enterprise unions grew out of the factory- and company-based war-time production committees. Since most Japanese unions

Figure 10.2 Trend of union members by the size of enterprise

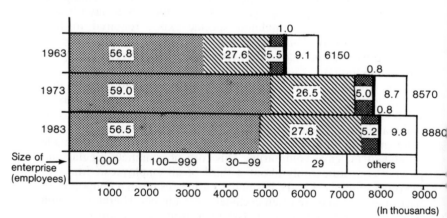

Note: Others denotes unions not based on enterprises.
Source: Shimizu (1984)

are organised separately for individual enterprises or plants, there are many unions: more than 74 000 at one recent count (Rodosho, 1983). Although there are also other types of union organisations such as industrial, craft and general unions, these are exceptions. *Kaiin*, the Seamen's Union is a rare example of an industrial union.

Most of the enterprise unions within the same industry join an industrial federation of unions. There are more than 100 such federations. The major functions of the industrial federations are: co-ordinating the activities of the member enterprise unions with the aim of increasing wages and improving working conditions; dealing with problems common to a whole industry; guiding and assisting member unions in specific disputes, etc.; and political lobbying in the interest of workers. These industrial federations themselves belong to confederations (national centres) such as Sohyo and Domei, or units within the multi-industrial joint councils such as Kinzoku Rokyo (Japan Council of Metalworkers' Unions: IMF–JC) or Zenkoun (all Japan Council of Traffic and Transport Workers' Unions), as illustrated in Table 10.1.

What is the political alignment of the confederations? Sohyo-affiliated unions support many political candidates. Domei, and the other confederations support rather fewer. The public-sector unions affiliated with Sohyo exert a major influence in general elections. Although the number fluctuates in each election, JSP has the largest number of successful union-supported candidates, with a success rate of 50–60 per cent. Other parties have lower success rates.

The JCP usually has no successful union candidates, because of the single-party-support system, in which Sohyo only supports the JSP and Domei only supports the DSP. Thus, JCP candidates are unable to obtain formal support from any major nation-wide unions. Consequently, JCP has endeavoured for many years to break up the single-party-support system, especially the Sohyo–JSP relationship, under the slogan of 'freedom in party support'. In recent years, however, this has aroused resistance from Sohyo's main faction and thereby intensified antagonism between Sohyo and the JCP.

After the two oil crises, unions waged what they called a 'policy-oriented struggle' with the aim of ensuring stable employment and maintaining their members' standard of living. In the course of such labour activities, another movement 'to unite the labour front under the initiative of private sector unions' emerged in December 1982: Zenminrokyo, the Japanese Private Sector Union Council. It was formed by the labour federations in the private sector and reflected their enthusiasm for further consolidation of their unity and strength.

Table 10.1 Membership distribution among major labour organisations

	Total		Private sector		Public sector	
	'Tan-sans' (federations)	Membership (1,000 persons)	'Tan-sans' (single industry federations)	Membership (1,000 persons)	'Tan-sans' (single industry federations)	Membership (1,000 persons)
Sohyo (General Council of Trade Unions of Japan)	49	4,508	30	1,459	19	3,050
Domei (Japanese Confederation of Labour)	32	2,193	24	2,036	8	157
Churitsuroren (Federation of Independent Unions of Japan)	10	1,480	10	1,480	—	0.05
Shinsanbetsu (National Federation of Industrial Organisations)	5	64	4	61	1	3
Others Independent unions which are not affiliated with the above four national centres	—	4,839	—	4,607	—	232
Zenminrokyo (Japanese Private Sector Trade Union Council)	54	4,843	54	4,843	—	—

Source: Rodosho (1984).

218

Table 10.2 **The number of employees, union members and union density since 1945**

Year	Employees (10 000)	Union members (10 000)	Estimated density[a] (%)	Growth rate over the previous year[b] (%)
1945	—	380 677	—	—
46	931	3 679 971	39.5	966.7
47	1 256	5 692 179	45.3	54.7
48	1 259	6 677 427	53.0	17.3
49	1 193	6 655 483	55.8	−0.3
50	1 251	5 773 908	46.2	−13.2
51	1 336	5 686 774	42.6	−1.5
52	1 421	5 719 560	40.3	0.6
53	1 631	5 927 079	36.3	—[c]
54	1 712	6 075 746	35.5	2.5
55	1 764	6 285 878	35.6	3.5
56	1 931	6 463 118	33.5	2.8
57	2 014	6 762 601	33.6	4.6
58	2 134	6 984 032	32.7	3.3
59	2 248	7 211 401	32.1	3.3
60	2 382	7 661 568	32.2	6.2
61	2 422	8 359 876	34.5	9.1
62	2 582	8 971 156	34.7	7.3
63	2 693	9 357 179	34.7	4.3
64	2 803	9 799 653	35.0	4.7
65	2 914	10 146 872	34.8	3.5
66	3 042	10 403 742	34.2	2.5
67	3 100	10 566 436	34.1	1.6
68	3 159	10 862 864	34.4	2.8
69	3 196	11 248 601	35.2	3.6
70	3 277	11 604 770	35.4	3.2
71	3 388	11 795 570	34.8	1.7
72	3 469	11 888 592	34.3	0.8
73	3 659	12 097 848	33.1	1.8
74	3 676	12 461 799	33.9	3.0
75	3 662	12 590 400	34.4	1.0
76	3 710	12 508 731	33.7	−0.6
77	3 746	12 437 012	33.2	−0.6
78	3 796	12 382 829	32.6	−0.4
79	3 899	12 308 756	31.6	−0.6
80	4 012	12 369 262	30.8	0.5
81	4 055	12 471 270	30.8	0.8
82	4 102	12 525 529	30.5	0.4
83	4 209	12 519 530	29.7	−0.1
84	4 282	12 463 755	29.1	−0.4
85	4 301	12 417 527	28.9	−0.4

Notes: a Estimated density denotes the ratio of the number of union members divided by the number of employees. See Appendix Table A.17 for a slightly different set of such data.

b '−' indicates decrease.

c There is a discontinuity of definition in 1953, which makes it difficult to make a genuine comparison.

Source: Rodosho (1984).

Zenminrokyo is seen as merely the first step in a movement towards greater union unity, and its leaders are determined to continue efforts to develop the organisation into a national centre, eventually integrating public sector unions. Public sector unions used to have more power, compared with those in the private sector. However, in general, union membership has decreased since 1978 and the centre of gravity has shifted towards unions in the private sector (Table 10.2).

Although the national confederations have important roles, the enterprise unions are much more powerful. Moreover the latter are autonomous in running their organisations and in promoting their members' interests. Furthermore, they are financially independent and self-supporting. Most union activities occur at the enterprise level, rather than at federation level.

Since most workers in the unionised sector are employees and union members based in the same firm, enterprise unions tend to consider the competitive position of the company in product or service markets. As the company's success greatly influences members' working conditions and employment opportunities, enterprise unions generally have a co-operative attitude toward management. Employees generally identify with their employer in making decisions which would, for instance, enhance the employer's competitiveness. Thus, a key aspect of the work environment in the Japanese company is this interdependence and the belief that the company is a 'community of fate' (i.e. 'everyone is in the same big family').

In addition, the relatively modest wage differential between managers, white-collar and blue-collar workers tends to reinforce the worker's sense of identification with the firm. This situation is quite different from that in some Western countries where there is a more rigid class structure.

Beside wages or salaries, most Japanese workers receive seasonal bonus payments worth about 4.8 to 5.2 months' salary a year. (In Japan most blue-collar workers are paid on a monthly salary basis, as are white-collar workers.) This practice originated from the employers' consideration of the extra expenditure required for the Bhuddhist 'bon festival', a kind of ancestor worship ritual observed in summer, and of the year-end and New Year celebration. The amount of bonus fluctuates according to the performance of the company or industry, and according to the merit of employees. However, it does not fluctuate much, and workers assume that the bonuses are a necessary part of their annual income.

The employers During the period immediately after the Second World War, there were many violent labour disputes in Japan, as a result of the economic disorder and the shortage of food and daily necessities. At that time, neither the employers nor workers had much industrial relations experience. To cope with this labour offensive and to establish industrial peace and order, employers organised regional and industrial associations. However, partly because of the so-called 'democratisation' policy of GHQ, employers were often obliged to yield to union pressures, thus facing an erosion of their managerial prerogatives.

Although most bargaining takes place at the enterprise level, some industries engage in collective bargaining at industry level, for example, in private railways, bus services and textiles. Apart from these few examples, none of the other national or regional employers' organisations are engaged in collective bargaining.

Nikkeiren, the Japan Federation of Employers' Associations, was founded in 1948. It is the most important employers' organisation from an industrial relations point of view and it has many functions. It co-ordinates and publicises employers' opinions on labour problems, selects employer representatives to the various government commissions, councils and ILO delegations, and provides its member organisations with advice and services on labour conditions and employment practices. Every year at the time of the *shunto* (the Spring Labour Offensive), Nikkeiren releases guidelines to be followed in dealing with demands from the various unions during collective bargaining. Thus although most of them do not have a direct role in bargaining, the employers' associations seem to have an important role behind the scenes (Levine, 1984:318 ff.). The role of employers' associations in industrial relations is, however, decreasing. The main determinant of the outcome of collective bargaining is the individual company's business performance.

Collective bargaining

Pay agreements may often be concluded separately from agreements on other matters. Most unions conduct pay negotiations during the Spring Labour Offensive in April and May each year, while negotiations on comprehensive labour agreements may be conducted in other periods. However, an increasing number of unions also make other claims during the Spring Labour Offensive, for example, for increases in overtime rates, revisions of allowances, shorter working hours, raising the retirement age and expansion of private pensions.

The structure of enterprise unions usually corresponds to the organisation of the enterprise (i.e. plant, department or divisional groupings). Grievances are often settled informally. Formal procedures are rarely used. Management often attempts to subdue tensions and conflict and to reinforce a feeling of community, following the pre-war tradition of paternalism. This does not mean that Japanese industrial relations are free from disputes. There were many large-scale and long disputes in the 1940s and 1950s. Some strikes were led by radical leaders. Most of these disputes left deep wounds on industrial relationships which would not easily heal.

Such disputes taught the unions and employers some important lessons. Although there was a high number of stoppages in 1974, there was a substantial reduction after that. Disputes are usually settled directly between the parties concerned, but sometimes a third party conciliates. Conciliation machinery for the private sector is provided by the Central and Local Labour Relations Commissions. Special commissions act for public sector employees and for seamen. Nearly all the disputes brought before these commissions are settled either by conciliation or mediation. Few disputes go as far as arbitration.

Contemporary Japanese industrial relations are relatively stable and relations between the parties can be characterised as co-operative. Some see this in a positive light. Others have a more negative view, arguing that enterprise unions are too dependent on employers, and that the relationship is one of collaboration and incorporation.

Unions represent sectional interests. Enterprise unions are no exception. Since most workers are expected to work for many years as employees in the same enterprise, they tend to place much emphasis on the improvement of their working conditions, but do not pay so much attention to the interests of the temporary workers at the same establishment.

Why has the relationship between unions and employers changed so fundamentally between the 1950s and the 1980s? There has been increased competition among firms, improved standards of living, a shift toward a service-oriented economy and also public opinion is more conservative in the 1980s than it was in the 1950s. But are co-operative industrial relations desirable under all circumstances? These relations may come under severe stress when labour and management have to face a serious depression, along with inevitable redundancy.

Issues of current and future importance

The social and economic environment in Japan is still changing. There is an ageing population, an increase in the proportion of highly educated workers, increased participation by women in the labour market, and a change towards an 'information society'.

Job security and employment practices   In the midst of the post-1973 recession, many countries experienced increases in unemployment. Looking at the trend of unemployment in Japan, it was 1.1 per cent in 1964 and remained less than 1.5 per cent until 1974. Since then, the unemployment rate has increased to 2.0 per cent in 1980 and 2.7 per cent in 1983, the highest rate since these statistics were first collected in the early 1950s. Unemployment has increased particularly among those less than 24 years old and those over 40 years old.

Total employment has continued to increase, despite the increase in unemployment. In the 1975–80 period, overall employment rose by 3 million, from 34.7 million to 37.7 million employees. The industries which created most jobs were retailing, business services, construction, medical services, and wholesaling. The new high-technology industries also expanded. Heavy manufacturing industries contracted, however, including textiles, shipbuilding, steel and nonferrous metals, lumber and industrial machinery. In such declining industries, unions, especially the industrial federations, participated almost for the first time in the reorganisation of industry by asking the government to establish industrial policies which take the unions' viewpoint into account. It is important to stress that, unlike the popular view in many other countries, the development of the service-based economy and the introduction of new technologies are not generally seen as leading to a reduction in job opportunities.

The stagnation following the oil crisis taught employers some important lessons, for example, about the difficulties of laying off redundant workers. Companies generally do not dismiss permanent employees, since there is no institutionalised lay-off system comparable to that of the USA. One of the strategies adopted in Japan was to increase flexibility by minimising the number of permanent employees, and by employing temporary and part-time workers instead. On the other hand, raising the mandatory retirement age from 55 to 60 or even to 65 years old is expected to increase the commitment of employees to particular organisations. Since the retirement allowance and private pensions are generally related to length of service, employees want to stay in companies for as long as they are allowed. Moreover, if firms did lay off people, this could destroy the 'high trust relations' which currently exist between managers and employees (Fox, 1974:171 ff.).

Nevertheless, many companies are modifying their traditional employment and wage system to introduce more flexible personnel management practices. Some of the measures being taken are 'plateauing' the age–wage profile after a certain age, say 45 years old, and introducing selective career paths which induce early retirement.

Some firms have reduced their total number of employees by 'natural wastage' or attrition.

Small and medium-sized enterprises   The practices mentioned above are typical of most large employing organisations, but are also found, albeit to a lesser extent, in small and medium-sized enterprises (SMEs). In 1981, some 88 per cent of all Japanese employees worked in the SME category, defined as firms with less than 300 employees (see Table 10.3).

Table 10.3   Private establishments and number of people employed by size of establishment and by industry (1981)

Size of establishment	Number of establishments (distributions %)		Number employed (distributions %)	
All sizes	6 269 071	(100.0)	45 720 190	(100.0)
1–4 people	4 349 060	(69.4)	9 389 701	(20.5)
5–29	1 696 519	(27.0)	16 981 109	(37.1)
30–99	183 297	(2.9)	8 976 915	(19.6)
100–299	32 714	(0.5)	5 137 389	(11.2)
300 or more	7 181	(0.1)	5 326 076	(11.6)

Source: Prime Minister's Office *Census of Establishments* (1982).

There are wide differences in wages and working conditions, depending upon the firms' size, although the shift from large to smaller ones is gradual. These differences reflect different capital–labour ratios and other factors resulting in higher value-added productivity in large firms. SMEs are not an inefficient and declining sector. SMEs account for a wide range of economic activity and increasing support for them is emerging today from many diverse quarters because they can be innovative and more flexible.

It is difficult to generalise about the characteristics of industrial relations in SMEs because of their wide variety. Subcontractors are one type of SME which play an important role in manufacturing industries (but the percentage of subcontractors is low in other industries). Although it is hard to obtain an exact picture, in 1981, about 66 per cent of manufacturing firms were subcontractors of one type or another. Industries which have many subcontractors are: the car, textiles, clothing, general machinery, electrical machinery and metal industries. The percentage of subcontractors increased in each of these industries between 1976 and 1981. However, as a firm increases in size, it tends to be more independent (see Table 10.4).

The independent firms constitute another type of SME; they compete with each other in the market. In this category, there are a

Table 10.4 **Percentage share of subcontractors**[a]

	1976 %	1981[b] %
Total manufacturing	61	66
Size of firm		
1–19	62	67
20–299	51	55
(20–49)	50	55
(50–99)	52	58
(100–299)	51	54
Industry		
Textiles	84	85
Clothing	84	68
Wood	43	48
Chemicals	37	38
Steel	70	72
Metal products	75	79
General machinery	83	84
Electric machinery	82	85
Cars	86	88
Precision machinery	72	81

Notes: a Percentage share of subcontractors = number of subcontracting SMEs/total number of SMEs.
  b 1981 figures are provisional.
Source: Chusho kigyo cho *Chusho kigyo hakusho* (White Paper on SMEs, 1983).

growing number of SMEs based on high technologies. This category of firm typically combines high technology with high levels of business acumen and technical ability. There are still relatively few of these firms, compared with the traditional type of SMEs. However, they are expected to have a great impact on both their product and labour markets.

Since union density is low in SMEs, the terms and conditions of employment are generally determined by market factors. In the case of the very competitive subcontractors, profit margins are low. Wage levels determined in the primary labour market do not correspond with the wage levels in SMEs, although there is a spillover effect.

The number of workers who work part-time increased by about 30 per cent between 1973–83. Most of them are married, middle-aged women. About 21 per cent of women workers are part-timers (Table A.3). The mobility of such workers who enter and leave the labour force has increased. The motivation of such employees is changing. Increasing numbers of them are entering the labour market not only for economic reasons but also for socio-cultural reasons: for example, to escape from the tedium of being a 'housewife'. And employers have increasingly wanted to employ more part-time workers, to win more flexibility in their labour force.

When considering these recent changes—the dynamic role of SMEs and the characteristics of Japan's part-time or temporary workforce—we should not apply the simple stereotype of a dual labour market to the Japanese situation. Current Japanese labour markets are more complex and segmented. Even the so-called primary labour markets are not completely stable because of structural changes. Employment in the manufacturing sector has stagnated since the oil crisis, especially in basic industries such as steel, nonferrous metals and chemicals. On the other hand, a variety of SMEs have emerged which are more dynamic, but are often in the secondary labour market category.

The role played by SMEs is increasing. The growth of the service sector means that there is an increasing diversity of workers' conditions depending upon specific business conditions. By the 1990s, 60 per cent of the total number of civilian employees will be in the service sector. The future of trade unionism in Japan greatly depends on whether unions can recruit such employees.

Technological change New technologies and their impact upon employment are also a current concern (Kuwahara, 1983; 1985). Both labour and management feel that technological change is inevitable in such a capitalist, market-oriented economy where much depends on market forces. Sometimes this feeling is intensified into a belief of 'no technology, no growth'. Unions and management have tried to utilise and adjust to new technology. 'Technological unemployment' has not become an acute social issue. This is largely because employers have not generally used new technology to displace their permanent employees. Although technological change has displaced some jobs, it has also been used to create new jobs.

However, we are approaching a difficult stage. Various new technologies are now being introduced into workplaces. In addition, union density has fallen. Therefore, perhaps before long there will be calls for an ombudsman or similar agency of social control, equipped with investigative and remedial powers, which can deal with the adverse effects of new technology on employment.

Conclusion

The pre-war paternalist traditions still influence the views and behaviour of older people, but these are increasingly being questioned among the younger generations. Before the 1970s, some union leaders and left-wing academics saw the main characteristics of the

Japanese model (e.g. lifetime employment, seniority-based wages and enterprise unions) as 'feudalistic' practices which should be abandoned. There was, however, a dramatic change of view in about 1973. Such characteristics came to be seen as increasingly important explanations of the post-war Japanese economic miracle.

In comparison with most other OECD countries, Japan has enjoyed high rates of economic growth. This may be an unexpected result of the war which destroyed almost all of the special interest organisations, which, as Olson (1982) argued, may hinder the growth of an economy. In the mid-1980s, Japan entered a stage of slower growth, though its situation may continue to be more favourable than some of the other developed countries. But, various bottlenecks in the supply of oil and other raw materials have impeded growth, particularly since 1973.

One of the most important characteristics of Japanese society, which is also reflected in industrial relations, has been its adaptability to change. There are various other characteristics of Japanese industrial relations which help to maintain flexibility, and thus, to facilitate adaptation to change. Some examples of these are: the relatively vague and wide job descriptions and the flexibility of personnel allocation in organisations, lack of rigid work rules which are often found in other developed countries, the bonus system, and long-term merit-rating for both managers and employees.

Increasingly, such constraints as low economic growth and the ageing of the population have induced some rigidities into Japanese society. There has been a narrowing of promotion opportunities within organisations. Above all, the diminution of opportunities for managers is becoming a serious issue among the prime age group (i.e. those who are 35–45 years old). The position of white-collar workers is also a major concern. Their status in enterprises and society is undergoing substantial changes. However, unlike some countries in Europe, in Japan we do not envisage the emergence of radical white-collar trade unionists.[4]

The future of the Japanese model of industrial relations depends upon its ability to continue to adjust to change by eliminating barriers to economic growth, with the help of various innovations. The model is changing, as there is continuing structural change in the face of strong competitive forces. New technologies are being used widely as a means to thwart rigidities in the labour market and in the wider society. Hitherto, the process of 'creative destruction' has generally had a positive impact on the Japanese labour market and has had favourable consequences for employers and most workers. However, there is increasing concern in Japan about the uncertainties which may lie ahead.

Abbreviations

Domei	Japanese Confederation of Labour
DSP	Democratic Socialist Party
GDP	gross domestic product
GHQ	General Headquarters of the Allied Powers
ILO	International Labour Organisation
IMF–JC	Japan Council of Metalworkers' Unions
JCP	Japan Communist Party
JSP	Japan Socialist Party
LDP	Liberal Democratic Party
Nikkeiren	Japan Federation of Employers' Associations
OECD	Organisation for Economic Co-operation and Development
Rodosho	Ministry of Labour
SMEs	small and medium-sized enterprises
Sohyo	General Council of Trade Unions in Japan
Zenkoun	All Japan Council of Traffic and Transport Workers' Unions
Zenminrokyo	Japanese Private Sector Union Council

A chronology of Japanese labour–management relations

1868	Meiji Restoration ended the feudal era.
1880	Early government factories sold to family groups, the genesis of *zaibatsu*, holding companies.
1887	Unionisation movement among printers, iron-workers and other craft workers (which soon disappeared).
1892	Formation of National Federation of Chambers of Commerce.
1894–95	Sino–Japanese War.
1897	Founding of Rodokumiai-kiseikai, the first successful union in Japan.
1900	Enactment of Chian-iji-how (Maintenance of the Public Order Act) with provisions to prohibit workers' rights to organise.
1904–05	Russo–Japanese War
1906	Founding of Nippon Shakaito (Socialist Party).
1907	Violent strikes at Ashio and Besshi copper mines.
1911	The first Factory Act.
1912	Founding of Yuaikai (Friendly Society).
1914–18	First World War.
1919	Record number of strikes (497).
1920	Great Depression.
1921	Founding of Nippon Rodo Sodomei (Japan Labour Federation).
1922	Founding of Nippon Kyosanto (Communist Party).
1937	Founding of Sangyo-hokokukai (Association for Services to the

	State through Industry)—a labour–management co-operative association.
1940	The government dissolved all independent labour organisations.
1941–45	Second World War.
1945	Japan's unconditional surrender.
1946	New Constitution. Labour Relations Adjustment Law. (Old) Trade Union Law.
1947	GHQ's injunction against a general strike. Formation of Katayama cabinet (Coalition of Socialist, Democratic, and People's Co-operation Parties). Labour Standards Law. Ministry of Labour set up.
1948	Introduction of nine principles of economic stability by GHQ.
1949	New Trade Union Law. Public Corporation and National Enterprise Labour Relations Law.
1950	Korean War. Formation of Sohyo.
1951	Peace Treaty concluded in San Francisco. Japan's readmission to the ILO.
1954	Strike at Ohmi Silk Company.
1955	Beginning of *Shunto* (Spring Labour Offensive).
1956	Japan joins the United Nations.
1959	Minimum Wage Law.
1960	Revision of Japan–US Mutual Security Treaty. Strikes at Mitsui-Miike mines and Ohji Paper Company.
1964	Japan joins the OECD. Formation of Domei.
1965	Japan ratifies ILO's Convention 87.
1973	Oil Crisis.
1974	The biggest strike in the history of the Spring Offensive—about 6 million participants.
1980	The American United Automobile Workers (UAW) asks for Japanese direct investment in the USA.
1982	Founding of Zenminrokyo (Japanese Private Sector Trade Union Council).

Notes

1 After the First World War, there was also a rapid growth of unions and of socialist and communist political activity. Such writers as Littler (1982) argue that employers also introduced lifetime employment in an attempt to screen out 'troublemakers' from their own work force.

2 The Japanese life expectancy in 1983 was 74.2 years for men and 79.8 years for women (Kosei Sho, 1984). By around year 2020, the Japanese ageing ratio (population of those 65 years old and over, divided by the total population) will be the highest among the major developed countries, according to an estimate by the Economic Planning Agency.

3 This is a rough estimate of the percentage of employees working for the big organisations listed in the major stock exchanges and the public sector. However, even in smaller establishments there are many regular employees

who stay in the same company for most of their working lives.
4 Since enterprise unions usually include both blue-collar and white-collar workers as members, the union density among white-collar workers is relatively high in Japan.

References

Abegglen, J.C. (1958) *The Japanese Factory: Aspects of Its Social Organisation* Glencoe, Ill.: Free Press
—— (1973) *Management and Worker: The Japanese Solution* Tokyo: Sophia University Press
Chusho Kigyo Cho (Small and Medium-sized Enterprise Agency) (1983) *Chusho Kigyo Hakusho* (White Paper on SMEs) Tokyo
Clark, R. (1979) *The Japanese Company* New Haven: Yale University Press
Cole, R.E. (1971) *Japanese Blue Collar: The Changing Tradition* Berkeley: University of California Press
—— (1979) *Work, Mobility and Participation: A Comparative Study of American and Japanese Industry* Berkeley: University of California Press
Dore, R.P. (1973) *British Factory—Japanese Factory: The Origins of National Diversity in Industrial Relations* London: George Allen & Unwin; Berkeley: University of California Press
Fox, A. (1974) *Beyond Contract: Work, Power and Trust Relations* London: Faber
Ford, G.W. (1983) 'Japan as a Learning Society' *Work and People* 9, 1, pp. 3–5
Fuerstenberg, F. (1984) 'Japanese Industrial Relations from a Western European Perspective' *Work and People* 10, 2, pp. 11–14
Hanami, T. (1979) *Labour Relations in Japan Today* Tokyo: Kodansha-International
Kamata, S. (1983) *Japan in the Passing Lane: An Insider's Account of Life in a Japanese Auto. Factory* ed. and T. Akimoto, London: George Allen & Unwin
Keizai Koho Centre (Japan Institute for Social Economic Affairs) (1984) *Japan 1984: An International Comparison* Tokyo: JISEA
Kosei Sho (Ministry of Health and Welfare) (1984) *Kani Seimei Hyo* (Simplified Life Expectancy Table)
Kuwahara, Y. (1983) 'Technological Change and Industrial Relations in Japan' *Bulletin of Comparative Labour Relations* 12, pp. 32–53
—— (1984) 'Employment and Japan's High-tech Industries' *Euro-Asia* 3, 2 (April), pp. 41–4
—— (1985) 'Labour and Management Views of and their Responses to Microelectronics in Japan' Paper presented to the International Symposium on Microelectronics and Labour, September 1985
Levine, S.B. (1984) 'Employers' Associations in Japan' in J.P. Windmuller and A. Gladstone eds *Employers Associations and Industrial Relations: A Comparative Study* Oxford: Clarendon, pp. 318–56
Levine, S.B. and Kawada, H. (1980) *Human Resources in Japanese Industrial*

Development Princeton, N.J.: Princeton University Press

Littler, C.R. (1982) *The Development of the Labour Process in Capitalist Societies* London: Heinemann

Nakayama, I. (1975) *Industrialisation and Labor: Management Relations in Japan* Tokyo: Japan Institute of Labour

Nihon Rodo Kyokai (Japan Institute of Labour) *Japan Labor Bulletin* (monthly) Tokyo: JIL

—— (1979–83) *Japanese Industrial Relations Series* nos 1–11

Olson, M. (1982) *The Rise and Decline of Nations: Economic Growth, Stagflation, and Social Rigidities* New Haven: Yale University Press

OECD (1977) *The Development of Industrial Relations Systems: Some Implications of Japanese Experience* Paris: OECD

Rodosho (Ministry of Labour) (1984) *Rodokumiai Kihon Tokei Chosa* (The Basic Survey on Trade Unions) Tokyo: Rodosho

Shimada, H. (1983) 'Wage Determination and Information Sharing: An Alternative Approach to Incomes Policy?' *Journal of Industrial Relations* 25, pp. 177–200

Shimizu, N. (1984) 'Rodokumiai Soshikiritsu no Choki Bunseki' (An Analysis of Union Density in Long-term) *Rodo Tokei Chosa Geppo* (Monthly Labour Statistics and Research Bulletin) 36, 4 (April)

Shirai, T. ed. (1983) *Contemporary Industrial Relations in Japan* Madison, Wisconsin: University of Wisconsin Press

Sumiya, M. (1981) 'The Japanese System of Industrial Relations' in P.B. Doeringer et al. eds *Industrial Relations in International Perspective: Essays on Research and Policy* London: Macmillan, pp. 287–323

Thurley, K.E. (1983) 'How Transferable is the Japanese Industrial Relations System? Some Implications of a Study of Industrial Relations and Personnel Policies of Japanese Firms in Western Europe' *Proceedings of the International Industrial Relations Association Sixth World Congress* Geneva: IIRA, pp. 116–31

Appendix: Comparative international data

As mentioned in chapter 1, it is extremely difficult to collect international data which are both up-to-date and fully comparable. The method of collecting data and the definitions used often vary enormously between countries. Therefore, wherever possible the data in this book are derived from such agencies as the International Labour Organisation (ILO), Organisation for Economic Co-operation and Development (OECD) or the US Department of Labor's Bureau of Labor Statistics (BLS). These agencies generally make an attempt to standardise in most of the data series, though, unfortunately, there is a time lag before such data become available. Some of the following tables are based on hitherto unpublished data.

When our international data are inconsistent with national sources, it is often because of the attempts to standardise. Even national sources may be merely approximations. Also, some sources may wish to 'massage' data for reasons of political expediency. For example, politicians in charge of a national source may be tempted to change definitions or publication dates or otherwise to exaggerate or understate the rates of unemployment, inflation or industrial stoppages, for electoral reasons.

Another difficulty is to find time series which do not have a break of consistency and which include all of the nine countries. Many sources omit one or more of the countries, so we have tended not to use these series, even though they are excellent for other purposes. Thus for making comparisons within Europe, a good source is the Statistical Office of the European Communities, Eurostat (e.g. Walsh, 1985).

To illustrate the importance of definitions, note that Table A.1

232

Table A.1 Population, labour force and working women

	Population (millions)				Total labour force (millions)				Percentage of women in the total labour force (percentages)		
	1963	1973	1983	1984	1963	1973	1983	1984	1963	1973	1983
Australia	11	14	15	16	4.5	6.0	7.1	7.2	24[a]	30	34
Canada	19	22	25	25	6.9	9.4	12	12	21[e]	30	40
France	48	52	55	55	20	22	24	24	28[f]	30	35
Germany (FR)	57	62	61	61	27	27	27	28	33	31	33
Italy	51	55	57	57	21	21	23[i]	23[i]	25	22	27[i]
Japan	96	109	119	120	47	53	59	59	38	37	38
Sweden	7.6	8.1	8.3	8.3	3.7	4.0	4.4	4.4	36	40	48
United Kingdom	54	56	56	56	25	26	27	27	30	32	37
United States	189	212	234	237	74	91	113	115	26	32	40

Notes: a 1964 data e editors estimate f 1968 data i data after 1980 have been revised.
Source: OECD (1985b); OECD Observer, March 1986; numbers greater than 10 are rounded in most of our tables.

233

cites data on the total labour force, while Table A.4 refers to civilian employment. What is the difference between these two concepts?

Total labour force = civilian employment + unemployment + armed forces.

Civilian employment includes all those above a specified age in self-employment (own account), as well as employees in paid employment. Also included are those temporarily absent due to illness, holidays, bad weather or industrial disputes etc. and unpaid family members currently working for at least one third of the normal working time. Thus many part-time workers are included, but not calculated as fulltime equivalents. To simplify this Appendix, we do not include full definitions. For precise definitions, which vary slightly between the various agencies, see the official BLS, ILO and OECD publications (e.g. ILO, 1984; OECD, 1985).

Women workers are increasingly important in the labour force. Table A.1 shows that, by 1983, at least 40 per cent of women were in the labour force in four of our countries. However, many women are employed part-time (see Table A.3) and even 'full-time' women workers tend to be employed for fewer hours than men.

Participation rates for each country are shown in Table A.2. The participation (or activity) rate is the total labour force divided by the population of working age (in most countries 15–64). Column 4 of Table A.2 shows that the participation rate for men in 1984 varied only between 77 and 88 per cent. The differing total participation rates largely reflect the differing propensities for women to work in each country. The participation rates for women varied more, from 41 per cent to 77 per cent. The Scandinavian countries generally have high total participation rates, largely because they have a high proportion of part-time workers, most of whom are women (see Table A.3). The low rate in Italy may reflect the relatively large informal economy of 'clandestine employment' there. Many Italians are 'discouraged' from engaging in 'active search for work' and it is difficult for the authorities to measure the size of the labour force accurately, particularly in the large rural sector in such southern European countries.

Table A.2 Labour force participation rates

	Men				Women (percentages)				Total			
	1963	1973	1983	1984	1963	1973	1983	1984	1963	1973	1983	1984[e]
Australia	94[a]	92	86	86	39[a]	48	52	53	67[a]	70	70	70
Canada	88[c]	86	85	85	40[c]	47	60	61	63	67	72	73
France	87[f]	85	78	77	46[f]	50	54	55	68	68	66	66
Germany (FR)	95	89	80	79	49	50	50	49	71	69	65	64
Italy[i]	92	85	80	80	37	34	40	41	63	59	60	60
Japan	90	90	89	88	57	54	57	57	73	72	73	73
Sweden	92	88	86	86	55	63	77	77	74	76	81	82
United Kingdom	97	93	88	88	47	53	58	59	72	73	73	73
United States	89	86	85	85	43	51	62	62	66	68	73	73

Notes: a 1964 data   c 1966 data   e OECD secretariat estimates   f 1968 data   i population data 14–64 years, data after 1980 has been revised.
Source: OECD (1985a; b)

235

In most of the nine countries, the long-term trend is towards a lower participation rate for men, which reflects the expansion of tertiary education and the increasing level of incomes and pensions which enable men to retire earlier. By contrast, the trend is towards higher participation rates for women, except in Japan, where employers generally prefer men; Japanese employers do hire a large number of young women, but often not in permanent jobs. Moreover, there has been a sharp drop in the number of female family workers in Japanese agriculture (ILO, 1984:55).

Although we do not present participation rate data analysed by age, it is worth noting that there are significant differences between the participation rates of people in different age categories. For example, in 1966, the male participation rate in Australia was 96 per cent for the 45–54 age group, but only 79 per cent for the 60–64 age group. Such differences tend to be magnified in periods of economic recession. By 1979, the rate was 92 per cent for the 45–54 age group, but it had fallen to 54 per cent for the older age group. This suggests a high level of 'hidden unemployment' among older people, especially when there are fewer jobs available, so some people are forced into early retirement (Carter and Gregory, 1981: Table 1; also see ILO, 1986).

Part-time employment has grown in most of the countries in recent years. The definition of part-time working varies greatly between countries, so inter-country comparisons are difficult. Nevertheless, we can infer from Table A.3 that part-time working is much more usual in Sweden and the UK than in France and Italy (but it seems likely that there are also many part-timers in the informal economy in Italy).

In all the countries, a large majority of part-timers are women. In Europe and Japan, part-time work is associated with the life-cycle phase when women's domestic work tends to be at its height. In Canada and the USA, however, part-timers tend to be younger than full-timers and are often single people, who are combining such employment with education.

Table A.3 Part-time employment

| | Part-time employment as a percentage of: | | | | | | | | | Women's share in part-time employment | | |
| | total employment | | | male employment | | | female employment | | | | | |
	1973	1978	1983ᵃ	1973	1979	1983ᵃ	1973	1979	1983ᵃ	1973	1979	1983ᵃ
Australia	11	16	17	3.4	5.1	6.1	27	34	36	80	79	78
Canada	11ᵇ	12	15	5.1ᵇ	5.7	7.6	20ᵇ	23	26	70ᵇ	72	71
France	7.2	8.2	9.7	2.6	2.5	2.6	15	17	20	78	82	85
Germany (FR)	10	11	13	1.8	1.5	1.7	24	28	30	89	92	92
Italy	6.4	5.3	4.6	3.7	3.0	2.4	14	11	9.4	58	61	65
Japan	7.9	9.6	10	4.6	5.2	4.8	15	18	21	61	64	71
Sweden	18	24	25	3.7	6.5	7.3	39	46	46	88	85	85
United Kingdom	16	16	19	2.3	1.9	3.3	39	39	42	91	93	90
United Statesᶜ	14	14	14	7.2	7.4	7.6	24	24	23	68	70	70
	(17)	(18)	(20)	(9.4)	(10)	(12)	(28)	(28)	(29)	(66)	(67)	(65)

Notes: a The number of non-declared persons in the 1983 data for the EC countries is distributed proportionately between full-time and part-time employment.
b 1975
c Short-time workers for economic reasons are excluded from both part-time and total employment. Data in brackets show the results of including this group in the calculations.

Source: OECD (1985a:26)

237

Structural shifts in employment are illustrated in Table A.4. The structure of employment is conventionally divided into three broad sectors: agriculture (including: hunting, forestry and fishing); industry; and services. Industry is broader than manufacturing, as it also includes mining and construction, for example. The distinctions between these three sectors are defined by the United Nations (1971). These distinctions are becoming outdated, however, especially as the agricultural and industrial sectors tend to contract, while the service sector is expanding in most of the nine countries. The service sector is now too heterogeneous, as it includes all the categories which do not fit one of the first two sectors, including public administrators, shop assistants, truck drivers, computer specialists, doctors, teachers and many more. Therefore Barry Jones (1982) suggests that it would be appropriate to sub-divide the service sector into: a tertiary sector consisting of tangible economic services; a quaternary sector comprising data processing; and a quinary sector covering unpaid work, homework where pay is secondary, and professional services of a quasi-domestic nature. However, unfortunately we do not yet have a sufficiently comprehensive set of such data.

As an additional complication, the sectoral distinctions are not always precise, because some people work in more than one sector. An individual may be engaged in clerical work in the mornings, but agricultural work in the afternoons. Furthermore, if that individual is employed by a manufacturing company, he or she would probably be classified as working in the industrial sector. However, if supplied by an agency, he or she is classified as in the service sector! Thus, to some extent, the trend towards subcontracting and the growth of employment agencies has exaggerated the growth of the service sector.

Table A.4 Civilian employment by sector

	Civilian employment (millions)				Agriculture (percentages of civilian employment)				Industry				Services			
	1963	1973	1983	1984	1963	1973	1983	1984	1963	1973	1983	1984	1963	1973	1983	1984
Australia	4.3[a]	5.8	6.3	6.5	10	7.3	6.6	6.2	38	35	28	28	52	57	65	66
Canada	6.5	8.8	11	11	12	6.5	5.5	5.3	33	31	26	26	56	63	69	69
France	19	21	21	21	20	11	8.0	7.9	40	40	34	33	40	49	58	59
Germany (FR)	26	26	25	25	12	7.3	5.6	5.6	48	47	42	41	40	45	52	53
Italy[i]	20	19	20	20	27	18	12	12	38	39	36	35	35	43	52	54
Japan	46	53	57	57	26	13	9.3	8.9	32	37	35	35	42	49	56	56
Sweden	3.7	3.9	4.2	4.2	13	7.1	5.4	5.1	41	37	30	30	46	56	65	65
United Kingdom	24	25	23	24	4.4	2.9	2.7	2.6	46	42	34	33	49	55	64	64
United States	68	85	101	105	7.1	4.2	3.5	3.3	35	33	28	28	58	63	68	68
Total OECD	270	303	326	332	19	12	9.5		36	36	32		45	52	59	

Notes: a OECD secretariat estimate   i data after 1980 have been revised.
Source: OECD (1985b); OECD Observer, March 1986.

The unemployed includes all those above a specified age without a job and currently seeking work. Also included in the BLS data are those laid-off indefinitely or temporarily without pay except in Europe or Japan. Excluded, however, are those intending to start a business, but who have not yet arranged to do so and who are not seeking paid work.

Unemployment levels are a crucial influence on the relative power of workers and employers. Table A.5 shows that the unemployment rates have generally been lower in Japan and Sweden, for example, than in the other countries. Before the 1970s, Australia and Germany also had comparatively low rates. But unemployment is particularly difficult to compare between countries, due to major differences of definition and methods of calculation. Also, the social security legislation and the benefits to be gained from registering as un-employed vary greatly between countries (Kaim-Caudle, 1973:238ff). In short, as in several of the other tables, the data in Table A.5 are reasonably valid for vertical comparisons (within a country), but horizontal comparisons (between countries) are only of limited validity, in spite of all the attempts at standardisation.

There is a major difference between the BLS and ISTAT series of Italian data in Table A.5. Of those not currently in employment, many report that they had not actively sought work in the last 30 days, so are excluded from the BLS definition of unemployment. As this definition was devised for the USA, it may be rather restrictive for Italy, where it generally takes longer to find a job.

Table A.5 Unemployment

Year	Australia	Canada	France	Germany (FR)	Italy[a] BLS	(ISTAT)	Japan	Sweden	United Kingdom[b]	United States
					(percentage of the labour force)					
1959	2.1[c]	5.5	1.7	2.0	4.1	(7.0)	2.3	1.6	2.6	5.3
1964	1.4	4.3	1.3	.4	2.3	(4.3)	1.2	1.5	2.3	5.0
1969	1.8	4.4	2.2	.6	3.0	(5.7)	1.1	1.9	2.9	3.4
1971	1.9	6.1	2.6	.6	2.8	(5.4)	1.2	2.5	3.8	5.8
1973	2.3	5.5	2.6	.7	3.2	(6.4)	1.3	2.4	3.1	4.8
1975	4.8	6.9	4.1	4.1	3.0	(5.9)	1.9	1.6	4.4	8.3
1977	5.6	8.0	4.9	3.4	3.5	(7.2)	2.0	1.8	6.2	6.9
1979	6.2	7.4	5.9	2.9	3.8	(7.7)	2.1	2.0	5.2	5.8
1980	6.0	7.4	6.3	2.8	3.8	(7.6)	2.0	2.0	6.8	7.0
1981	5.7	7.5	7.4	4.0	4.2	(8.4)	2.2	2.5	10.2	7.5
1982	7.1	10.9	8.1	5.8	4.7	(9.1)	2.4	3.1	11.7[d]	9.5
1983	9.9	11.8	8.3	7.3	5.2	(9.9)	2.7	3.4	12.7[d]	9.5
1984	8.9	11.2	9.8[d]	7.7[d]	5.8[d]	(13.2)	2.7	3.1	12.8[d]	7.4
1985	8.2	10.4[f]	10.3	7.9[d]	6.0[d]	(12.4)	2.6[d]	2.8[d]	13.3	7.2
1986	7.8[e]	9.7[f]	10.0[f]	7.7[f]	NA	(13.5)[e]	2.9[e]	2.7[e]	13.2[e]	6.6[f]

Notes: a The national source Italian data (ISTAT) is included in brackets, because it is so different from the BLS data; see text.
  b Great Britain only
  c National source Australian data
  d Preliminary
  e Data from the *Economist*, 26 January 1986, based on different (national) definitions
  f January data from BLS, March 1986.
Source: US BLS *Monthly Labor Review;* unemployment rates approximating US concepts.

Gross domestic product (GDP) is a measure of the total sum of final goods and services produced by an economy at market prices. GDP includes the cost of capital goods for replacement purposes. Intermediate products are not counted separately, as their value is already included in the prices of final goods and services. Income from abroad is excluded; hence the term gross *domestic* product.

Gross national product (GNP) equals GDP plus net property income arising from foreign investments and possessions. These two measures are indicators of the relative prosperity of each country. Table A.6, columns 3 and 4 show that Japan had much the most rapid annual rate of growth of GDP (1978–85), while column 6 shows that in 1984 the GDP per capita (person) was highest in the USA (US $15 000) and Canada (US $13 000).

In 1984, the average GDP per capita was US $10 280. However, such data obviously fluctuate enormously, according to vagaries of currency exchange rates (see columns 7–9).

Table A.6 Gross domestic product and exchange rates

	GDP[a] (billion US $)		Average annual GDP increase		GDP per capita[a] (thousand US $)		Currency exchange rate per US $		
	1984	1985	1978–83	1984–5	1982	1984	31 Dec 1983	31 Dec 1984	31 Dec 1985
Australia	174	154	2.2	4.2	10	11	1.1	1.2	1.5
Canada	334	342	1.3	4.0	12	13	1.2	1.3	1.4
France	490	503	1.5	1.0	10	8.9	8.4	9.6	7.6
Germany (FR)	613	612	1.2	2.2	11	10	2.7	3.2	2.5
Italy	348	354	1.4	2.2	6.1	6.1	1660	1934	1678
Japan	1255	1308	4.1	5.0	9.0	10.4	232	251	200
Sweden	95	99	1.7	2.5	12	11	8	9	7.6
United Kingdom	423	438	0.8	3.2	8.5	7.5	0.7	0.86	0.7
United States	3635	3865	1.1	2.5	13	15	1	1	1
Average	—	—	1.7	3.0	10.25	10.28	—	—	—

Note: a current prices and exchange rates
Source: *OECD Observer*, March 1984; March 1985; March 1986.

Comparative international data

Cost of living increases are a major influence on pay settlements, union growth and other aspects of industrial relations. Table A.7 shows that Italy, France and Sweden experienced a 'double digit' rate of increase in their cost of living (consumer-price inflation) in the early 1980s. By contrast, the rate was less than 5 per cent in both Japan and Germany. In all the countries the inflation rate was less during 1984–85 than the average for the period 1979–84.

Table A.7   Increase in consumer prices

	Average annual increase 1979–84 (percentages per year)	Percentage increase (Dec 1983– Dec 1984)	(Dec 1984– Dec 1985)
Australia	9.0	2.6	7.6[a]
Canada	8.7	3.8	4.4
France	11.1	6.7	4.7
Germany (FR)	4.5	2.0	1.8
Italy	16.1	9.2	8.9[b]
Japan	3.9	2.6	1.8
Sweden	10.2	8.2	5.6
United Kingdom	9.5	4.6	5.7
United States	7.4	4.0	3.8
Average	8.9	4.9	4.9

Notes: a third quarter   b Nov.
Source: *OECD Observer*, March 1985; March 1986.

Real wages can be estimated by dividing the average wage levels by consumer price indices. This gives a constant price measure of wages. This measure is only approximate, however, as it does not take into account the changing structure of the economy or changing participation rates; nor does it take into account *disposable*, rather than gross pay, or other influences on living standards. Table A.8 shows that real wages rose in the 1970s in all nine countries, with the apparent exception of the USA. There, the apparent decline reflected the rapid increase in the numbers of women and young people in the labour force. If we allowed for this increase, there would also have been a small improvement in real wages in the USA (Flaim, 1982). Real wages generally rose to a greater extent in the 1960s, than in the 1970s. But in the early 1980s, in most countries, there was no significant increase (ILO, 1984:137).

Table A.8 also shows that national rates of pay increases generally did not deviate substantially from the rates of growth in national output, as reflected in changes in real per capita GNP.

Table A.8   Growth rates of real wages and GNP per capita

	Real wages[a]	GNP per capita
	(annual average percentages in the 1970s)	
Australia	3.1	1.4
Canada	1.4	2.9
France	4.2	3.0
Germany (FR)	2.9	2.6
Italy[b]	5.6	2.3
Japan	3.8	3.9
Sweden	2.2	1.1
United Kingdom	2.0	1.9
United States	−0.4	2:2

Note: a calculated from data on non-agricultural wages   b based on an index of wage rates
Source: ILO (1984:136)

Comparative purchasing power calculations provide a way of overcoming some of the problems in comparing living standards. Such calculations aim to evaluate the relative purchasing power of workers' pay in different countries. For example, we have unpublished BLS data on 'purchasing-power-parity exchange rates', but unfortunately, they exclude Australia and Sweden. However, the International Metalworkers' Federation (IMF) publishes surveys of metalworkers' purchasing power, based on average hourly net wages (i.e. after deduction of workers' social security contributions), expressed in working time required for the purchase of selected consumer items. In an attempt to obtain comparable data, the price levels used are for medium quality goods, in a major industrial town. Table A.9 presents such an analysis for the automobile industry. These calculations are particularly difficult, so may not always accurately reflect reality, even though much of the data are derived from the West German Federal Statistics Office, which aims to take into account the cost of living and the different patterns of consumption in the various countries.

Table A.9 The purchasing power of working time

	Bread (per kilo)	Coffee (per kilo)		Men's shoes (per pair)		1 litre petrol (super)		Rent 3–4 rooms[a] (monthly)		Colour TV (0.5 m screen)	Annual income tax[b]	Net hourly earnings
	mins	hrs	mins	hrs	mins	hrs	mins	hrs	mins	hrs	hrs	Swiss Francs
Australia	9.5	2	46	5	45		3.5	61	00	78	332	17.50
Canada	5		45	5	15		2.5	55	00	52	424	22.29
France	43	2	39	17	15		10	135	15	151	108	8.55
Germany (FR)	12	1	36	6	15		6	34	30	107	NA	12.09
Italy	17	1	43	8	30		11	60	45	157	288	9.39
Japan	15	4	28	5	45		6[c]	32	00	98	202	15.54
Sweden	32	1	36	10	15		8	57	00	148	NA	9.81
United Kingdom	13.5	3	35	7	00		7	29	00	69	522	11.00
United States	6		28	4	00		2	37	15	44	NA	31.53

Notes: a plus kitchen and bathroom   b for a metalworker with two dependent children and an unemployed wife   c ordinary, not super
Source: IMF (1985:42ff)

247

Women should receive equal remuneration for work of equal value, according to the ILO constitution adopted in 1919 and its 1951 Equal Remuneration Convention (no.100), which has been ratified by 104 member countries. Nevertheless, as shown in Table A.10, there is a substantial gap between men's and women's earnings in manufacturing. In 1975, this gap was narrowest in Sweden and widest in Japan. By 1982 the gap had narrowed further in Sweden, but widened in Japan. Since public policies to promote 'equal pay' often seem to have had little impact, the USA, for example, has moved towards a notion of 'comparable worth' in an attempt to close the earnings gap between men and women (see chapter 3).

These data must be interpreted cautiously, because, in comparison with men, on average, women are employed for fewer hours per week, retire earlier, have fewer qualifications and often work in different jobs and sectors from men. Women workers are concentrated in lower status occupations and industries which are generally low paid, such as retailing and catering. Conversely, there are relatively few women managers. Women workers still shoulder most of the home-making responsibilities, which can adversely affect their work performance. In short, women workers are caught in a vicious circle.

Table A.10 also shows that there is a higher level of unemployment among women than men, in most of the countries. These data understate the reality, because more women than men are generally 'discouraged' from 'active search for work' or from registering as unemployed. In 1982, there were about 1 million women in the USA in this category (1 per cent of the labour force). Also, much female

Table A.10 Women's pay and unemployment

	Women's pay as percentage of men's in manufacturing		Unemployment 1982 (percentages)	
	1975	1982	women	men
Australia	78.5[h]	78.2[h]	8.4	6.2
Canada	NA	NA	10.8	11.0
France	76.4[h]	77.7[h]	11.6	5.6
Germany (FR)	72.1[h]	73.0[h]	7.7	6.0
Italy	NA	NA	14.7	6.0
Japan	47.9[m]	43.1[m]	2.3	2.4
Sweden	85.2[h]	90.3[h]	3.4	3.0
United Kingdom	66.5[h]	68.8[h]	7.1	12.6
United States	NA	NA	9.4	9.7

Notes: h hourly wages   m monthly wages
Source: ILO (1985:216ff) for pay data; OECD (1985a:88) for unemployment data.

unemployment is 'hidden' in part-time working. Although many women prefer to work part-time, some part-timers would prefer to work full-time. In 1983, in the USA, there was a total of at least 6.5 million non-agricultural workers involuntarily on part-time schedules (ILO, 1985:216; also see our Table A.3).

Social security was recognised in the Universal Declaration of Human Rights adopted by the United Nations in 1948. Public social security schemes developed rapidly after the Second World War. They may include medical care, pensions, family benefits and other elements, which have increasingly been the subject of bipartite or tripartite consultation and sometimes formal negotiation between unions, employers and governments.

In some countries, private schemes play an important role, especially company pension funds and insurance. None the less, such non-legislated schemes are excluded from Table A.11, as are statutory impositions on employers. This Table shows that, in the late 1970s, the public social security receipts as a percentage of GDP varied widely from a high of 34 per cent in Sweden to a low of 15 per cent in the USA and Australia. The USA has no comprehensive public medical care scheme, but Australia re-introduced a 'Medicare' scheme in 1984.

Normal retirement ages vary between 55 and 65 in the nine countries. However, many people retire earlier, especially if they experience ill health, and particularly in economic recessions. The current trend in Australia and Europe is towards lower retirement

Table A.11 Social security and retirement ages

	Social security receipts, 1977 (percentage of GDP)	Normal retirement age in 1981 men	women
Australia	15[e]	65	60
Canada	17[ab]	65	65
France	26[ad]	65[f]	65[f]
Germany (FR)	24[ad]	65	65
Italy	21	60	55
Japan	14[ab]	60	55
Sweden	34[ad]	65	65
United Kingdom	19[ab]	65	60
United States	15[ac]	65	65

Notes: a provisional figures   b 1979–80   c 1978–79   d 1979   e 1976–77   f subsequently changed to 60
Source: ILO (1984:211ff).

ages, largely to alleviate high levels of unemployment. By contrast, in Japan, there is a trend towards the retirement ages moving up from 55 to 60; and in the USA, the compulsory retirement age has been increased from 65 to 70.

Hours of work are also difficult to compare between countries because the data are not consistent, but generally include part-time workers. In brief some countries collect data on (a) average hours *actually worked*, while others' data are (b) of average *hours paid for*. Hours actually worked include normal hours of work, overtime, stand-by hours at place of work and short rest periods at the workplace including tea or coffee breaks. Hours paid for comprise hours actually worked and, depending on national practices, paid annual leave, paid public holidays, paid sick leave, meal breaks and time spent on travel from home to work and vice versa, etc. These broad differences are indicated by the summary notes against each country in Table A.12.

In 1983, among the countries for which we have reasonably comparable data in manufacturing industry (total), the Australians appeared to work on average the least hours, while the Japanese and British appeared to work the most. However the Japanese take fewer holidays, so, in total, they tend to work most hours per year.

Indices of average weekly hours indicate the general long-term trend towards a reduction in the average working week. Table A.13 shows that there was almost a 30 per cent reduction in the working week in Sweden between 1950 and 1980. On the other hand, in this period, there appeared to be scarcely any reduction in the USA.

Table A.12   Hours of work per week in manufacturing

	men		women		total	
	1980	1983	1980	1983	1980	1983
Australia[a]	39.1	38.0	34.4	33.5	38	36.9
Canada[b]	NA	NA	NA	NA	38.5	38.4
France[a]	NA	NA	NA	NA	40.7	38.9
Germany (FR)[b]	42.2	40.8	40.0	39.1	41.6	40.5
Italy[b]	NA	NA	NA	NA	38.6[c]	38.5[c]
Japan[j]	42.4	42.3	38.4	38.6	41.2	41.1
Sweden[b]	39.4	39.6	32.9	32.7	37.7	37.9
United Kingdom[a]	41.9	42.5	33.7	34.6	39.6	41.0
United States[b]	NA	NA	NA	NA	39.7	40.1

Notes: a hours actually worked   b hours paid for   c calculated on a daily basis   j excluding temporary workers

Source: ILO *Bulletin of Labour Statistics* 1985/4: 65ff;
ILO *Yearbook of Labour Statistics* 1984:540ff;
BLS unpublished data, 4 April 1986.

Table A.13 Average weekly hours in manufacturing (Index 1950 = 100)

Year	Australia	Canada	France	Germany (FR)	Italy	Japan	Sweden	United Kingdom	United States
1950	NA	100.0	100.0	100.0	100.0	100.0	100.0	100.0	100.0
1955	NA	96.0	102.1	100.1	102.5	104.8	99.3	101.3	100.3
1960	NA	95.7	106.9	90.2	103.6	109.5	94.0	99.0	98.3
1965	100.0	96.9	105.3	84.5	92.2	101.5	89.8	95.8	101.7
1970	97.3	94.9	103.1	83.1	91.1	99.1	83.2	92.5	98.7
1975	89.6	92.1	96.5	75.3	77.0	89.5	76.9	85.9	98.0
1980	90.2	91.7	94.2	74.5	79.2	94.2	71.4	82.7	98.3

Source: Hart 1984:41 (after BLS data), but, for Australia calculated from ILO *Yearbook of Labour Statistic* various years (data for men, hours paid for, Index 1965:100).

(However, note that the 1950 base varied between countries. The American and Canadian data are not fully comparable, mainly because they are based on hours paid, whereas the data are hours worked in the other countries.) By contrast with the USA, in most of the other countries, there has been a substantial reduction in the number of hours worked per year, due to an increase in holiday entitlements.

Hourly labour costs vary a great deal between countries. Table A.14 presents an index of the relative costs per hour of work in manufacturing, compared to those in Germany. Note that a positive sign shows a relative increase vis-à-vis *German* hourly labour costs, while a negative sign shows the opposite. This table shows that differentials in relative hourly labour costs in the nine countries narrowed in the 13 year period. However, this was largely due to the declining value of the US dollar in the 1970s coupled with the relatively low pay increases in the USA, and to the rapid rate of pay increases in Japan.

These hourly labour costs can be divided into two components: wage costs and non-wage costs; the latter includes employers' social security contributions. Column 6 of Table A.14 shows the differing percentages of total employment costs which are non-wage costs. Note the relatively low percentage in Japan, in particular.

Table A.14   Relative hourly labour costs

	Index Germany = 100		Changes relative to Germany (FR)		Total hourly costs 1983 (DM)	Non-wage costs per hour 1983 (percentage of column 5)
	1970	1983	1970–83	1982–83		
Australia	84	100	+18	− 1.6	27.3	30
Canada	135	112	−17	+ 7.9	30.8	26
France	68	74	+ 7.3	− 7.1	20.2	45
Germany (FR)	100	100			27.4	44
Italy	74	77	+ 4.1	− 3.4	21.0	48
Japan	42	70	+66	+11.4	19.0	22
Sweden	118	86	−27	−11	23.7	41
United Kingdom	62	62	+ 0.5	− 6.0	17.1	29
United States	168	114	−32	+ 3.9	31.1	28

Source: *IW—trends* Koln: Institute der Deutschen Wirtschaft 2/84, 29 May 1984, pp. 30–39, reported in ILO *Social and Labour Bulletin*, 3–4, 1984:476ff. (These data relate to manufacturing.)

Productivity can be measured in terms of output per worker-hour. Although this measure relates output to the number of people employed in manufacturing, it does not measure the specific contribution of labour as a single factor of production. Rather, it reflects many other influences too, including the use of new technologies, capital investment, capacity utilisation, energy efficiency, and the skills and efforts of management as well as workers. Like many of the other indicators, this one is only an approximation, because the type, quantily and quality of the output varies greatly from one country to another, and between industries and firms (Smith et al., 1982). Nevertheless, we can infer from Table A.15 that the productivity growth in Japan far exceeded that in any other country, while the USA had the lowest rate of growth.

Unit labour costs reflect changes in hourly labour costs and productivity. Therefore, unit labour costs are a more important indicator than hourly labour costs. Table A.15 also summarises the average annual rates of change in unit labour costs, on a US dollar basis. It shows that unit labour costs rose most in the UK and least in Japan and Sweden during the 1973–84 period. In 1984, unit labour costs did not appear to increase in any country.

Table A.15 Manufacturing productivity and unit labour costs (annual average rate of change)[a]

	Output per worker-hour		Unit labour costs (in US dollars)	
	1973–84	1984	1973–84	1984
Australia	NA	NA	NA	NA
Canada	1.7	4.0	6.3	− 7.0
France	4.6	5.0	4.5	− 9.5
Germany (FR)	3.3	4.7	4.4	−11.2
Italy	3.7	6.3	4.8	−10.1
Japan	7.3	9.5	3.1	− 5.7
Sweden	2.9	6.8	2.7	− 3.7
United Kingdom	2.3	3.9	9.2	− 8.4
United States	2.0	3.5	6.7	0.1

Note: a In columns 1 and 3, rates of change computed from the least squares trend of the logarithms of the index numbers.
Source: US BLS *News*, 10 June 1985:2, as later revised for Sweden.

Exporting and importing goods may be reflected in the traffic of industrial relations policies and practices. The pattern of world trade does not tend to change dramatically from year to year, but there have been major changes during the post-war period. These changes are especially due to the emergence of the newly industrialising countries and the growing importance of the oil trade. For example, when Britain became a substantial oil producer after 1975, oil became an import substitute. The decline in its imports tended to mask the increase in its imports of manufactured goods.

In absolute terms, the USA was by far the biggest exporter in 1953 even though Europe had largely recovered from the war by then. By 1984, however, the USA was no longer so dominant. West Germany and Japan, in particular, had greatly expanded their exports. Of the top 20 exporters in 1953, only fourteen were still in the list in 1984. Australia was among the departures. The newcomers were led by Saudi Arabia, Taiwan and South Korea (see the *Economist*, 18 Jan. 1986:91).

International trade is proportionately more important in some countries than others. Table A.16 shows that, as a percentage of their GDP, imports and exports are greatest for Sweden and least for the USA and Japan. These differences reflect the small home market in Sweden and the huge ones in the USA and Japan. Nevertheless, international trade is vital for all nine countries.

Table A.16 International trade

	Imports as a percentage of GDP, 1983 (current prices)	Growth of imports 1978–83 (percentages per year)	Exports as a percentage of GDP, 1983 (current prices)	Growth of exports 1978–83 (percentages per year)
Australia	12	−1.0	13	2.4
Canada	19	0.9	23	2.5
France	20	3.1	18	3.1
Germany (FR)	23	1.5	26	2.2
Italy	23	1.6	21	2.0
Japan	11	0.5	13	6.3
Sweden	28	4.6	30	4.8
United Kingdom	22	2.4	20	1.4
United States	7.9	0.1	6.1	−0.2

Source: *OECD Observer*, March 1985.

Union membership is a crucial variable for students of industrial relations. Bain and Elsheikh (1976) explain the rise and fall of union membership in terms of the business cycle. They cover only four of our nine countries, however, and focus on data up to 1970. Bain and Price (1980) is one of the most authoritative sources; unfortunately, however, it covers only six of our nine countries and has little post-1976 data. Walsh (1985) is a good source on our four EC member countries and for a useful discussion, see ILO (1985:5ff). For more comprehensive data, again we turn to the BLS.

Comparative union membership (density) data are even less reliable than most other comparative data. Union density is given by the formula:

$$\frac{\text{actual union membership}}{\text{potential union membership}} \times 100$$

The numerator is usually based on membership figures supplied by the unions themselves. Many unions do not collect precise membership details centrally. For various purposes, moreover, they may either wish to exaggerate or understate their membership. The numerator also depends on the working definition of a union. Does it include employee associations (USA), staff associations (UK) and professional organisations of doctors and lawyers, for instance, which may have some union functions?

The denominator (bottom line) depends on the definition of potential union membership. This raises many questions. The BLS data use civilian employees, which excludes the armed forces. The BLS generally exclude other groups who rarely belong to unions, such as employers, the self-employed, the retired, the unemployed and those employed in agriculture, forestry and fishing in most countries, unless the notes to Table A.17 specify otherwise. Therefore this BLS series tends to imply that union density is rather higher than other series which exclude fewer such groups.

It is important to note that within each country, the aggregate union density data conceal enormous variations between men and women, and between different occupations and sectors (see chapter 4, Table 4.2; also see Bain and Price, 1980).

Table A.17 Union membership

Year	Australia[a]	Canada[b]	France[c]	Germany (FR)	Italy[d]	Japan[e]	Sweden	United Kingdom	United States[b]
				(percentage of wage and salary employees)					
1955	64	32	23	46	NA	38	70	46	34[f]
1960	61	31	24	41	NA	34	68	45	32[f]
1965	59	28	23	38	NA	36	71	46	29[f]
1970	52	32	22	37	41	35	79	51	31
1975	58	35	23	41	49	35	84	54	29
1976	57	36	NA	41	51	34	87	56	29
1977	57	37	NA	41	52	33	89	58	27
1978	57	37	NA	42	52	33	92	59	27
1979	58	NA	21[g]	42	51	32	89	58	25
1980	58	36	21[g]	42	50	31	90	57	25
1981	57	36	20[g]	42	49	31	91	56	23[g]
1982	58	38	20[g]	43	48	31	93	55	20[g]
1983	58	38	19[g]	43	48	30	94	54	20[h]
1984	57	38	18[g]	NA	NA	29	NA	50[g]	19[h]

Notes:
a Women in domestic service excluded.
b Forestry and fishing employees included.
c Agricultural employees included; source Eurostat.
d Agricultural employees included; members of 'autonomous unions' and other employee organisations are included in the numerator; denominator source: the Italian national source, ISTAT.
e Fishing employees included.
f Excludes members of employee associations. In 1970, union membership excluding members of employee associations as a percentage of non-agricultural wage and salary employees was 28 per cent.
g Editors' estimate.
h Includes agricultural employees; source Flaim (1985:208) also see Adams (1985:25ff).

Source: BLS January 1986 estimates based on ILO, OECD and national sources, except where otherwise specified above.

257

Industrial disputes

What is the relative strike-proneness or incidence of industrial disputes in the nine countries? As mentioned in chapter 1, international
comparisons of this aspect of industrial relations are also very difficult. Given that studying industrial disputes is so central to industrial
relations, we offer more comment on these data than in the earlier
sections. In making a broad international comparison, we cannot
maintain any of the many idiosyncratic national definitional distinctions, because they are not adopted consistently across any two of the
countries, let alone across all of them (see Table A.18; also Fisher,
1973).

Of course work stoppages are only one form of sanction. There are
many others including working-to-rule, working without enthusiasm,
banning overtime working and so on, but there are no comparative
data available on such forms of collective sanction. Nor are there any
comparable data available on the many forms of individual sanction
such as absence, apathy, industrial sabotage and quitting.

There are various indicators of strike-proneness, including the
number of working days lost in stoppages per 1000 employees, number of stoppages per 100 000 employees, number of workers involved
per 1000 employees, and the average stoppage duration (Creigh
et al., 1982). However, none of the agencies standardise these indicators. Mining, manufacturing, construction, and transport and communication tend to account for a large proportion of the working days
lost in most countries. Furthermore, stoppages in these industries
may have a particularly serious impact on an economy. Therefore the
ILO has a series of international comparisons based on these four
sectors, which reduces the effect of national differences in industrial
structure. The number of working days lost in stoppages per 1000
employees in these four sectors is probably the most useful
international measure of 'strike-proneness': the best of a rather
dubious bunch of strike activity measures.

Walsh (1983) is an excellent source of comparative data on strikes.
However, as it does not cover all of the nine countries, Table A.19 is
derived from ILO data. Using average data for the decade 1974–83 as
a whole, it shows that Australia, Canada, Italy and the USA were
relatively strike-prone. In spite of the myth about Britain being
particularly strike-prone, it was in an intermediate position. Japan,
West Germany, Sweden and France were less strike-prone. These
relative positions may vary from one year to another. For example,
there was an unusually high number of days lost in France in 1968, in
Sweden in 1980 and in West Germany in 1984.

On an average basis in the medium-term, there is a general stability

Table A.18 Industrial disputes: comparisons of coverage and methodology

	Minimum criteria for inclusion in statistics	Political stoppages included?	Indirectly affected workers included?	Sources and notes
Australia	10 or more days lost	Yes	Yes	Information from arbitrators, employers, and unions
Canada	10 or more days lost or of more than a half day's duration	Yes	No	Reports from Canada Manpower Centres also Press and Provincial Labor Depts
France	No restrictions on size. However, public sector and agricultural employees are excluded from statistics	Yes	No	Labour inspectors' reports
Germany (FR)	More than 10 workers involved and more than one day's duration, unless 100 or more working days lost	Yes	No	Compulsory notification by employers to Labour Offices
Italy	No restrictions on size	Yes, since 1975	No	Local police reports sent to ISTAT
Japan	More than half a day's duration	No	No	Interviews by Prefectorial Labour Policy section or local Labour Policy Office of employers and employees
Sweden	More than one hour's duration	Yes	No	Press reports compiled by State Conciliation Service are checked by employers' organisations and sent to Central Statistical Office
United Kingdom	More than ten workers involved and of more than one day's duration, unless 100 or more working days lost	No	Yes	Local unemployment benefit offices make reports to Department of Employment, which also checks press, unions, and large employers
United States	Before 1982: more than one day or more than five workers; from 1982: more than one day's or shift's duration and more than 1000 workers involved	No	Yes	Reports from press, employers, unions and agencies, followed up by questionnaires

259

Source: UK Department of Employment *Employment Gazette,* April 1985:152.

in the relative position of most countries. Japan, however, has changed its position. In the 1950s there were more working days lost per 1000 employees in Japan than in Britain. Also, in the early 1950s, France was more strike-prone than Australia, while Sweden was one of the most strike-prone countries, before its long period of Social Democratic government which began in the 1930s.

There appear to be huge differences in strike-proneness between countries; for example, compare Italy and Germany. How can we explain such differences? Shalev (1980) considers three types of explanation: institutional, infrastructural and political. In the terms of chapter 1, the first two are pluralist approaches, while the third has something in common with both the radical and political economists' approaches.

Institutional explanations   Ross and Hartman's classic study argued that 'the existence of a labour party with close trade union affiliations is perhaps the greatest deterrent to the use of the strike' (1960:68). They also argued on the basis of 1900–56 data, that the use of strikes was 'withering away'. Both arguments have subsequently been discredited. Australia has a labour party, and in most countries strikes have hardly withered away.

In an attempt to explain why the USA generally seems to be more strike-prone than five other countries, Clegg (1976) uses three explanatory variables: the level of bargaining, the presence of disputes procedures and the indirect effect of the level of bargaining through factional bargaining. He argues that the American-style decentralised (plant) bargaining structure promotes factionalism within the unions and hence recourse to unofficial strikes for internal political reasons. Moreover, American unions can call official strikes at particular plants at far less cost to themselves, in contrast with unions in countries which generally engage in industry- or regional-level bargaining.

This is hardly a satisfactory type of explanation. As Shalev comments, 'collective bargaining arrangements are reflections of the distribution of power and the outcomes of conflicts between labour movements (unions and parties), employers and the state at the time these arrangements came into being' (1980:29). Shalev admits that such institutions may subsequently acquire a degree of 'functional autonomy'. None the less, they are no more than intervening variables in comparative theories.

Infrastructural explanations   For a causal explanation, we have to look to the social, political and economic environment, as do some Marxists. For instance, Ingham (1974), in his comparative study of strikes in Sweden and Britain, focusses on industrial concentration, in particular, and the structure and strategies of employer organisations.

Table A.19 Working days lost per thousand employees in selected industries[a]

	1974	1975	1976	1977	1978	1979	1980	1981	1982	1983	Average 1974–78	Average 1979–83	Average 1974–83
Australia	2630	1370	1440	610	850	1580	1360	1710	910	590	1400	1230	1320
Canada	2600	2780	2560	830	1930	1650	1510	1870	1410	600	2140	1430	1770
France	250	390	420	260	200	350	170	160	260	160	300	220	260
Germany (FR)	60	10	40	—	360	40	10	10	—	—	90	10	50
Italy[b]	1800	1730	2310	1560	880	2560	1590	950	1920	1490	1650	1700	1680
Japan	450	390	150	70	60	40	50	20	20	20	220	30	130
Sweden	10	20	20	20	10	20	2250	60	—	10	20	480	240
United Kingdom	1280	540	300	840	840	2410	1160	330	460	330	760	1000	870
United States[b]	1480	990	1190	1100	1100	910	850	670	NA	NA	1172	(810)c	(1036)c

Notes: a Mining and quarrying, manufacturing, construction, and transport, storage and communication

b Includes electricity, gas and water industries (estimates) ('—' indicates less than 5 days per thousand employees)

c (Brackets) indicate averages based on incomplete data for USA, which no longer colelcts such data in a comparative form (see chapter 1).

Source: UK Department of Employment *Employment Gazette*, March 1984; April 1985 (using ILO data though several national sources have since revised their data, which the ILO has subsequently endorsed).

He argues that, in Sweden, the powerful and cohesive employers' confederation negotiated centralised regulatory procedures with a similarly potent union confederation. This infrastructure provided a means of settling disputes and a way of exerting control on both sides of industry.

Ingham attributes too much importance to the employers in the formation of industrial relations institutions. It is more realistic 'to conceive of the development of worker and employer organisations dialectically, that is, as an ongoing process of challenge and response' (Shalev, 1980:30). An examination of the infrastructure alone cannot adequately explain the differences between other countries, nor does it explain the dramatic change in the pattern of Swedish industrial disputes in the late 1930s.

Political explanations Another school of thought does offer such an explanation, in terms of political exchange. Thus in Sweden, the employers were face with a highly unionised work force holding a firm grip on political power in the late 1930s. This induced the employers to a policy of accommodation with the labour movement (Korpi, 1981).

The fundamental difference between the earlier 'industrial relations' approaches and this political approach is that the latter emphasises that strikes are merely one working-class strategy, while political action is another. Thus political economists see the role of governments and labour political action as important independent variables. Since the unions have a powerful position in the polity in Sweden, this provides an alternative to action in the industrial arena. This explanation appears also to apply to Germany, Austria and Norway, which lose a relatively low number of working days. The explanation also applies to Italy, Canada and the USA, which are all strike-prone and in each case the unions have relatively little power in the political arena.

However, the relatively low number of days lost in France and Japan are less easily explained. The unions have not consistently been powerful in the polity in these countries. Another weakness is that this theory does not differentiate between types of strikes. Surely a wildcat stoppage about piece-work rates in the USA is less politically-motivated than a widespread demonstration stoppage in France?

Stoppage duration There is a different cleavage between these countries in terms of the average duration of stoppages. Why is Australia, for instance, near the top of the strike-prone league (Table A.19), but near the bottom of the average stoppage duration league (Table A.20)? In common with the French unions, few Australian unions prescribe strike benefits in their rules and in both countries there are statutory ways of dealing with grievances, 'where they con-

Table A.20 Annual average duration of stoppages
(All industries and services 1970–79) working days lost, per worker involved

USA	17.4
Canada	16.0
Italy	15.4
UK	8.1
Sweden	5.6
Japan	2.5
West Germany	3.9
Australia	2.3
France	2.1

Source: Creigh et al. (1982:19).

cern failure to observe the law, or to observe regional agreements in France and arbitration awards in Australia' (Clegg, 1976:74).

Conclusion   In any country, the current institutions, infrastructure and working-class representation in the polity reflects a mixture of economic, social and political variables. Therefore, as Creigh et al. point out 'it is not perhaps surprising that any attempt to relate developments to two or three explanatory variables can be faulted' (1982:20).

   Although we can criticise most of the various theories which have been put forward, attempting to formulate comparative explanations is still worthwhile as a way of beginning to understand the complex differences between national patterns of industrial relations. This look at the pattern of industrial disputes in our countries hardly lends support to the notion of convergence outlined in chapter 1. If anything, it implies that there is a continuing divergence between these countries, with some of them being strike-prone and others much less so.

Abbreviations

BLS	Bureau of Labor Statistics, US Department of Labor
EC	European Communities
EUROSTAT	Statistical Office of the EC
GDP	gross domestic product
GNP	gross national product
ILO	International Labour Organisation
IMF	International Metalworkers' Federation
ISTAT	Instituto Centrale di Statistica (Italy)
NA	not available
OECD	Organisation for Economic Co-operation and Development

References

Not all of these sources are cited explicitly in this Appendix. The following list includes others, as an initial guide to sources of data relevant to the study of international and comparative industrial relations data. The ILO and OECD also publish many other useful works (including the twice-yearly OECD *Economic Outlook* and the OECD annual economic surveys of trends and prospects for each OECD country)

Adams, L.T. (1985) 'Changing Employment Patterns of Organized Workers' *Monthly Labor Review* (Feb.) pp. 25–31

Australia, Department of Employment and Industrial Relations *Bulletin of Labour Market Research* Canberra: Bureau of Labour Market Research (quarterly)

Australian Bulletin of Labour Adelaide: National Institute of Labour Studies, Flinders University (quarterly)

Bain, G.S. and Elsheikh, F. (1976) *Union Growth and the Business Cycle: An Econometric Analysis* Oxford: Blackwell

Bain, G.S. and Price, R.J. (1980) *Profiles of Union Growth: A Comparative Statistical Portrait of Eight Countries* Oxford: Blackwell

Bratt, C. (1982) 'International Statistical Comparisons' *Labour Relations in 17 Countries* Stockholm: Swedish Employers' Confederation (SAF) (intermittently)

Carter, M. and Gregory, R. (1981) 'Government Pensions, Benefits and the Distribution of Employment for Males during a Recession' Working Paper, Canberra: Research School of Social Sciences, Australian National University

Clarke, R.O. (1980) 'Labour-Management Disputes: A Perspective' *British Journal of Industrial Relations* 18, 1 (Mar.), pp. 14–25

Clegg, H.A. (1976) *Trade Unionism and Collective Bargaining: A Theory Based on Comparisons of Six Countries* Oxford: Blackwell

Creigh, S.W. et al. (1982) 'Differences in Strike Activity between Countries' *International Journal of Manpower* 3, 4, pp. 15–23

EC (1985) *Report on Social Developments Year 1984* Brussels – Luxembourg: European Communities Commission (annually)

EC *EEC Labour Costs Survey* Brussels: Eurostat (triennially)

Economist 'Economic and Financial Indicators' London (weekly)

Fisher, M. (1973) *Measurement of Labour Disputes and their Economic Effects* Paris: OECD

Flaim, P.O. (1982) 'The Spendable Earnings Series: Has it Outlived its Usefulness' *Monthly Labor Review* (Jan.)

—— (1985) 'New Data on Union Members and Their Earnings' *Employment and Earnings* (Jan.)

Hart, R.A. (1984) *Shorter Working Time: A Dilemma for Collective Bargaining* Paris: OECD

ILO (1976) *International Recommendations on Labour Statistics* Geneva: International Labour Organisation

—— (1984) *World Labour Report Vol.1: Employment, Incomes, Social Protection, New Information Technology* Geneva: ILO

—— (1985) *World Labour Report Vol.2: Labour Relations, International*

Labour Standards, Training, Conditions of Work, Women at Work Geneva: ILO

—— (1986) *Yearbook of Labour Statistics 1986* Geneva: ILO (annually)

—— *Bulletin of Labour Statistics* Geneva: ILO (quarterly)

—— *Social and Labour Bulletin* Geneva: ILO (quarterly)

IMF (1985) *The Purchasing Power of Working Time: An International Comparison, 1985* Geneva: International Metalworkers' Federation

Ingham, G.K. (1974) *Strikes and Industrial Conflict* London: Macmillan

Japan Institute for Social and Economic Affairs (1985) *Japan 1985: An International Comparison* Tokyo: Keizai Koho Center (annually)

JIL (1985) *Japanese, Working Life Profile: Statistical Aspects* Tokyo: Japan Institute of Labour (annually)

Jones, B. (1982) *Sleepers, Wake! Technology and the Future of Work* Melbourne: Oxford University Press; Brighton: Wheatsheaf

Kaim-Caudle, P.R. (1973) *Comparative Social Policy and Social Security: A Ten Country Study* London: Martin Robertson

Korpi, W. (1981) 'Sweden: Conflict, Power and Politics in Industrial Relations' in P. Doeringer et al. eds *Industrial Relations in International Perspective: Essays on Research and Policy* London: Macmillan

OECD (1985a) *OECD Employment Outlook* Paris: Organisation for Economic Co-operation and Development (annually)

—— (1985b) *Labour Force Statistics 1963–1983* Paris: OECD (annually, with a 20-year historical abstract)

—— *Quarterly Labour Force Statistics* Paris: OECD (quarterly)

—— *OECD Observer* Paris: OECD (bimonthly; the March issue usually includes an invaluable supplement, a set of summary tables, 'The OECD Member Countries', with most data only two years old)

Ross, A.M. and Hartman, P.T. (1960) *Changing Patterns of Industrial Conflict* New York: Wiley

Shalev, M. (1978) 'Lies, Damned Lies and Strike Statistics: The Measurement of Trends in Industrial Conflict' in C. Crouch and A. Pizzorno eds (1978) *The Resurgence of Class Conflict in Western Europe Since 1968, Vol. 1: National Studies* London: Macmillan, pp. 1–20

—— (1980) 'Industrial Relations Theory and the Comparative Study of Industrial Relations and Industrial Conflict' *British Journal of Industrial Relations* 18, 1 (Mar.), pp. 26–43

Smith, A.D. et al. (1982) *International Industrial Productivity: A Comparison of Britain, America and Germany* Cambridge: Cambridge University Press/ National Institute of Economic and Social Research

UK Department of Employment *Employment Gazette* London: HMSO (monthly)

United Nations (1971) *Indices to the International Standard Industrial Classification of all Economic Activities* New York: Department of Economic and Social Affairs, UN (intermittently)

US Bureau of Labor Statistics *Handbook of Labor Statistics* Washington DC: US Department of Labor (intermittently)

—— *Monthly Labor Review* Washington DC: US Department of Labor (monthly)

—— *News* Washington DC: Bureau of Labor Statistics Press Releases, US

Department of Labor (intermittently)

Walsh, K. (1983) *Strikes in Europe and the United States: Measurement and Incidence* London: Frances Pinter

—— (1985) *The Measurement of Trade Union Membership in the European Community* Luxembourg–Brussels: Eurostat

Walsh, K. and King, A. (1986) *Handbook of Comparative Labour Market Indicators* London: Macmillan

World Bank (1981) *World Bank Atlas* Washington DC: International Bank for Reconstruction and Development (annually)

—— (1982) *World Development Report* Washington DC: International Bank for Reconstruction and Development

Author index

Subject index